STRANGE CUSTOMS
OF
COURTSHIP
AND
MARRIAGE

STRANGE CUSTOMS

OF

COURTSHIP

AND

MARRIAGE

By

WILLIAM J. FIELDING

Author of *Sex and the Love Life*
The Caveman Within Us, etc.

The New Home Library

NEW YORK

COPYRIGHT 1942, BY GARDEN CITY PUBLISHING CO., INC.

An Original Publication of THE NEW HOME LIBRARY, SEPTEMBER, 1942
REPRINTED OCTOBER, 1942
REPRINTED FEBRUARY, 1943
REPRINTED SEPTEMBER, 1943
REPRINTED APRIL, 1944

THE NEW HOME LIBRARY, 14 West Forty-ninth Street
New York, N. Y.

CL

PRINTED IN THE UNITED STATES OF AMERICA

Contents

v

STRANGE CUSTOMS

OF

COURTSHIP

AND

MARRIAGE

Introduction

THE FAR-REACHING IMPORT OF COURTSHIP.—Courtship, with its connotations of romance and love, with its glamorous appeal to the mind of youth—and those not so young—with its alluring promise of fulfilment of the heart's desires, is an intriguing experience in nearly every life; possibly, in every normal life that has fully expressed itself.

Its influence is so far-reaching, and its presence as a social institution is so taken for granted, that we do not begin to realize the extent of its ramifications until we stop and take account of some of its tendencies.

Every newspaper has whole pages—and Sunday editions whole sections—devoted to its activities, highlights and culminations. It has been perhaps the theme of more novels, stories and poems than any other inspiration, as it is love in its supreme moment.

The *boy meets girl* motif is the mainstay of stage and screen. Likewise, on the stage of life it is an ever-present drama in our midst—among the young people in our own homes, in the neighborhood, in the parks, on the street, in the automobile, wherever people live, move or congregate. Objectively, we are often amused by its comic aspects, and sometimes shocked by its tragic implications.

Business and industry profit by its whims, necessities and

demands. The shops of fashion, jewelry, confections, flowers, and many other products cater to its needs. To what extent the mighty cosmetic and beautifying industries are stimulated by its dynamic impulse, we can only hazard a guess.

But courtship was not always so! While man has always wooed and won the woman of his choice, the method of wooing has varied as greatly as the conditions of primordial life have varied from our own. Different ages of time, different races of people, different periods of development, have produced a multiplicity of customs which have governed the mating of man and woman.

A DEFINITION OF MARRIAGE.—This great urge has had as its impetus the bringing together of the couple in sexual union. With it ultimately came the establishment of marriage, of varying periods of duration, depending upon the conditions which determined the arrangement, the most important of which has been the raising of children.

The situation as gleaned by the anthropologists—those tireless students of the history of mankind—is of course too complex to be related in a few pages. In primitive life, precise and orderly forms of mating could scarcely be expected, nor did they exist. There have been countless sorts of variations and many contradictions.

According to the great authority on the subject, Professor Edward Westermarck, author of *The History of Human Marriage,* human beings have always lived in what may be broadly described as a state of marriage. Not in the definitely formulated sense that we now know this institution, but in a recognizable and definable form.

Westermarck thus defines marriage as a relation of one or more men to one or more women which is recognized by custom or law and involves certain rights and duties both in the case of the parties entering the union and in the case of the children born of it.

Continuing, Westermarck says that marriage always implies the right of sexual intercourse; society holds such intercourse allowable in the case of the husband and wife, and, generally speaking, even regards it as their duty to gratify in some measure the other partner's desire. But the right to sexual intercourse is not necessarily exclusive. He adds, as an alternative definition: a more or less durable association between male and female lasting beyond the mere act of propagation till after the birth of the offspring.

In support of this theory, it is argued that marriage has developed out of primordial habit—the habit of a man and a woman (or several women) to live together, to have sexual relations with one another, and to rear their offspring in common. The man became the protector and supporter of the family, the woman his helpmate and the nurse of their children. This habit in time became sanctioned by custom, and eventually by law, and thus was transformed into a social institution.

It is shown that many of the higher animals have a family life analogous to human marriage in its primitive form. Indeed, it has been observed that the highest form of paired mating—not excluding man—is to be found among many species of birds.

Among the great majority of birds, the male and female keep together even after the breeding season, and in a great many species the parental instinct has reached a high degree of intensity on the father's side as well as on the mother's. So true is this that Brehm, the naturalist, has remarked that "real marriage can be found only among birds."

So the terms "marriage" and "family" are used to describe a definite human and sub-human relationship, and our modern marriage and family are a development of this process which began at a very primitive level of life.

Comparatively early in its development marriage became an economic institution, affecting the proprietary rights of the parties.

Among certain peoples, as we shall see in later chapters, plurality of wives is legally permissible; among others, more primitive, the marriage is a loose and temporary union, lasting little beyond the birth of the offspring. This situation accounts for Westermarck's qualifying definition.

On the other hand, higher in the social order, we find an established condition wherein marriage means something more than sexual congress. In this order man and wife maintain a household together. They may have a community of goods. There is a common interest and responsibility in the care of the children. It is upon this basis that there has developed the system of monogamous marriage now prevalent throughout most of the modern world.

ORIGIN OF THE WORD "WEDDING".—When we look into the origin of certain words we get an intimation of the development or transformation of the system described by the word in question. This is characteristically true of the word "wedding". It derives from the barbaric stage of wife purchase through which marriage passed. The *wed* was the purchase money or its equivalent, horses, cattle or other property, which the groom gave to the father to seal the transaction.

In the early days of the Anglo-Saxons children were often betrothed by the parents, the bridegroom's pledge of marriage being accompanied by a security, or *wed,* furnished by the father of the groom. Thus originated the term *wedding,* or *pledging the troth* of the bride to the man who secured her by purchase.

It is said that traces of the ancient legal procedure connected with wife purchase remained in England as late as the middle of the sixteenth century. In France, even until the time of Louis XVI, it was the custom to pay down thirteen *deniers* upon conclusion of a marriage contract. This latter practice was doubtless merely a symbolic relic of the time when marriage was an outright cash transaction.

THE ANTIQUITY OF MARRIAGE.—As we have already seen, marriage appears to have had its origin at the very dawn of human society, perhaps being a continuation of an analogous relationship in subhuman life. There are, however, different schools of thought on this subject, as we shall presently see.

Among many species of the animal kingdom, the male and female remain together not only during the pairing season, but until after the birth of the offspring. It seems reasonable to assume that they were induced to do so by an instinct which had been acquired through the process of natural selection. This tendency preserved the next generation, and thereby perpetuated the species.

Confirmation of this theory is found in the fact that in such cases the male not only stays with the female and young, but also takes care of them. Prince Peter Kropotkin, the great Russian naturalist, cites numerous instances of devotion, loyalty and self-sacrifice among the denizens of the animal world in the wild stage that would be a credit to humanity at its best.

Among mammals the young are dependent for a considerable time upon the mother, who consequently is concerned for their welfare, attending to them with much affection. While in most cases the relations between the sexes are restricted to the pairing season, there are however certain species in which they are of a more permanent character, and the male acts as guardian of the family.

The family consisting of parents and children prevails among the lowest savages, as well as among the most civilized races of men. It may therefore be assumed that the factors which led to marital and parental relations among the higher animals, about which we know, also operated among our earliest human and nearest subhuman ancestors.

Furthermore, as the period of infancy among human beings has always been comparatively long, and the number of children very small, as well as the hazards of primitive life very great, a family relationship with joint parental protection was quite a necessary factor for the continuation of existence of human life in its early stages.

That the functions of the father and husband are not merely sexual and procreative, but involve the duties of supporting and protecting the wife and children, is confirmed by an array of facts relating to peoples in all parts of the world and in all stages of civilization.

Many savages do not permit a man to marry until he has given satisfactory proof of his ability to fulfil these duties. Marriage and the protection of the family are thus intimately connected, even in primitive life.

Among some peoples, true married life does not begin for couples who are formally married, or marriage does not become final, until a child is born or there is evidence of pregnancy. In other cases, sexual relations, even when not entered into with the view to marriage, are followed by the obligation to marry when pregnancy or the birth of a child results.

These facts led Westermarck to conclude that marriage is rooted in the family, rather than the family in marriage.

Some authorities of note, such as Morgan, Lubbock, McLennan, Bachofen, Bastian and others, disagree with this premise, and are convinced that man lived at first in a state of promiscuity. This implies that the earliest men and women lived together indiscriminately, with no bond to unite them except the fact that they lived together.

In the opinion of Iwan Bloch, whoever knows the nature of the human impulse has learned how the race developed, and whoever has studied the conditions still existing in the sexual field among primitive races and among modern civilized races, can have no doubt that a condition of sexual promiscuity prevailed in the beginning of human development.

Of course, we have no proof of who was right about the ways of cohabitation in the dim, distant twilight of human life. Perhaps even primitive life was complicated enough to afford some basis for both hypotheses. Again, it may be largely a matter of interpretation and emphasis.

We are living today in a country in which monogamy is the legally and socially accepted standard of the marital relationship, to which the great majority conform. But if some sociologist thousands of years hence should attempt to determine our prevailing sexual relationship, say by referring to the files of the tabloid newspapers or certain literature of this period, he might be justified in concluding that twentieth-century America was a cavalcade of unbridled licentiousness and promiscuity.

THE TREND TO MONOGAMY.—Regardless of the prevailing types of the family relationship at earlier periods of human society, and notwithstanding the continuation of the multiple marriage in many parts of the world, which in some areas exists to this day, there nevertheless developed a definite trend to monogamy.

What brought about this change? In the first place, with the evolution of society from a comparatively simple to a more complex structure, or organism, plurality of wives led to increasing complications and conflicts. As society became more complex, so too the individuals responded to the environmental changes. The minds of men and women developed from experience, and began to question the values of old practices—although ancient traditions always die hard.

Furthermore, with increased knowledge and sharpened intelligence, there were emotional reverberations of far-reaching consequence. Certainly jealousy, among other of the elementary emotions, must have become increasingly important at some stage of human development, and with greater opportunity for the unfoldment of this primordial impulse, multiple marriage became increasingly difficult.

The complications relative to numerous children from several wives also in time became a serious problem as society developed from a pastoral to a more advanced stage. In a purely pastoral society, several wives and many children would be an asset as it would assure many hands to perform the arduous drudgery required in that form of economy. There was then little time to dwell upon personal considerations, and no energy left to expend itself or explode in the emotional channels of jealousy.

With the next step in the social organization leading into primitive commerce and the crafts, a smaller unit of family life became inevitable. There was, of course, no abrupt transition from polygamy to monogamy, but the trend became marked, even though plural wives continued as a survival in the new era, for those who were willing to pay the price—in nerve strain as well as in wealth—for the luxury.

As monogamy gained a foothold, women sensed the advantages and were hardly willing to become the second wife to a man already married, or her parents would be reluctant to compel her to marry such a man, unless some unusual advantages, economic or social, were gained thereby.

The smaller home of the post-pastoral period made it increasingly impractical to raise two or more broods of children from the several wives under one roof, and a practical adjustment of this matter was tried by providing each wife with a separate dwelling. This required much extra expense, so that polygamy became a prohibitive luxury to all men except the very wealthy.

Westermarck states that the custom of giving a separate home to each wife was intended to prevent quarrels and fights, but even when this end was achieved—which was not always the case—female jealousy is an obstacle to the practice of polygamy.

When monogamy rose into the prevalent status of family life, it became sanctioned by custom, law and morals, and therefore in the Western World any open violation of this accepted code of marital life is usually subject to penalty.

THE MARRIAGE CEREMONIAL.—Marriage has progressed through three general stages in its evolutionary development. Each of them has contributed its share, which is readily identifiable, to the ceremony of modern marriage.

Marriage through force, or by capture (which will be the subject of a subsequent chapter) was the first important stage. It was literally stealing and carrying off a desirable woman, usually of another tribe, and making her the wife of the captor.

Marriage through contract or purchase succeeded marriage by capture. One stage gradually overlapped upon the other. It is probable, as tribal strength and solidarity increased, that more and more effort was made to avenge the women stolen from the group. A raid was made against the tribe which held the woman captive, and to avoid a disastrous war compensation was offered. From this, the idea arose of arranging compensation beforehand, or, more prosaically, buying the bride.

"Giving the bride away," in the modern marriage ceremony, is a symbolic survival of the time when the bride was really sold. The bride's veil is a modified survival of the days when she was literally shrouded from head to foot. The "best man" is the modern counterpart of the fellow-warrior who assisted the would-be bridegroom to carry off the bride. The honeymoon symbolizes the period during which the bridegroom found it necessary to hide away with his prize until her family or kinsmen grew tired of searching for her. Carrying the bride over the hearth, and other playful suggestions of force in modern marriage, are relics of the time when force was used in its pristine form.

The next great stage is marriage through mutual love, which has been an undying theme of romantic poets and singers down through the centuries since the first attempt was made to separate sordidness from the sexual relationship. Although the process has not yet been completed at this late date, that does not alter the fact that love came upon the scene at a comparatively early period in the development of man's psycho-intellectual life as distinguished from his immensely longer biological background as a human being.

It is from this long history of human marriage that have been drawn the numerous elements that make up the formalities of the marriage ceremony. They vary in many lands and among peoples of different social traditions, but through most of them run the thread of a common heritage based on the patterns of marriage in the past, even the very distant, long forgotten past.

Marriage denotes a great and fundamental change in the way of life of the individuals concerned. It means leaving the hearthstone or protection of the parents, and venturing upon a new experience, a new existence as the potential progenitors of a new generation.

Even the primitive mind saw the importance of the step, and surrounded the event with rites and ceremonies considered appropriate for the occasion. Among those peoples obsessed with magic or other weird superstitions, marriage received its full share of magical and superstitious implications. As it was associated with, or closely followed the advent of puberty among many groups, its culmination in the breaking down of the sexual taboo was a subject for solemn rites essential to appease the tribal deities. It was perhaps the most highly dramatized event in primitive life where there existed a traditional background of any note.

In our modern world, besides the legal aspects of the ceremony that are indispensable for the conclusion of a valid marriage, we find the conventional rites peculiarly paralleling the practices of the past, making due allowance for the difference in culture, and the symbolization of forms that once had literal meaning. That these survivals of the past are not considered empty formalities is evidenced by the fact that the modern bride rarely chooses to dispense with them. When they are now dispensed with, in the case of impromptu marriages or elopements, it is usually a matter of expediency rather than choice. Such is the influence of tradition upon the human mind.

MARRIAGE AS A SACRAMENT.—In the ages preceding Christianity, after marriage had been elevated to the status of a ceremony, it may have been a solemn religious ordinance or a purely civil contract.

Marriage customs, like all others, change very slowly, and it was not until the Council of Trent, in the middle of the sixteenth century, that the Roman canon was drastically revised. It was then decreed that a Catholic marriage, to be valid, must be celebrated by a priest of the parish, or by some other priest delegated by him for the purpose, in the presence of two or three witnesses.

Up to the time of the Council of Trent, the marriage ceremony was one which the couple themselves could perform, and the clandestine, unconsecrated marriage was completely valid. Thus, for upward of the first fifteen hundred years of Christianity—or for three-quarters of the entire Christian era—it was the custom for most Christian couples entering marriage, simply to ask the blessing of the priest. Even this was not absolutely necessary to make the tie valid in the eyes of Church and State.

There were few other ceremonials connected with marriage, especially in the first centuries, as the primitive Christians were for the most part a humble people, often hunted or persecuted by their pagan contemporaries, and had little time for formalities. Furthermore, the founders of Christianity did not prescribe any particular ceremonies in connection with marriage.

Gradually, however, as Christianity came into ascendancy, and as it became accepted more and more as the state religion, the religious phase of marriage became increasingly emphasized. In medieval times, the priest was called in to bless the marriage bed, a custom that still prevails in many European countries. The object of this ceremony was partly to bestow upon the couple a long life, progeny and other desirable things, but more especially to protect them against evil influences, as the Latin formula spoken on the occasion indicated.

The practice of religious marriage, performed in the church, or by a clergyman in the home, gradually became general. It was made obligatory in 1563 by the Council of Trent.

Luther's opinion that all matrimonial affairs should come under civil jurisdiction, and not that of the Church, was not

accepted in the main by the legislators of the Protestant countries. Marriage continued to be regarded as a divine institution,
and the sacerdotal nuptials became obligatory on Protestants
and Catholics alike.

The French Revolution brought about the first change in
this respect. The Constitution of September 1791 made civil
marriage mandatory, although this could be supplemented by
a sacerdotal benediction, if the parties so desired. A religious
ceremony alone, however, would not be a valid marriage.

Civil marriage eventually became the accepted legal form in
most European countries, although in some of them, as in the
United States, the parties may choose either the civil or religious rite, either being equally valid under the law. Thus the
state became an interested party in the marriage contract.
Even though a clergyman officiates at the ceremony, as in the
United States, a license must be secured from the city or other
political subdivision of the government, and in an ever increasing number of states a medical examination of the contracting
parties has been made obligatory by legislative enactment.
Furthermore, a prescribed lapse of time between the issuance
of the license and the performance of the marriage is often
required to prevent too hasty or rash marriages.

Governmental supervision of marriage serves several purposes. It tends to reduce the possibility of force or fraud. It is
intended to prevent polygamous unions and those that may be
considered incestuous. In states where the racial question is an
acute problem, miscegenation through marriage is usually prohibited by law. The control of the state over marriage also
assures more accurate and complete vital statistics, which are
becoming increasingly important in our complex civilization.

CHAPTER I

Curious Mating Customs

A BROTHER-IN-LAW COMPLEX.—The marriage customs of the Southern Slavs and people of the Balkan peninsula take on some peculiar forms. Young married women enter into a very intimate relation with their bride attendants, two of whom attend a bride on her wedding day. The bride is a very young girl, and in accordance with the local custom she is given to a man she has never seen before, and, by the logic of the circumstances, does not like and seems determined never to like.

She comes into a strange house where it is incumbent upon her for the rest of her life, or their lives, to show her parents-in-law the greatest humility and submission. This is an in-law situation that is not altogether unique, as it prevails to a greater or lesser extent in many parts of the orient and elsewhere.

To make her position more difficult, she is forbidden by custom to approach her husband freely. She seems ashamed of her marital relation, and thinks it indecent to address her husband in public, even after she is the mother of his children. Likewise, he remains a stranger to her, and their relationship is limited to the sexual sphere, without any evidence or pretense of affection. Even in death, it would be a shame for a woman to mourn for her husband.

As nature is said to abhor a vacuum, she is however not without some consoling attentions. She may converse freely with her husband's brothers, who were her bride attendants. The elder one, if he is married—which means that he shows no interest in his wife—may become her best friend. She also remains deeply attached to her own brothers.

The Albanian who has been away on a journey will not return with a present for his wife. He will reserve this token for the wife of his eldest brother.

In former times, among these peoples, it was considered improper for the groom to start conjugal life immediately after marriage. The bride attendants, brothers of the groom, spent the first night by the side of the bride. Custom demanded that the groom show reluctance. A Serbian woman is looked down upon if she becomes a mother within a year after marriage.

THE COUVADE.—A most peculiar custom that has existed among peoples in various parts of the world is the *couvade*. This provides that at the time of childbirth, the husband takes to his bed and simulates the pains that the wife actually undergoes. Following the birth of the child, he keeps to his bed and receives all the attentions commonly bestowed upon the mother.

The term is derived from the French verb, *couver,* to brood, to hatch, and was first used by Sir E. B. Taylor.

While the custom has tended to disappear with the advance of civilization, it has prevailed from time immemorial down to comparatively recent years. Writers as remote as Plutarch have described the man imitating the cries of the woman in travail. The practice has been reported from various regions of the White Nile, India, Japan and Chinese Turkestan. Butler had it in mind when he wrote:

> For the Chinese go to bed
> And lie-in, in their ladies' stead.

The *couvade* has also been described by explorers and missionaries among some of the aborigines of North, Central and South America. It appears in Celtic legend, and is bound up in certain elements of witchcraft, with the forceful transference of pain to the father by nurse or midwife, as noted in Scotland and Ireland.

The rite is said to be practiced still by the West Indian Caribs, in the Pearl Islands, in the Gulf of Panama, and by a number of South American tribes.

Various reasons have been ascribed to account for the origin of the custom, one of the most logical being that it is an expression of the physical bond between father and offspring, emulating in a symbolic manner the actual physical bond between mother and child. Symbolism and magic have a place of tremendous importance in primitive life, and the *couvade* undoubtedly comes within this sphere.

DOWRY EARNED BY PROSTITUTION.—Among various peoples it has been considered proper for a young woman to earn her dowry by prostitution. Some cases doubtless were prompted by an economic motive, the poverty of the family, but more usually the reason was superstitious. Either a sacrifice to the divinity of love and fertility was intended, or it was considered that evil spirits could be driven away from the newly wedded couple in this way, as the custom was usually a preliminary to the woman's prospective marriage.

This practice prevailed among certain Algerian tribes, and anciently among the Phoenicians, Cyprians, Lydians and Etruscans. In the New World, it has been described among the Natchez of Louisiana, and the aborigines of Nicaragua and Guatemala.

There is undoubtedly some connection between this institution and an earlier age when freer sexual relationships generally existed. It has been especially found among races or in regions where forms of defloration by somebody other than the husband have been prevalent. The *Testament of Judah* remarks that "it was a law of Amorites that she who was about to marry should sit in fornication seven days by the gate."

Customs such as these seem quite inexplicable to the conventional modern mind, and indeed even the most profound writers on the subject seem hardly to reveal much light, aside from presenting the evidence. The fact is, of course, that modern investigators have been able to understand only very imperfectly the workings of the primitive mind.

We know that magic is very important to the savage and the barbarian, and that the commands and taboos of a religious nature which have been transmitted from previous generations are accepted and obeyed without inquiring into the reasons why.

ARTIFICIAL DEFLORATION OF MARRIAGEABLE GIRLS.—Another custom having a bearing on the foregoing, or possibly derived from similar magical sources, is that whereby girls are artificially deflowered before marriage by someone else than the future husband.

It is based on the taboo against the husband deflowering his bride, which in the reasoning of many primitive tribes might lead to all sorts of evil results. This reluctance on the part of the bridegroom is a fact widely attested in the lore of anthropological research.

Often it was the mother, or other older women of the tribe who performed the rite as an initiation ceremony preliminary to marriage. It signifies that the subject had passed from the condition of childhood, and was now a woman with the responsibilities and duties incumbent upon her new position in life.

In some sections of ancient Peru, when a girl was sought in marriage she was deflowered by the mother in the presence of the relatives who made the betrothal arrangement, to demonstrate to all present the care that had been taken of her. It was proof of the honor and respectability of the bride, and at the same time relieved the future husband of the necessity of defloration in the manner indicated by nature.

Among the Kamchadal the bride's mother was blamed if the man found his wife to be a virgin, so it became the practice of the mother to perform the defloration in the girl's early youth.

The Todas of the Nilgiris, in Southern India, considered it most essential that the defloration should take place before puberty, and few things were regarded as more disgraceful than that this ceremony should be delayed beyond this period. It might subject a woman to reproach and abuse for the remainder of her life, and it was even said that men might refuse to marry her if this ceremony had not been performed at the proper time.

Whether these rites are performed by the mother or other women of the tribe, or by extra-matrimonial intercourse through arrangements made by the bride's family, they are always considered a very serious matter, bound up with the most sacred beliefs of those who participate in the practice.

THE MATCH-MAKER.—The mind of twentieth-century American youth, used to choosing his own mate, finds it difficult to contemplate seriously the function of a professional matchmaker. Nevertheless, the matrimonial middle-man has been an important institution among many peoples in various parts of the world, and even in our own country among certain groups of immigrants, and their children of the first and second generation, until the process of assimilation has outmoded the custom.

Primitive and civilized people alike have found this practice an expedient way of bringing together marriageable young men and young women, who otherwise would have little opportunity to meet eligible prospects for marriage. It is common among the Mohammedans and Arabs; it prevailed in ancient India, and it has existed in European countries down to the present time.

Insufficient opportunity for eligible young people to meet and enter into a mutually satisfactory marriage contract seems to be the impetus that brought this system into being. Higher up in the social scale the problem is made more complex by the economic factors, material means or wealth, that may be involved.

The connection between marriage and money is an old one, and since the beginning of the institution of private property, the problem of marrying off daughters and sons advantageously has been one that has caused concern to innumerable fathers and mothers.

In the more primitive periods of human society, before the acquisition of private property became the established feature of social organization, this factor did not enter into the prospects of marriage. There were many peculiar customs, some of which have been touched upon and others of which will be related in subsequent chapters, but marriage for money or kind, with or without the influence of a match-maker, was not one of them. Marriage for money must therefore be regarded as a by-product of civilization.

Insofar as the match-maker deals with the medium of money or other wealth, he is an agent or broker performing his function like any other commercial go-between in our own business world. On this basis, he usually receives a commission, representing a percentage of the dowry as his fee. Consequently, it is to his interest to see that the dowry is as large as can be exacted.

There are people among whom it is customary for the father to think of his daughter as a piece of desirable or valuable property. His whole interest in her is to receive as much as possible for her in cattle, merchandise or money. What his daughter will think of her husband is for him a matter of no importance. The purchaser must be able to pay for value received, and his trustworthiness must be assured if the bride is to be purchased on deferred installments. It is true that the tribe or community may limit the circle from which the husband may be drawn, but it may limit still further the marketability of property other than daughters.

The opposite of this situation—where the husband is "bought" and the bridal price is paid—often introduces the factor of the desirability of the marriage from points other than the pecuniary one. In this case, the bride's family is buying rather than selling, and the element for which they are paying is usually position, title or social prestige of some sort. The match-maker in instances of this kind becomes something more than a mere business agent. He may act by virtue of his position in the community. That is, he officiates because he is a person of special social, political or religious importance, or he may be a relative whose tact and diplomacy make him eligible for this delicate duty. He may not receive pecuniary compensation, but the successful culmination of his efforts assures him of the rewards of obligation and respect of influential people, and thus enhances his position and increases his prestige.

Throughout the Middle Ages and right down to our own

time a professional class of match-makers existed among European Jews, known as *shadḳans* or *shadchans*. In the early days these men were mostly rabbis and persons engaged in the study of Talmudic law and theology. It was considered improper for them to derive pecuniary gains directly from their leaning, but the match-making profession offered a dignified way for them to earn a livelihood.

Probably the principal reason why the institution of the professional match-maker continued among the Jews through the centuries, while it tended to disappear among other Europeans, is found in the ostracism of the Jews in a predominantly Christian society. During the medieval period of constant oppression and periodic massacre, the Jewish people were almost exterminated in certain localities, and the isolated survivors found it necessary to take unusual means to arrange for desirable marriages of their sons and daughters in at best a latently hostile environment.

In the course of time the haggling and indecorous competition which arose drove most of the learned men from the profession, no longer held to be so honorable as in the past.

The *shadchan* has survived, particularly among Slavonic and other Jews of Eastern Europe. In this way the institution reached America and enjoyed a period of successful transplanted life, created largely in the East Side of New York and other large Jewish communities. The *shadchanim* advertised in the Yiddish newspapers, announcing their office hours and setting forth their ability to provide professional men, business men and honest workingmen for maidens and widows.

Of course, the practice was prompted by conditions in the old world, which had diminishing application here, except perhaps in the instance of more or less wealthy Jewish merchants with marriageable daughters in non-Jewish communities. As the American-born Jew has ample opportunity to meet girls freely both within and without his own circle, the institution of the *shadchan* seems destined to fall into desuetude, although the professional match-makers can be depended upon to wage a vigorous fight against assimilation—and the loss of his commission.

And lest the non-Jewish American should think this custom altogether alien to our native way of life, it might be well to point out that we have a large and ever growing number of matrimonial papers (journalistic match-makers) and correspondence bureaus (mail order go-betweens) to perform a similar service, although, unfortunately, less expertly. The amply dowried daughter and the rich widow are offered as crowning inducements to the acquisitive American male with the price of a subscription, or even return postage. The results, of course, would cause the humblest *shadchan* to blush for shame over the status of his once honorable profession.

CHAPTER II

Modern Survivals of Ancient Customs

ECHOES FROM THE PAST.—The betrothal, or engagement, is a custom that harkens back to remote antiquity. In primitive life there was little courtship or wooing, except possibly as a prelude to the sexual act, which is more or less prevalent throughout the animal world. In a word, the wooing of early man was perhaps a brief episode which precipitated almost at once into marriage of the kind that prevailed in the given period.

With the development of tribal life and organized communities, following the period of marriage by capture, mating took place on another basis. Savage people took considerable pains to make themselves attractive to, and attracted by, the opposite sex by ornamenting, painting and tattooing themselves, or even by grotesquely mutilating certain features.

The long period of marriage by purchase, or by contract, must have lent encouragement to these expressions of sexual interest. An attractive daughter, possessing the qualities most desired according to the existing standards, made her a valuable marketable asset to the father when the time came to arrange for her marriage. And the dynamic sexual impulse of the male, normally the one to take the initiative in this sphere, assured sustained interest and activity from the beginning of puberty.

Romantic courtship, of course, did not exist—that is, the

pre-marital love of one individual for another of his choice. But the mating urge that is inherent in all forms of life above the asexual prompted youth to react with erotic interest toward the members of the opposite sex in general, at least within its own group or approved circle.

The boy looked forward to the day when he could have his mate, the same as his elders. The girl just as eagerly hoped for the fulfilment of her biological destiny. The manner in which this object was to be accomplished could hardly ever have been a matter of personal choice, but was rather a business arrangement between the families of the couple, or more especially between the respective fathers or other male acting head of the family.

Nevertheless, the very nature of the arrangement brought about the function of the betrothal. It may have seemed desirable to the families concerned to seal the betrothal during the infancy or childhood of the bride and groom-to-be.

In some of the islands of the Pacific, it was common for fathers to betroth their unborn children. In New Caledonia the girls were betrothed at birth. In the Fiji Islands it was the custom until recently, and perhaps still is to some extent, to marry the children when the infant bride and groom are only three or four years old. Though the marriage is only a ceremony, it is strictly binding and the couple start living together when they reach maturity. When infant betrothal is practiced, the bride may not see her future husband until the day of their marriage.

Where there were mutual family property rights to be considered, or social advantages to be secured, the betrothal of children at an early age was a likely procedure to effect the desired results. Even in modern times, in the heyday of royalty in Europe, this practice was often followed to advance what was considered to be the interests of the regal houses, or, sometimes, to improve the national position of the countries represented in the union.

Not infrequently a royal personage in love with a woman of inferior rank or position, who wished to establish the relationship on a quasi-legal basis, has entered into what is called a morganatic marriage. This form of marriage did not give the royal rank of the husband to the morganatic wife or her children, nor did it entitle them to inherit the father's property. It was usual, however, to make an adequate settlement upon the woman who entered into such a relationship, both for her support and for the maintenance of their offspring.

Thus love will assert itself, in spite of the rigid restrictions imposed upon the blood royal. Unfortunately, the royal princess was denied the same freedom as the male members of her class in entering into a morganatic alliance with a commoner. Women of high royal caste on occasion have married men of lesser rank, usually of the nobility, but this has been more for political expediency than for love. The amorous princess and the neglected queen who sought romantic diversion outside of the limited royal circle usually had recourse to a lover—and they have been legion in the history and annals of the royal courts.

Tokens of Engagement.—Sealing the engagement pact with a ring or other token is a usage of great antiquity. It probably derives from the very old custom of using the ring as a pledge in any important or sacred agreement.

In the first book of the Old Testament it is stated: "And Pharaoh said unto Joseph, See I have set thee over all the land of Egypt. And Pharaoh took off his ring from his hand, and put it upon Joseph's hand" (*Genesis* xli, 41, 42).

An ancient custom among the common people was to break

a piece of gold or silver to seal the marriage pact. One half of the token was kept by the man, the other half by the woman. This practice preceded the exchange of rings, with which it has a close affinity in the use of precious metals for the purpose.

In ancient Ireland it is said to have been the custom for the man to give the woman he wanted to marry a bracelet woven of human hair. Her acceptance of it was symbolic of accepting the man, linking herself to him for life. The use of some strands of hair in love-lockets, usually curled into a circle, has been a custom down to modern times. In the bracelet, as in the ring, we have the circle—the link—symbolizing union, unbroken and without end.

Throughout the Middle Ages, it was quite customary to seal the betrothal pact by means of a ring. In England rings were exchanged to solemnize the verbal contract of betrothal. In Southern Europe, the use of the ring was also widespread. The joint ring—made in two parts and linked together in a seemingly solid circle—has had much favor as a token of love uniting the betrothed couple.

A Greek engagement or betrothal ring of the fourth century B.C. bears the following exalted inscription, "To her who excels not only in virtue and prudence, but also in wisdom." Another early example carries an inscription as modern as today's colloquialism—the single Greek word meaning "Honey".

THE DIAMOND RING.—With the development of the artistic crafts, the enhancement of esthetic taste, and the greater commercial facility in transporting objects of value about the world, it was only natural that the betrothal ring should eventually be ornamented by precious stones.

All the well-known precious gems have been used for this purpose, but it is significant that the diamond—and especially the solitaire—has come to be generally accepted as the ideal engagement ring, most highly prized by the modern maiden.

There are other stones of exquisite beauty, faultlessly colored in nature's matchless laboratory, and often of greater value, size for size, than the diamond—the ruby, the emerald, the oriental sapphire—but none can hope to compete in popularity with that sparkling carbon-crystal known as the diamond.

How much superstition has to do with this—the superstitious fancy or sentiment that seems to be an inborn trait of feminine intuition—we may only guess. But we do know there is an ancient superstition that the sparkle of the diamond originated in the alchemistic fires of love Sentiments associated with certain ideas seem to be ageless and immutable, and regardless of time or the state of cultural or social advancement we find a particular sentiment associated with a particular object So the diamond ring, the portent of love, and the betrothal, ever hopeful portal to a new life of happiness, are found inseparably linked by sentiment and tradition.

THE WEDDING RING.—While there is no exact history of the origin of the wedding ring, it is believed to have evolved from the older betrothal ring. The earliest record of the wedding ring appears in Egyptian literature. The idea fitted in with Egyptian thought, as in hieroglyphics the circle represents eternity. By applying the name to a plain band or circle for the finger, marriage was thus identified with a tie through eternity.

According to tradition, the early Hebrew wedding rings were usually plain gold, without setting They were permitted to be of silver, and even base metals were acceptable. It is apparent that the Jewish wedding ring was of ceremonial or symbolic meaning because it was often too large for wearing as a finger ornament.

The Christian form, on the other hand, has always been the true finger ring, usually of gold, and generally devoid of ornament. The use of the wedding ring among Christians has been traced back to the year 860. It is said that when a marriage settlement had been properly sealed, rings bearing the names of the newly married couple were passed around for inspection among the guests.

There have been many variations of wedding or marriage rings—such as double rings joined by a pivot (gemmal rings), rings set more or less elaborately with gems, and even so-called puzzle rings, in which several individual loops were so shaped as to form together an apparently indivisible ring—but the single unadorned band has been the most common form of wedding ring.

Marriage rings have been made of a great variety of materials. Besides the various metals, such as gold, silver, iron, steel and bronze, wood, rush and leather have also been used. The Romans used iron, which had an appropriate significance because of the traditional strength and durability of this metal. Medieval peasants used circlets of rush, wood or leather because they could afford no better, but they insisted upon some sort of a ring to seal the union. At the beginning, the use of gold bore the association of purity, and its value indicated it as a token of the wealth the husband brought to the consummation of the marriage contract.

Platinum has come into extensive use in later years for wedding rings as in other jewelry, and the wedding ring set with a row, or forming a circle, of small diamonds has had considerable vogue. Among the novelties have been the "Orange Blossom" ring, bringing the symbolism of one of nature's most prolific fruits into association with the marriage, and the "Venus" ring, harking back to the goddess of Love.

Aside from the symbol of unity and eternity associated with the wedding ring, it has been maintained that the finger circlet of marriage developed from the circular fetters or bracelets placed upon the captive woman of primitive times, thus being a symbolic relic (although an unconscious one) of her ancient status of subjection and servitude to the master.

The exchanging of wedding rings has likewise symbolized loss of freedom—the "ball-and-chain" concept, in another form —bondage for the man and subjugation for the woman. These associations of servitude and inferiority undoubtedly sprang in part from the language of the Christian marriage ritual, when it took over the traditionally secular marriage contract. The sacramental view of marriage, with its emphasis on the permanent spiritual union, denotes the surrender of freedom. The use of the phrase "to obey" in the woman's vow, so long a feature of the Christian marriage rite, but now more and more omitted by mutual wish, was a further note of her subjugation to the husband's will.

THE RING FINGER.—Further evidence of the concept of servitude, symbolized in the use of the wedding ring, is indicated by the wearing of the ring on the left hand. From earliest times, the right hand has symbolized power and authority; the left hand, subjection.

The particular digit upon which the ring is worn—the fourth finger—once had special significance. It was thought in ancient times that a certain vein or nerve in the fourth finger of the left hand ran directly to that time-honored seat of the affections— the heart. This significance is no longer known by the great majority of women who wear the ring, and it is known to be an anatomical fallacy. Nevertheless the old custom continues. Many women would consider themselves something less than properly married if they wore the wedding ring on any other finger.

The utilitarian argument has been presented that the fourth

finger is a logical choice because it is guarded by the fingers on either side, that of all the fingers it is the least used, and, furthermore, that the left hand, as the hand less used, is the place of least wear. As in most cases of trying to prove a point, where tradition, sentiment and superstition are involved, this seems like a choice bit of rationalization.

As a matter of fact most fingers of both hands, including the thumbs, have been used for wearing rings. During the Elizabethan period in England, the wedding ring was worn on the thumb, as is shown in portraits of ladies of that time.

BRIDAL CUSTOMS.—It is inevitable that numerous customs should have grown up and centered about the bride, to whom the anticipation of marriage has meant so much. There are bridal showers and hope chests, the preparation of the trousseau and other intimate things for the wedding and honeymoon, the significance of the bridal veil, the now obsolete custom (except among certain savages) of cutting the bride's hair, the bridal escort, and many others.

It is believed that the idea of the "hope chest" grew out of the ancient custom of the dowry, which in turn grew out of the much older custom of marriage by purchase. As the usages of society departed further from their coarser and more sordid beginnings, it became desirable to use symbols or subterfuge for the original practices, so as still to keep something of the traditional past.

Thus the dowry was an indirect way of compensating the bridegroom for the bride-price paid to the parents. It tended to take away the stigma from a transaction that originally had been strictly a business deal—the purchase of the bride. With the passing of marriage by purchase, the bridegroom no longer gave money or goods to the father, but the latter nevertheless furnished the daughter with her dowry.

There is something romantic, comforting and, naturally, *hopeful* about a hope chest, so that the idea survived as a sentimental relic of other days. The old tradition was that for the girl—and she may have begun at a very early age—to make every item of personal finery and household linen that went into the hope chest was to earn everlasting marital happiness.

This belief, of course, originated in a more frugal and thrifty age, when for generation after generation mother taught daughter the virtues of discipline, patience and industry. Father made the chest, mother inspired the daughter with its meaning and traditions, and the handiwork of the daughter constituted its contents. Today, of course, the hope chest is bought in a department store, and its contents generally represents a *pot pourri* from all sources except the handicraft of the owner.

The bridal shower is a custom perhaps centuries old, about which there are related some amusing legends. And like many legends that seem farfetched, or preposterous, they may have some basis of fact. Its merit lies in its being a delightful way for friends and acquaintances to present gifts that would seem too trifling if they were independently presented.

Also intimately concerned with the bride's preparations for marriage is her *trousseau.* The term is from the word *trusse,* meaning a little bundle. It originally constituted the dowry, and with the decline of marriage by purchase, became a tactful way of compensating the bridegroom for the money or goods which he paid to the girl's father. The trousseau, or dowry, was handed over to the daughter as her marriage portion.

At one time it was the privilege of the prospective bridegroom to examine the trousseau in order to determine whether or not in his opinion it was adequate or complete. Not infrequently, we are told, the decision of the suitor depended upon the value of the girl's trousseau. The term then included not only the personal apparel appropriate for her wedding and honeymoon, but also all kinds of household items, such as gold and silver tableware, china, linens, tapestries and what not.

Among the superstitions concerning the trousseau is that it is unlucky to try on any of the wedding garments before the actual day of marriage. A widespread belief prevails that to do so will result in disappointment and unhappiness.

According to the old Grecian custom the sons of a family were not supposed to marry until the daughters had found husbands. To facilitate the marriage of their sisters the brothers made it a point to help provide their trousseaux. Such is brotherly love!

THE BRIDAL VEIL.—The veil, of all the bride's marriage outfit, has special symbolic significance, and is still the most conspicuous feature of her dress at a formal wedding. There are various reasons advanced to account for this old and widespread custom. It is said to have originated in ancient times as a symbol of the bride's submission to the husband.

Credence is given to this opinion by the analogous custom of sisters in ecclesiastical orders, who universally wear veils as a symbol of their submission to the absolute authority of their religious order. The analogy to the bride or marriage is further indicated by the fact that the sisters are said to be "Brides of Christ", or "married to God" (i.e., to the service of God).

The veil is unquestionably a symbol of submission. This thought, however, is far from the mind of the modern bride as she marches serenely to the altar, draped in yards and yards of the symbolic vestment of bygone centuries.

Among peoples of the Near East and elsewhere, it was and still is in some cases customary to keep the bride hidden from her future husband until the day of the wedding. On this occasion, he goes through the solemn ceremony of uncovering the face. Great must be the surprise that meets his eyes after the long months, or even years, of wondering and anticipating what this moment would bring forth. How often delight? How often disappointment?

THE BRIDESMAIDS.—Again, in the matter of the bridesmaids, we find the origin of the custom in the pretense to struggle, as a survival of the time of marriage by capture, or its immediately succeeding period. This was considered the modest and maidenly thing to do.

There is a great mass of evidence from the marriage customs of peoples all over the world—which will be referred to in greater detail in the chapter on *Marriage by Capture*—of the simulation by the bride of struggle against conquest by the groom.

Fitting into this allegory, the bridesmaids may be considered a modification or survival of the bride's militant attendants, assigned to protect her from the impending fate that awaits. Certainly, in formal marriages, especially church weddings, the bride has an impressive escort, and there seems to be a conspiracy to keep the bride and groom apart until they meet at the altar.

It has been suggested, less convincingly, we believe, that the bridesmaids had their origin in the old Roman custom of having ten witnesses at the solemn marriage ceremony. On this theory, the bridesmaids developed from the ancient practice of having the required witnesses, usually friends of the bride's family. This hypothesis completely overlooks the common symbolism that runs through the marriage ceremonies of almost all peoples, whether or not there has been any traditional Roman influence. It does not account for the numerous devices tending to simulate the evasion or reluctance of the bride in connection with the completion of the rites.

Other customs have had long vogue in various parts of the world, some having become passé because of a more enlightened viewpoint, and others having become almost unrecognizable because of symbolic representation. Cutting the bride's hair, for instance, was a widespread ancient practice. This was doubtless associated with the idea that newly married women should be deprived of their principal charm, so as to make them unattractive to other men.

The cutting of the hair also symbolized the bride's submission and subjugation to the husband; as the identical practice in ecclesiastical orders symbolizes the submission of the novitiate to the authority of the order. In male religious orders a similar symbolism is found in either clipping the hair completely off the head, or shaving a so-called "crow's nest" on the crown of the head. In the modern marriage the symbolism of the bride's submission is accomplished, without the sacrifice of her charms, by the use of the veil.

Among the Egyptians, it was the custom to tie up the bride's hair upon the conclusion of the wedding ceremony. The practice also prevailed in ancient Britain, the bride going to the wedding with her hair hanging loosely, signifying freedom, and after the ceremony, the hair was bound up as a sign of her subjugation. This was a desirable modification of the older custom of shearing off the hair, for while it symbolized the surrender of freedom, it did enable the bride to keep her "crowning glory," which must have contributed to the maintenance of her integrity as a personality.

In ancient Japan, where heavy eyebrows were considered one of woman's greatest charms, the brows were shaved off at the time of marriage, thus presenting the physical evidence of the wife's new status of subordination to her lord and master. The position of women in oriental life was and largely is one of accepted subjugation anyway, so this merely identified her as a married woman, as distinguished from her unmarried sisters.

THE BRIDEGROOM AND HIS TRADITIONS.—A groom no less than a bride is also identified with an assortment of traditional practices. He has his best man, and if the wedding is a formal one, the groomsmen. He is permitted to have, and if he fulfils all the formalities, he is expected to give, a final bachelor's dinner.

In modern times, of course, he is subordinated and almost lost sight of in the focusing of interest and attention upon the bride and her activities. In contrast to the self-assurance and poise of the bride, he is invariably nervous and evinces the attitude of having consciously, or self-consciously, resolved to see the thing through. It is not without reason that the competent, experienced clergyman carries as standard equipment for all wedding ceremonies a spare wedding ring, unobtrusively to slip into service when and if the absent-minded groom should mislay, lose or forget the ring that seals the nuptial bond.

The best man, like so many of the mainstays of the ceremonial wedding, is considered a relic of marriage by capture. When the primordial bridegroom started out to capture a bride he was usually accompanied by an able-bodied friend who intercepted the pursuit by the girl's kinsmen or protector.

Groomsmen, likewise, were originally attendants of the stalking bridegroom when he needed a small contingent to cover his adventure and escape, instead of depending upon his one strong-armed aid—the forerunner of the best man.

We are told that in medieval times the groomsmen were

known as *bride knights*. Thus, it would seem that with the disappearance of the original purpose of these stalwarts, the custom of having them was retained, but their function was diverted to another ceremonial use. They now served the bride, led her to the church, accompanied her to the altar, and after the ceremony relinquished her to the groom.

As a matter of fact, this symbolism appears to suggest a survival from marriage by purchase. A delegation from the bride's family, under the latter arrangement, accompanied the bride from her home to the place of the ceremony, saw that the terms of the contract were carried out in all details and, this accomplished, turned her over to the husband-to-be.

The name "bridegroom" has been attributed to the custom among various peoples of having the newly married man, on his wedding day, wait at table on his bride. "Groom" signified one serving in a menial position. Thus, "bridegroom" was one who served the bride. The term may have a still more literal meaning.

It is said that the custom of the bachelor dinner originated in Sparta. The bridegroom in that country customarily entertained his friends at supper on the eve of the wedding. The event was known as the "men's mess." The widespread practice of this custom, however, indicates that it may have started spontaneously in many lands, as so many early customs seem to have done. Well it might, as it is only natural for a group of friends to be invited to a little stag party at which the bridegroom-to-be bids farewell as a bachelor to his old cronies.

MISCELLANEOUS WEDDING CUSTOMS.—Among the early Anglo-Saxons, before the Church made it compulsory for the marriage to be performed by a priest, certain secular marriage vows were repeated and certain rites were performed, out of which developed the traditional rites and ceremonies of the present day. The bride was taken "for fairer or fouler, for better or worse, for richer or poorer." She promised, among other things, to be "buxom and bonny" to her future husband.

The ceremony was a simple but solemn, self-administered rite, requiring no clerical intermediary. After the mutual pledge, the bridegroom put the ring in turn on each of the fingers of the bride's left hand. At the first he would say, "In the name of the Father," at the second, "In the name of the Son," at the third, "In the name of the Holy Ghost." Upon reaching the fourth and final ring finger, he said simply, "Amen," and the wedding ceremony was finished. The Church, as well as the State, recognized the validity and legality of this form of marriage.

It was an age of comparative simplicity. Marriage was a fundamental way of life, and it was necessary to make provisions for its fulfilment with the simple means at hand. And yet we recognize in their homely pledges and ritual the essential features of the marriage ceremony that have come down through the centuries, a few obsolete words only being changed. The orthodox Quakers, staunch individualists always, have continued this practice of solemnizing their own marriage without benefit of clergy, requiring only witnesses to attest the ceremony.

BRIDAL FLOWERS.—Orange blossoms have been carried by brides and associated with weddings from time immemorial, and many are the legends relating to this bloom and its fruit. As a tree that blooms and bears concurrently, and in all seasons, the analogy to fruitfulness is obvious. One good trait calling for another, the blossoms soon came to portend good luck and happiness (which, after all, were synonymous with fertility in the long ago). Today, perhaps, the good luck portent is cherished, but the original motive is forgotten.

The use of the orange blossom as a bridal flower is said to have been introduced into Europe by the returning Crusaders. It was customary to use sprigs of the blossoms as a crown on the bridal veil, a practice of Saracenic origin. Spenser and Milton interpreted the orange as the "golden apple" presented to Jupiter by Juno on their wedding day.

Lilies-of-the-valley and roses have likewise been favorite wedding flowers, their delicacy and fragrance making them especially appealing to the bride. By tradition the red rose has been dedicated to Venus, and is a symbol of love, joy and beauty. There is also the mythological legend that Cupid gave a rose to Hippocrates to bribe him on his celebrated oath, not to reveal the indiscretions of Venus.

The ancients favored the myrtle which, because of its enduring freshness, they considered the flower of the gods, and was used by them to symbolize constancy in duty and affection.

The flower girl of today's formal wedding harkens back to medieval times. It was the custom for two little girls, preferably sisters, dressed identically and carrying garlands of wheat, to walk before the bride in the marriage procession. This symbolism presaged the fruitfulness of the union and an abundance of happiness.

The throwing of the bridal bouquet is doubtless a substitute for the old custom of scuffling for the bride's garter. In France in the early fourteenth century it was considered a lucky omen to secure the bride's garter, and there was a general rush for it at the conclusion of the wedding ceremony. Notwithstanding that brides considerately left one garter dangling where it could readily be reached, they were often injured or roughly handled in the scramble.

"Stocking throwing" directly succeeded the contest for the

garter. As stockings, however, are not among the easiest and most convenient things to remove and cast to the wedding guests for luck, some inspired bride thought of throwing her bridal bouquet as a substitute. This custom has come down through the centuries. Tradition says that the lucky maiden who catches the bouquet will be the next to marry.

THE SYMBOLISM OF RICE.—The custom of throwing rice, or other grain, after a departing bridal couple goes back to very ancient times and is almost worldwide. Rice is traditionally symbolic of fertility or productiveness, and its use at weddings evidences the wish of fruitfulness for the union.

Among peoples to whom rice was not available, wheat, corn, or other grain served the same purpose, the symbol of fecundity. The ancient Greeks were accustomed to pour flour and sweetmeats over the bride and groom as an expression of a wish for an abundance of all that is good and sweet and desirable. Fruits and nuts have likewise been widely used, especially in the Mediterranean countries, as a symbol of fruitfulness.

In India the throwing of rice can be traced from its earliest literature down to the present day. The poet Kalidasa describes how Prince Aja and his bride, sitting on a golden chair, were strewn with wet grains of barley, first by young Brahmans, then by the King and all his relatives, and finally by noble women.

It was the custom in seventeenth-century England to cast wheat over the head of the bride when she came from church. In the north of England one of the oldest inhabitants of the neighborhood, who has been stationed on the threshold of the bride's new home, throws a plateful of short-bread over her head, so that it falls outside. A scramble ensues among the

friends of the married couple for the pieces, as it is deemed
very fortunate to get a piece of the short-bread. In Gloucester-
shire, at the beginning of the eighteenth century, a large cake
was broken over the heads of the couple.

In northeastern Scotland, when the bride passed over the
threshold, there was held over her head a sieve containing
bread and cheese, which were distributed among the guests or
sometimes scattered around her, in which case there was a
scramble by the young folks to secure a piece. At times an
oatmeal cake was broken over her head, and in later days a
thin cake of short-bread, called the bride-cake, was substituted
for it. This, too, was distributed among the guests, who carefully preserved it, particularly the unmarried.

Variations of these customs persist to this day in England,
Scotland and Ireland. They are of course closely related to the
throwing of rice or grain, ingredients from which the objects
thrown are made. The sieve, of which frequent use is made in
marriage ceremonies, is also regarded as a symbol of fecundity.

Among more primitive savages, the throwing of rice is
thought to have originated in the desire to appease evil spirits
and keep them from doing injury to the bridal pair. It was the
primitive belief that evil spirits were always present at a marriage, so food was offered to propitiate these unseen malignant
influences.

Numerous devices have been employed to drive demons and
wicked genii from the house where the wedding takes place,
and from the nuptial bed. In old Russia, doors, windows and
chimneys were tightly closed at a wedding in order to keep
out witches. Shooting off guns and fireworks to remove the
power of evil spirits is an ancient practice of people as far removed as the Southern European and the Chinese.

Other primitives offer rice as an inducement to the soul of

the bridegroom to remain with the bride. A widespread belief prevails in Celebes that the soul of the bridegroom, unless bribed, may fly away at marriage and never return. Rice is thus scattered over him to prevent the flight of his fickle soul.

Even the act of eating rice together out of a common bowl constitutes marriage among some primitives. Among nearly all savages the function of eating together symbolizes friendship, kinship and peace. To eat with a stranger automatically made him a kin. Eating together out of the same bowl or dish signified the closest possible relationship, a spiritual or physical union, or marriage. Marriages generally in some of the Malayan and neighboring communities are completely carried out by the mutual eating of rice.

The idea that eating or drinking together signifies an essential part, or even the whole, of the marriage ceremony is widely entertained. In Japan the traditional wedding ceremony in its entirety consisted of drinking wine together, exchanging cups nine times, when the rites were completed. Among the Jews, the bride sips from a goblet of wine and gives it to the bridegroom, who, after drinking from it, throws it down and breaks the glass. This act may symbolize that the husband and wife share something in common, of which no other person may partake.

The breaking of dishes, glass vessels, eggs and various other objects is common in marriage ceremonies. The origin of the custom is believed to be in the notion that malignant spirits are thus driven off. Some primitives consider it a magic act to make child-bearing easy. The shattering of a glass, or analogous article, is sometimes said to represent the bride's loss of virginity; also to insure the easy consummation of the marriage. As we have seen, customs continue long after their original motive has been forgotten.

THROWING THE SHOE.—The casting of sandals, shoes and slippers at bridal couples is one of the most common of all practices. The throwing of shoes may represent the battle between the bride's kinsmen and tribesmen, and the bridegroom's party which is carrying her off. Westermarck here sees a defense against malign spirits and other evil influences.

The shoe has also been acknowledged from ancient times as a symbol of authority. Its evidence at weddings as an object to shower the bridal couple may well combine the symbolization of transfer of possession and authority, with the significance already mentioned.

The Assyrians and Hebrews, when closing a bargain, gave a sandal as a token of good faith and to signify the transfer of property. The Egyptians exchanged sandals to indicate that property had been transferred or authority granted. Symbol of possession was shown by flinging a sandal upon a piece of property newly acquired. Thus:

> Upon the land of Edom do I cast my shoe.
> *Psalms* 60:8; 108:9

In old Britain it was the custom for the father to give his new son-in-law one of the bride's shoes, in token of the transfer of authority. The bride was at once made cognizant of the change by a tap on the head given with the shoe. For his part the husband took an oath to treat his wife well. If he failed to do so, she might leave him, but the law and public opinion of the time gave him considerable license.

Among the Arabians, as with many peoples of the East, it was once customary for a man to have first right to marry his cousin—a survival of endogamy, or marrying within a close family or tribal group. He was not required to marry her, but anyone seeking to do so had first to obtain his permission. If he relinquished his right to marry his cousin, he said, "She was my slipper. I have cast her off." Stripped of its symbolism, this statement meant: "I had first right to her as my cousin, but I have given up that right."

THE WEDDING CANOPY.—A wedding custom peculiar to a number of peoples is the canopy erected over the heads of the bride and groom. At Hebrew weddings it is the practice to cover the bridal couple with a square vestment of this kind, flowing with pendants. The canopy, or *chuppah,* is held over the heads of the couple by four intimate friends. Many Jewish marriages are still celebrated under the canopy.

In towns of Palestine and Egypt, the bride is described as walking under a canopy, escorted on either side by a man with a drawn sword. The protector symbolized here indicates a survival from the age of marriage by purchase—the kinsmen delivering the bride in accordance with the prearranged bargain.

Anciently, the bride occupied a canopied litter in the marriage procession. In other cases the canopied area was the actual compartment to which the couple retired when the wedding had been solemnized to consummate the union.

A similar custom prevailed among the Anglo-Saxons who utilized a "care-cloth." Remnants of this custom, and practices associated with it, are said to have survived in Britain until the reign of Henry VIII.

In some of the Teutonic countries of old, before a marriage was regarded as legally valid, it was necessary to prove that the couple had been together under the same blanket. The bride and bridegroom therefore went to bed together in the presence of the required witnesses. This custom survived in many localities until quite modern times.

In the Scandinavian countries and in France, a square piece

of cloth (in Sweden called *pāll;* in France, *carré*) was held over the bride and bridegroom at the benediction. This practice was continued in Swedish-speaking communities in Finland until recent times.

Among other peoples, the custom of introducing a coverage is thought to have originated in antiquity in connection with the belief in sympathetic magic. It indicated a particular care to protect the bride or groom against dangers from above. Thus, in China, when the bride ascends the bridal sedan she wears a hat of paper, and an old woman who has sons and grandsons holds an umbrella. Male children are highly desired in China, and girls traditionally unwanted; so we see the symbolism of cajoling the spirits in favor of male offspring by employing the old woman who had been signally honored with sons and grandsons.

Gifts in Courtship and Marriage.—The giving and receiving of presents are intimately bound up with the traditions of courtship and marriage. Among primitive peoples the tendering of gifts, and the expectation of receiving gifts, are elementary emotional responses. Even the distinction between making a gift and surrendering ownership of the object given may be hazy in the savage mind. Hence, we have the "Indian giver". Young children evince the same trait—to give a thing, with a string of ownership attached.

Gifts are made primarily to please or appease the recipient, and to win his or her favor. It is therefore natural that gift-making should occupy an important place in the role of courtship. This was probably true in the time when courtship was no romantic adventure; when, in fact, what passed for courtship as a prelude to marriage was largely a matter of physical force or purchase.

In any event, the tendency of gift-making fosters a feeling

of friendliness. The savage recognizes it as the quickest and surest way to win one's favor. And it is only necessary to win a person's favor when the attitude of the person is uncertain or antagonistic. When he or she is friendly it is no longer necessary to give or appease. The logic of the thing is elementary and readily grasped by the primitive mind—whether in the savage or the immature civilized individual.

Even during the period of marriage by capture, there was the necessity or the desirability of appeasing the indignation or vanity of the captured bride in an effort to live in something approaching amicable relations, as they were then understood. There was also the possibility of making a post-marital gift to the stolen bride's father to calm his wrath. This practice could easily have led to the succeeding practice of marriage by purchase—making a gift with the expectation of winning the daughter in return, or conducting an outright bargain for her, calling it a gift, if you will. Primitive people had more gift-sense than purchase-sense, anyway. The real meaning of purchase came with the establishment of private property on a solid basis and with it the responsibility of ownership.

Among the North American aborigines, when the young brave wished to court an Indian maiden he presented gifts, not to her, but to her father. If the gifts were accepted by the father, the betrothal was considered sealed. Again a form of marriage by purchase.

A similar custom prevailed among the Japanese people. The sending of specified gifts by the young man to the girl's parents was an important part of the ceremony. When the gifts were received and accepted, the marriage contract was considered effective. Neither party could then withdraw. There are other variations of this practice, in some cases the mere exchange of gifts constituting the entire marriage ceremony.

Today, in our Western World, the making of gifts likewise is an important feature of courtship and marriage; but no longer from the groom to the bride's parents, except as one friend or in-law to another, because the period of marriage by purchase is long past, and the relics of it that remain are otherwise symbolized in the ceremony.

Good judgment and the recognized rules of etiquette now govern the custom of giving presents by the various parties in connection with courtship and marriage. In any event, the one who makes a gift on these occasions, whether it be the bride or the groom, or a relative or friend of the bride, is carrying on a tradition whose origin is lost in the mists of time.

Wedding Superstitions That Linger.—Superstitions concerning weddings and marriage are associated with all peoples and all cultures. Many of them have been vital enough to come down through the ages to the present day. Few are the modern brides who will ignore all of them in making their wedding plans. Some of these associations are merely quaint rhymes or fanciful prose sayings; others are sentiments ingrained into the legends and lore of all civilized people. No treatment of the subject would be complete without mentioning the following superstitions, which still command attention, if only, in some cases, because they are constantly repeated:

If you marry on Wednesday you will be happy; if you marry on Friday or Saturday you will be unhappy.

The prospects for the whole week have been indicated in quatrain form as follows:

> Monday for wealth, Tuesday for health,
> 　Wednesday best day of all;
> Thursday for crosses, Friday for losses—
> 　Saturday, no luck at all.

A double wedding means unhappiness to one of the couples.

It is bad luck to try on a wedding gown before the ceremony.

To lose the wedding ring is an omen of unhappiness.

A bride to be happy should step over the church sill with her right foot.

The bride is the first to cut the wedding cake. If anyone else cuts into the cake first, the bride's happiness and prosperity are cut into.

June is the traditionally lucky month in which to marry. Incidentally, it is the month of more weddings than any other.

The bride is advised to wear "something blue", a sentiment said to have been carried down from the ancient Israelites which still commands popular notice. The Israelite brides were bidden to put upon the shoulders of their fringed garments a "ribband of blue"—blue being the color of purity, love and fidelity. This thought has been perpetuated in the couplet:

> Something old and something new,
> Something borrowed and something blue.

The weather is a factor that has not been overlooked! "Happy is the bride the sun shines on," is an adage of old that is still repeated. Even this seemingly trite comment has a logical basis in the language of symbolism. The fertilizing, life-sustaining power of the sun was recognized by primitive man. It was therefore an omen of happiness, a harbinger of fruitfulness, when the sun shone upon the bride on her nuptial day. The Hindu bride was expected to rise early on the day of her wedding and look into the face of the sun. In certain parts of Asia it was the custom for the bride and groom to greet the rising sun together on the wedding morn.

THE WEDDING CAKE.—The wedding cake is doubtless a development of the primitive practice of eating a special food as part of the marriage rites. Food and the wedding ceremony have been almost inseparable, and in certain instances, as we have seen, the partaking of food or wine together under a certain specified formula has constituted the entire marriage ritual. Among primitive peoples, eating together symbolized kinship and evidenced one of the strongest ties of life.

It is probable that the modern wedding cake, to consider it in its specialized form, is directly descended from the Roman *confarreatio,* a marriage ceremonial employed by the old patrician families, at which a particular kind of cake was used. At these marriage feasts, the cake of *confarreation* was broken over the bride's head as a symbol of fruitfulness and plenty. Each of the guests took away a piece of the cake to insure plentifulness for himself or herself.

We have the survival of this custom to the present day in providing pieces of the wedding cake neatly packed in small boxes and tied with white ribbon, for the convenience of the guest.

Some of the American Indians used a bride cake in marriage feasts. The Iroquois had a special kind of meal cake, made by the bride and presented to the groom, which played an important part in the marriage ceremony. Traces of the custom still remain.

The early English provided great baskets of small dry crackers for their marriage festivities. Each guest took one home. The remainder was distributed to the poor. It later became the custom to bring to the wedding small richly spiced buns which were piled in a great mound on the table. Custom called for the bride and groom to attempt to kiss each other over this mound, and if they succeeded they were assured lifelong happiness and prosperity.

We are told that the highly decorated wedding cake of the present day was the ingenious idea of a French cook who was traveling in England. Attending a wedding festival, he observed the inconvenience of piling a great number of small spiced cakes into one mound, and conceived the idea of icing the mound into one solid mass. This, at least, is the legend of the birth of the modern wedding cake.

A custom that once had considerable vogue, and is still extant, is to have a ring baked in the cake. According to the superstition, the person who gets the ring will be the next to marry.

THE HONEYMOON.—The honeymoon is essentially a period of seclusion of the couple, or absence from the familiar habitat, following the marriage. It is considered a relic of the remote time of marriage by capture, when it was necessary for the groom to remain in hiding with his bride until the search for her was given up.

The word derives from the custom which prevailed among some of the northern European countries for the newly married couple to drink metheglin or mead—a kind of wine made from honey—for a period of a month after the marriage. Thus, we have the combination of "honey" and "month" (moon). It seemed appropriate, too, to associate honey with a period of so much sweetness and delight for the parties concerned. According to tradition, Attila the Hun, once the scourge of Europe, drank so much mead at his wedding feast that he died from the over-indulgence.

Long after the period of marriage by capture, when love and romance and frequent elopement entered the picture, it often became necessary for the bride and groom to remain in hiding for a while until the parental wrath cooled down, and the olive-branch of forgiveness was extended. So the traditional honeymoon flight once more became a literal reality.

Aside from the historic necessity and the modern conventional desire to make the honeymoon a hide-out or a journey, certain peoples have made the seclusion of the newly married couple an integral part of the ceremonial rites. The Bulgarians commonly shut up the bride and groom for a week, during which time they were not permitted to see visitors nor to visit others. Other peoples have followed the same practice for various lengths of time, from two or three days and nights to ten days or more.

There is a common folk-saying that just as the moon begins to wane when it has reached its full, so does the honeymoon, and when the extreme of affection and love has been reached, then the turning point has come to a less violent emotional relationship.

As we are now living in a mobile, travel-conscious age, the modern honeymoon, of course, is usually spent in travel or sojourning at a romantic spot. Whether the taste and purse determine upon Niagara Falls or Honolulu, or some other point, the pilgrimage is nevertheless spiritually of a piece with the withdrawal of the primordial groom and his bride to a distant hide-out, safely away from all contact with alien, new-found kinfolk.

THE SHIVAREE.—It is a custom in many small communities in various parts of this country to serenade newly married couples in a rather boisterous, rowdy fashion, with the beating of tin-pans and kettles, miscellaneous noises, catcalls and by other hilarious means. If the village or town has a fife-and-drum corps, and the eminence of the couple seems to warrant it, this more formal serenading may also be provided.

This practice, called shivareeing, is of Latin origin and was introduced into America by the French people of Canada and Louisiana. It is an adaptation of an old French custom, practiced in rural France, where it is called the *charivari*.

It is said that this form of serenade was at one time universal in the ancient provinces that became modern France, and it was the custom to *charivari* all newlyweds. Being obviously an undignified procedure, its practice in the course of time became restricted to marriages among the peasantry, who were not so sensitive to the coarseness of the horseplay. It was esteemed an admirable vehicle for harassing unpopular marriages, for annoying newly wedded couples who had in any way defied or neglected the conventions, or to embarrass widows and widowers who remarried too soon to conform to what might be considered the proprieties.

The American version of the shivaree, however, is characteristically a harmless, playful outburst of the local youth, usually free of any malice. Its most disconcerting feature is the din and noise produced. As practiced in the childhood home community of the present writer the principal object of the leaders of the shivaree was to continue the hilarious serenading until the marriage party threw out some money, usually silver coins in the amount of a dollar or two. The resultant scrimmage for the coins broke up the shivaree.

WEDDING ANNIVERSARIES.—The celebrating of anniversaries has been a popular custom since man began to take note of eventful dates in the course of his life. At an earlier age, when the burdens of life were more arduous, the hours of labor longer and the routine more tedious, the occasion for a celebration of some kind was an opportunity not to be overlooked. It offered an interlude for merry-making in the serious business of life. Many of these festive days were connected with seed-time, harvest-time, the changing seasons and other important events in the cycle of nature.

In the realm of personal and family life, the wedding anniversary became a favorite occasion for celebration and merrymaking. Gifts were presented to commemorate the event, and it became a tradition to associate a certain article or material with the particular anniversary. Following are the customary wedding anniversaries as they are now generally accepted.

The First Anniversary	Paper
The Fifth Anniversary	Wood
The Tenth Anniversary	Tin
The Twelfth Anniversary	Silk
The Fifteenth Anniversary	Crystal
The Twentieth Anniversary	China
The Twenty-fifth Anniversary	Silver
The Thirtieth Anniversary	Ivory
The Thirty-fifth Anniversary	Jade or Coral
The Fortieth Anniversary	Ruby
The Forty-fifth Anniversary	Sapphire
The Fiftieth Anniversary	Gold
The Fifty-fifth Anniversary	Emerald
The Sixtieth Anniversary	Diamond

All lists of this kind, of course, are somewhat arbitrary, and in more recent years they have been considerably augmented and commercialized. The tradition, however, is a time-honored one, although through popular custom the silver and golden wedding anniversaries are celebrated more than any others.

CHAPTER III

Kissing Customs

ORIGIN OF THE KISS.—The contact of the lips in the kiss is an inspired discovery and development of the Western World. Strange as it may seem to us of European heritage, the kiss was unknown in many parts of the world until Western explorers, travelers and missionaries carried their customs to the remote parts of our planet. Even today it is not the preferred form of intimate expression of love or affectionate greeting among most peoples in Asia, Africa, the Eskimo domains, Polynesia and other distant lands where the aboriginal customs still hold sway.

Authorities tell us that the impulse to kiss is not innate to man; that it has been developed gradually, and has only acquired by degrees a relation to the erotic sphere. Havelock Ellis regards the love-kiss as a development from the primitive maternal kiss and from the nursing of the infant at the mother's breast, which are customary even where the erotic kiss is unknown. Out of these maternal caresses grew the kiss of love and affection, of devotion and reverence, that we know today.

Like many other quirks of human nature, the development of the kiss indicates a curious paradox in the pattern of human actions. Kissing as a manner of showing affection is said to have been comparatively a late development in mankind's repertoire of caresses. Certainly, the custom cannot be traced as a form of affection in antiquity with any degree of positiveness.

In all the Celtic tongues, we are told, there is no word for "kiss". The custom of kissing appears to have been acquired by the Celts long after it became a racial habit of most other Europeans. Homer scarcely knew it, and the Greek poets, faithful portrayers of the customs of their time, seldom mention it.

On the other hand, actions resembling and analogous to the kiss are found among a great many animals. Birds use their bills as a form of caress. Even snails and certain insects caress antennae. The dog who licks his master is expressing the physical attribute of the kiss, and perhaps the canine equivalent of the sentimental. Dogs also lick each other as a form of greeting. Man's closest relations in the animal world, the simians, are addicted to kissing. But, then, the subhuman primates are confirmed experimentalists and notorious sensualists, so they may have discovered its merits from the application of their tireless curiosity.

Anatomically, the kiss is the ideal mode of expression of love and affection, as the lips are the seat of a particularly sensitive area, or erogenous zone, especially subject to erotic stimulation. As a stimulus of love, of course, the kiss must carry the fire and force of conviction. Byron, himself no tyro in the arts of love, recognized this when he wrote:

> A long, long kiss, a kiss of youth and love,
> And beauty, all concentrating like rays
> Into one focus kindled from above;
> Such kisses as belong to early days,
> Where heart and soul and sense in concert move,
> And the blood's lava, and the pulse a blaze,
> Each kiss a heart-quake—for a kiss's strength,
> I think it must be reckoned by its length.

A Pledge of Love.—The kiss has a special significance as a pledge of love, or, as has been more euphoniously expressed, *the seal with which lovers plight their troth*. It has also been defined by the physiologist Burdach as the symbol of the union of souls, analogous to the galvanic contact between a positively and a negatively electrified body.

Even those who habitually treat the kiss lightly, perhaps scarcely less casual than a handshake, reserve a special place in their emotional potential for the kiss of fealty and affection.

In some communities, it was, and still is among certain people, considered improper for a girl to permit a man to kiss her until he has asked her to marry him, and she has accepted. In our present modern world, this extreme attitude is looked upon as a provincial one, more typical of another age.

The nuptial kiss of the bride and groom is an important feature of the marriage ceremonial. Aside from that, however, kissing the bride has had special significance among various peoples, and has been widely prevalent throughout Europe and among people of European derivation. It is still indulged in among all but the most dignified social groups.

Quoting from an old Scottish source, we are told that "the parson who presided over the marriage ceremony uniformly claimed it as his inalienable privilege to have a smack at the lips of the bride immediately after the performance of his official duties." It was firmly believed that the happiness of every bride depended in no small measure upon the pastoral kiss. As the pastor found the duty agreeable, he saw no reason to take issue with this popular belief.

The Scotch, in particular, were much impressed with the importance of the bridal kiss. In some parts of Scotland, after the marriage ceremony, the bride was expected to proceed around the wedding company, attended by her maidens, and kiss every one of the males present. A dish was then passed around, in which those so favored placed some money. This thrifty custom seems limited to Scotland. At Bourges, it was the practice for the brides on coming out of church to embrace all whom they met in the street, and in the province of Marche they were said to do so before the marriage service.

One of the earliest definite instances of kissing as an expression of love and affection is related by Leybard, the famous saint of Tours of the sixth century, who gave his betrothed "a ring, a kiss and a pair of shoes." The symbolism, in the order given, is thus indicated: The ring to bind them together; the kiss to seal the pledge of affection; the shoes, as a sign of his utter subjection to her.

Even in early medieval Europe, it seems probable that the kiss was not widely given as an expression of sexual or erotic sentiment. It appears to have been a refinement of love practiced only by the more cultivated social groups. It is only in a comparatively high stage of civilization that the kiss has been emphasized and cultivated in the art of love. Among rude and uncultivated peoples it was not developed.

Erasmus mentions that when he visited England he found kissing a widely practiced and general form of greeting. Upon his arrival at a house, the visitor kissed his host and hostess, all their children, and even the dog and cat—so relates the great Renaissance scholar.

From a fifteenth-century historian we learn that a young lady of rank in France, at that time, would rise in the midst of divine service, inconveniencing all those about her, in order to kiss on the mouth the cavalier who entered the church at the moment.

France proved a fertile field for the appreciation and development of the kiss, and it was soon firmly established in the pursuits of courtship and love. Montaigne remarked that in his country it was the privilege of any Jack with three lackeys to kiss almost any woman he chose. The dance embrace afforded an excellent opportunity, or excuse, and the popular dance figures were those that introduced a kiss in the proceedings.

Louis XII is stated to have conferred the royal benediction in the form of a kiss on every woman in Normandy. Perhaps that was a pleasant means of building up popularity and entrenching his throne. Today, politicians advance their cause and personal popularity by kissing babies. Kissing for popularity, however, is as old as Absalom.

The example set by France quickly spread over most of Europe. In Russia, not given to inhibitions, the kiss is said to have become epidemic in scope. A kiss from the Czar was esteemed as one of the highest forms of official recognition.

As a contrasting example, let us look at the status of the kiss among the urban Italians of the same period. The osculatory salutation was treated so seriously that if a maiden was kissed by a young man in public, it practically made marriage obligatory. Rowdies frequented the streets, which at best were no place for a young girl unless escorted. Historians of the period tell us that there was always the danger of a subtle sally from amorous eyes, or some familiarity, such as a kiss, from some undesirable admirer or needy youth who wished by this means to force a marriage.

We are told that even church was not a safe refuge for girls unescorted. In Venice young women of the wealthier classes always went to church hidden by long white veils, and accompanied by male escorts, or even armed retainers, according to their circumstances.

Early in the sixteenth century, Pierto Lando, afterwards doge, but then podesta at Padua, ordered his own natural son to be decapitated for the offense of kissing a girl, with whom he was in love, in the public street.

THE KISS AS A SACRED PLEDGE.—In the Eastern World, the kiss was early associated with sacred uses, which seems to account for its practical omission in the sphere of love and affection. The ancient Arabians made their devotions to the gods by a kiss. The house gods were so greeted upon entering and leaving.

There is evidence to indicate that the tactile kiss, whose usage has been our cherished heritage, originated in ancient times in Asia Minor—where the vassal kissed his suzerain and where the kiss of love held some sway, as is gleaned from the Hebraic *Song of Songs*—"Let him kiss me with the kisses of his mouth."

In ancient Rome, too, the kiss indicated the sentiments of reverence and respect far more than those of love. This influence left its impress on the early Christians, to whom it had almost sacramental meaning. It still retains its ancient and sacred significance to a great extent in the practices of both the Eastern and Western Churches. Thus, the kiss is bestowed upon the relics of saints, the foot of the Pope, the hands of bishops, just as the ancients kissed the images of their gods. Kissing the hand or the foot as a mark of homage or respect has been known from the very earliest times.

Even in our secular life, until comparatively recently, the sacredness of the kiss was legally recognized in the form of taking an oath by kissing the Bible, now generally superseded by laying the right hand on the book and raising the left hand. In taking the serious pledge of induction into high political office, the kiss is still sometimes preferred.

Kissing as a form of obeisance also existed among primitives, who did not know its significance in the realm of love—perhaps because love, as we know it, held little or no significance to them. Among some African tribes the natives kiss the ground over which a chief has trod, as a sign of their reverence. The Australian aborigines kissed the ground, or more literally, breathed upon it, as a form of greeting and show of respect. The olfactory sense, incidentally, is closely bound up with the kiss, or its analogous manifestation—such as nose-rubbing, etc.—in many parts of the world.

THE OLFACTORY, OR SMELL-KISS.—The kiss as known to man may involve either the sense of touch or that of smell, occasionally both. Our kiss of European origin is mainly tactile, or related to the sense of touch.

A form of salutation, however, that has much wider vogue throughout the world is the olfactory kiss, involving primarily the sense of smell, although it may at the same time in some instances simulate our tactile kiss. This type of kiss has representation even in Europe, among the Laplanders and the Russian Yakuts, both of Asiatic social heritage. It is the predominant form of kiss in Asia, Africa, Polynesia and other parts of the world, including some of the aborigines of the Americas.

There are variations of the olfactory kiss, but a typical form is practiced in these three phases: (a) the nose is applied to the cheek of the person kissed; (b) there is a long nasal inhalation accompanied by the lowering of the eyelids; (c) followed by a slight smacking of the lips without the application of the mouth to the recipient's cheek. The procedure is predicated on the sense of smell.

It is said that the Chinese who have not become enamored of Western ways consider the European kiss as highly objectionable from the esthetic standpoint, being suggestive of ravenous cannibals. Native mothers in French Indo-China frighten their children by threatening to give them a white man's kiss.

The Chinese regard their form of kiss as an expression of sexuality, appropriate only to lovers. Fathers refrain from kissing their children except when very young, and even mothers rarely indulge in the practice, and then surreptitiously.

In Japanese literature kisses and embraces simply do not exist, as they are unknown as tokens of affection in Nipponese life. Japanese mothers may hug and caress their young children, as mothers do the world over, but after babyhood there is no more hugging and lipping. Except in the case of infants, such actions are regarded as immodest. Girls do not kiss one another; nor do parents kiss or embrace their children after they are able to walk. This is true of all classes.

Among the tribes of southeast India who practice the olfactory kiss, instead of saying to the loved one, "kiss me", it is the custom to say in the native vernacular, "smell me."

Among other variations of olfactory osculation may be mentioned the following: The tribesman on the Gambia in Africa who greets a woman takes her hand and places it to his nose, twice smelling the back of it. The native mothers on the Niger coast rub their babies with cheek, nose and mouth, but do not kiss them. Lovers, likewise, do not kiss, although they cuddle, squeeze and embrace.

In Samoa kissing is analogous to smelling. The North American Eskimo practices only the olfactory kiss, as did the Blackfeet and some other Indian tribes, although kissing of any kind seems to have been unknown to many of the North and South American aborigines, as was also the case among the Dyaks of the Malay archipelago.

The smell kiss is typical of Polynesia. In New Zealand nose-pressing, or the *hongi,* is the native kiss of welcome and sympathy. It is said that in Borneo kissing is a kind of smelling, and the word interpretative of smelling is used to indicate the act. A visitor to that country states he never saw a native kiss a woman. It is always done in private, indicating its voluptuous character.

It has been suggested that the reason the olfactory kiss has prevailed almost exclusively among primitive peoples is that in the lower stage of humanity—as in the animal world—the sense of smell is a much more important factor than it is in the case of civilized man. The love zone of the primitive, as well as his nutritive zone, is more intimately related to his sense of smell. In the life of civilized man, on the other hand, the olfactory sense has been relegated to a relatively unimportant position among the senses. Being farther removed from primordial nature, the sense of smell is not so important as a life-sustaining factor, and its influence diminishes in all spheres of activity.

In civilized man, sight is the paramount esthetic sense with respect to sex, as well as to other phases of his cultural life. It is the first messenger of love. By means of this sense, color and form become the primary media of sexual stimulus. The sense of sight conveys the first total impression of the beloved personality. Sexual interest and attraction are always first dependent upon sight. Of all the factors that enter into the choice of the loved one, the sense of sight is unquestionably supreme.

THE EROTIC SIGNIFICANCE OF THE KISS.—As sexual love has been described by physiologists as a higher, specialized form of tactile sensation, the kiss plays an extremely important role in the refinement of the art of love.

It is impossible even to think of the tender, consummate embrace of two lovers without the lingering rapture of the kiss. But among human beings of baser disposition, the manifestation of their "love" may be no more than a crude expression of the sense of touch.

The kiss sets off the reverberating, electrifying spark of voluptuous sensation that permeates to the innermost parts of our being. It is part and parcel of the love-play that leads normally to the realization of the sexual acme. However innocent a lover's kiss may appear, it is never wholly asexual, and constitutes a stage between desire and possession.

Surfaced by a tissue of full-blooded, sensitive membranes, moistened by the honey of salivary sweetness, shaped at their loveliest into a curvature that has been likened to Cupid's Bow, the lips seem especially contrived by nature for their role of allurement into the labyrinths of love.

In its sensory impulses, the kiss is the most direct prelude and incitement to sexual fulfilment. It is for this reason that restraint and discrimination should be the watchword of those who understand the real meaning and importance of the kiss and hold in high regard the sacredness of the love forces which its casual bestowal may unwittingly release.

THE LOVE-BITE.—It may seem like a contradiction of terms to speak of the "love-bite", but the phrase has a place and a definite meaning in the story of the kiss. It is perhaps an intensification of the tactile kiss under the stress of voluptuous excitement. It is usually playful—a tantalizing, controlled "bite" to increase sexual feeling—but among peoples of ardent temperament and unrestrained impulses, it may assume the proportions of mild or extreme sadism.

The love-bite is essentially a primitive expression of sexual ardor, more typical of hardy-living, lusty peoples, but it is not unknown among highly cultivated individuals. It may be playfully enacted in connection with the familiar expression, "I could eat you," or the wild kisses of passionate love may take the form of uncontrolled frenzy.

Among the Southern Slavs, it is said the custom of biting one another is general. This indicates the presence of mutual masochistic tendencies, as evidenced by the patience with which pain is borne when it has a voluptuous tinge, as well as sadistic propensities.

Its place in the normal fulfilment of ardent love is indicated by the heroine of Kleist's *Penthesilea,* who aptly remarks: "Küsse (kissing) rhymes with Bisse (biting), and one who loves with the whole heart may easily confound the two."

It has been suggested that the erotic kiss is a sublimation of the amorous bite; the difference is quantitative rather than qualitative.

KISSING AS A PASTIME.—Kissing as a pastime, modernly known as *petting,* is by no means a modern innovation. The outward forms of old customs change, but inherently there is little difference in the nature of the practice. The twentieth-century automobile, with its comforts and conveniences, has done much to establish "petting" as a household term, and to create the legend of its modernity.

Kissing along the roadside, however, occurred in the horse-and-buggy days, whether known as "spooning" or "mooning"; nor was it exclusively associated with the equestrian-minded. Pedestrians, too, have strolled down lover's lane and its by-ways, have spooned and necked and petted and kissed from time immemorial.

The great Scottish bard of love, Robert Burns, in another era, posed the delicate question whether, "Gin a body meet a body coming through the rye; gin a body kiss a body, need a body cry?"

The answer may be in the length and ardor of the kiss, and

whether it ignited a spark of love that was, well, not wise! Like most of Burns' superb, immortal lines, it is likely that this query was prompted by an amorous episode from the book of his own life. If so, he doubtless knew the answer to his own riddle.

The literature of the Western World is without limit in its treatment of the subject of the kiss, and kissing. It is the inexhaustible theme of popular songs of our time. Stolen kisses, kisses that linger, kisses in the moonlight, kisses in June, kisses any time, anywhere—but kisses, kisses!

The motion picture has been a worldwide medium for publicizing the technique of the Hollywood kiss. Some State Boards of Censorship put a stop-watch on the film to make certain that the endurance of the osculation does not exceed the prescribed limit of time fixed by the Board. The communion of lips that does not linger beyond the specified time is deemed an innocent kiss that may properly be seen by all and sundry. The one that extends over the time limitation is banned as destructive to public morals!

Kissing as a forfeit is a part of many old games and customs. Catching a girl standing under the mistletoe is one of the most familiar instances. In colonial New England, if a man succeeded in gaining possession of a girl's gloves, according to custom, he could claim a kiss as forfeit for their return. There is an old English custom analogous to this, although acting somewhat in reverse: If a man is caught sleeping and is kissed by a woman, he is obliged to present her with a pair of gloves.

There are a number of so-called kissing games which were popular in the parlor entertainment era, in which the kiss takes place as a forfeit at some point in the game. Such games as "Post Office," "Pillow," "Drop the Handkerchief," and "In a Well" are representative of this group.

In the game of whist that was popular before its almost total eclipse by contract bridge, it was the custom in some circles that if the four cards played to a trick ever fell in the sequence of ace (one), deuce (two), three and four, the person playing the fourth card might claim a kiss of the dealer—if the dealer happened to be someone he wished to kiss!

Some of the old English folksongs, such as "The Farmer in the Dell," "King William Was King James's Son," and "The Needle's Eye" used as ring-games by children, have kissing as an integral part.

The old nursery remedy of "Kiss it and make it well" proves quite efficacious in drying the tears and assuaging the minor hurts and bruises of babyhood. Incidentally, it seems a natural instinct to put a hurt finger or hand to the mouth.

THE PLATONIC KISS.—There is the salutation of the kiss as a form of greeting, which may be either casual or formal, among men. This kiss, which may be given on both cheeks, or either cheek, is prevalent in France and certain other parts of continental Europe. It is often part of the greeting in formal ceremonies when eminent dignitaries meet. In itself, it probably has little more significance than the conventional handshake of the English-speaking world, but is an added gesture, expressive of the vivacity and effervescence of the Latin temperament. In any event it may be considered a platonic, or passionless, kiss. Probably in the case of the formal ceremonial salutation, particularly among high political dignitaries, it may sometimes turn out to be a Judas-kiss.

In the same countries, kissing among male relatives and intimate friends as a greeting, or even at casual meetings, is quite common. Kissing among adults as a form of greeting in countries of the English-speaking world is almost exclusively restricted to the female sex, or between men and women.

It is also customary in some of the continental European countries, in the more formal social circles, for the gentleman to kiss the lady's hand as a greeting. This form of salutation, which takes the place of the handshake, is sometimes seen in this country when practiced by visiting foreigners. Some of our own repatriated countrymen, after living abroad, may affect the usage, as evidence of their cosmopolitan manner.

KISSING BY CORRESPONDENCE.—No treatise on kissing would be complete without mention of the lover's kiss in the epistle of love. The row of crosses or "x's" at the foot of the letter is as unmistakable as the contact of the lips, if less satisfying. A more sophisticated method, however, for the modern maid to show the seal of her affection is to make it quite literal: Lips well rouged by the lipstick, when pressed to the page of the letter, leave an impression which the recipient will recognize as coming direct from the lips of the loved one.

CHAPTER IV

Bundling

A QUAINT CUSTOM OF COURTSHIP.—Bundling is one of the quaint practices that seems to have had independent existence among alien peoples in widely separated areas of many countries. As is now widely known from the rather amusing treatment of the theme on stage and screen, as well as from more serious presentations, the characteristic feature of the custom is for a man and woman to lie together in bed without undressing. Local traditions, national temperament and other factors introduced variations of one kind or another, including the dividing board, but the identifying feature remained.

It is commonly thought to have been a custom peculiar to early rural New England and some of the other Eastern Atlantic states, but it was not essentially Yankee either as invention or monopoly. The Yankees merely adopted an old custom.

This fallacy with respect to origin is due to some extent to misinformation from old sources, such as Grose's *Dictionary of the Vulgar Tongue,* which defined the practice as follows: *"Bundling*—A man and woman lying on the same bed with their clothes on; an expedient practiced in America on account of a scarcity of beds, where as occasion necessitated, husbands and parents frequently permitted travelers to bundle with their wives and daughters."

Scarcity of beds may have been something of a problem in

early colonial America, but it is doubtful if this had much to do with bundling. It was often necessary to double up, and perhaps triple and quadruple up, in bed in the early days, but this could ordinarily be arranged without bundling travelers indiscriminately with wives and daughters. Public inns also permitted several unassociated guests to sleep together in one bed, and to keep their clothes on for the sake of comfort and warmth—the only stipulation being that they should remove their boots. (Organ-grinders and tinkers slept in the barn.)

The phase of bundling under discussion is that relating to courtship—the practice as it involved the young woman and the young man in their courting days, or more literally *nights,* and as a normal but not inevitable preliminary to marriage.

The rigors of climate, no less than the limitation of household facilities, seem to have been a large factor in the custom, as it prevailed not only in New England and the adjacent states, but throughout the countries of Northern Europe, England, Scotland, Wales, the Netherlands, Scandinavia, Germany and Switzerland, and doubtless other countries of similar culture and climate.

Each country had its major or minor variations, and also its rules governing the ethics of the practice. These latter varied all the way from very strict regulations, with severe penalties for violations, to the greatest possible freedom of conduct.

In Holland, it is said that if the lover exceeded the limits set by custom, he was very harshly dealt with by the people of the village.

In New England the winters are long and cold, and at the period in question candlelight and fuel were not to be wasted. Dwellings generally were far apart. After the young swain had done a hard day's work around his father's farm and went calling on his sweetheart at perhaps a considerable distance, sitting in the chilly, dimly lighted room during the evening was certainly not conducive either to common comfort or romantic thoughts. Under the circumstances, relaxing together fully clothed in bed under a warm New England goose-down quilt was an understandable, and not illogical, thing to do.

Perhaps in some cases, as an observer has stated, the young man has walked ten or more weary miles on a Sunday evening to enjoy the company of his favorite lass. In the few brief hours which would elapse before the morning light should call him again to his homeward trek and his week's toil, was it not the dictate of humanity, as well as of economy, which prompted the old folks to allow the approved and accepted suitor of their daughter to pursue his wooing under the downy coverlet of a good feather bed—ofttimes in the very same room in which they themselves slept—rather than have them sit up and burn firewood and candles uselessly?

In the rural districts, where the practice of bundling chiefly occurred, many, perhaps the majority of the dwellings of early settlers, consisted of one large room, in which the whole family lived and slept. This fact alone would tend to keep abuses of the privilege down to a minimum.

Furthermore, before the intimacy had developed this far, it is likely that the couple were engaged, or it was tacitly understood they were entering that stage of courtship.

It is not very likely that every Tom, Dick and Harry called on successive evenings to bundle with the daughter of the homestead. Bundling was thus more or less a prerogative of the engaged couple, or of the couple who were accepted as courting with matrimonial intentions. In former times, too, the fact of having called at the home of a girl was in itself evidence of serious intentions.

Nevertheless, there were the natural factors of climate,

limited household facilities and hardy living that favored the custom. As evidence of this, it may be stated that bundling took place only in the cold seasons of the year.

Sociologists tell us that the practice in itself was never proof of licentious manners. Generally speaking, the proprieties seem usually to have been observed, although lapses in conduct, human nature being what it is, sometimes occurred.

Bundling was an old institution in both Holland and England, and it is likely that the custom was brought to this country by early settlers—the Dutch in New Amsterdam, and the English in New England, as reference to it goes back to the first settlement.

Early historians began to write upon the subject when the custom was being frowned upon as evidence of rustic coarseness and vulgarity, or downright bad form, although it continued in a decreasing measure long after their words were written. Some treated the matter critically; others heaped sarcasm upon it. Still others blamed the erring ways of a neighboring colony for introducing the custom into their own midst.

Ministers, particularly in the cities and towns, fulminated against the sinful custom. In order to lend discouragement to the practice, the more sophisticated element introduced sofas into the household. The country people thought the new device less proper—a heathen Turkish importation with the connotations of the harem—and maintained there was more sinning on city sofas than on rural beds.

The courts, too, were in due course drawn into the controversy to decide on the legal merits of seduction claims that grew out of the practice. By this time the custom was fast nearing its end, and the notice of the law was but a final gesture to a passing folkway.

Washington Irving, in his *Knickerbocker's History of New York,* humorously attributed the practice to the inventive genius of the Connecticut Yankees, implying that it fostered immorality. He wrote of "the curious device among these sturdy barbarians (the Connecticut colonists), to keep up a harmony of interests and to promote the population. They multiplied to a degree which would be incredible to any man unacquainted with the marvelous fecundity of this young country. This amazing increase may, indeed, be partly ascribed to a singular custom prevalent among them, commonly known by the name of *bundling*—a superstitious rite observed by the young people of both sexes, with which they usually terminated their festivities, and which was kept up with religious strictness by the more bigoted and vulgar of the community.

"This ceremony was likewise, in those primitive times, considered as an indispensable preliminary to matrimony; their courtships commencing where ours usually finish, by which means they acquired that intimate acquaintance with each other before marriage, which has been pronounced by philosophers the sure basis of a happy union. Thus early did this cunning and ingenious people display a shrewdness at making a bargain, which has ever since distinguished them, and a strict adherence to the good old vulgar maxim about 'buying a pig in a poke.'

"To this sagacious custom, therefore, do I chiefly attribute the unparalleled increase of the Yanokie or Yankee tribe; for it is a certain fact, well authenticated by court records and parish registers, that wherever the practice of bundling prevailed, there was an amazing number of sturdy brats annually born unto the state, without the license of the law or the benefit of clergy. Neither did the irregularity of their birth operate in the least to their disparagement. On the contrary, they grew up a long-sided, raw-boned, hardy race of whoreson whalers, wood cutters, fishermen and peddlers; and strapping corn-fed wenches, who by their united efforts tended marvelously toward populating those notable tracts of country called Nantucket, Piscataway and Cape Cod."

Washington Irving was undoubtedly amusing at the expense of being accurate. The Reverend Samuel Peters of the same Connecticut came heartily to the defense both of his state and the custom of bundling, testifying to the modesty and virtue of their women.

The beginning of the decline of bundling seems to have come about in New England and adjacent states in the late eighteenth century, when the more fastidious members of the population began to decry the custom and forbade the practice under their roof. As late as 1776, a clergyman from one of the more conventional towns went into the country and is said to have preached against the unchristian custom of young men and maidens lying together on a bed. Upon leaving the church, he was besieged by the women of the congregation who resented his strictures and their reflections upon themselves and their daughters.

Other defenders of the custom, testifying to the high esteem in which it was held, said there was something satisfying and homey to the domestic instinct in having the old ladies, as often happened, look in before retiring to see that the bundling couple were comfortable, and possibly tuck them in or put on more bed clothes, if necessary.

Most of the old timers who lived through the heyday of the practice and saw its decline insisted "there wasn't any more mischief done in those days than there is now."

Dr. Henry Reed Stiles, in his book on the subject, states that the custom was widely practiced among the Dutch settlers in Pennsylvania, and that traces of it continued down well into the nineteenth century. He cites the case of an old schoolmaster in his teaching experience in Southern Pennsylvania. The schoolmaster used to board around, and when it was not convenient to go to his usual boarding place for the time being, he was accustomed to stop at a tavern kept by an honest old Dutchman.

On one occasion, having asked the landlord if he could stay overnight, he was told he could, and after chatting with his host through the evening, was shown to bed. The landlord set down the candle and had gone out of the room, when the schoolmaster noticed that the only bed in the room was already occupied, and calling to his host, informed him of the fact. He replied over his shoulder: "Oh! dat ish only mine taughter, she won't hurt nopoty," and went on his way.

Visitors, unfamiliar with bundling, uniformly remarked how innocently those accustomed to it looked upon the practice. The open sanction of the custom by the parents and the community must have had the effect of inspiring in the young folks a sense of restraint from what was known to be wrong, and a strong incentive to doing right. There was, too, the close supervision by the elders that was inevitable on account of the limitation of space in the home.

TARRYING.—A somewhat similar custom, known as *tarrying,* is reported as having had a considerable following in certain parts of the colonies concurrently with and subsequent to the reign of bundling. Under this practice, when a young man wished to marry a girl, he made known his intention to the parents. If they were agreeable, he was allowed to tarry with her for one night, in order to pay his court.

At the usual time the parents retired to bed, leaving the

young folks to settle matters as best they could. After having sat up as long as the conventions seemed to require, they got in bed together, but without taking off their underclothes. If the parties were still of the same mind by morning, all was considered well. The banns were published and the marriage took place without delay. If the *tarrying* did not work out to the satisfaction of the couple, they parted, possibly never to see each other again.

The final disappearance of bundling as a social custom in America has been attributed to a number of causes. First and foremost, of course, was the gradual elimination of the principal factors which did so much to start it and make it popular. That is, housing and living facilities were much improved, dwellings became less isolated as the country became more thickly populated, and with the change in these physical elements, there gradually came a change of mind toward the practice.

With the development of a more fastidious and conventional viewpoint, what had been looked upon as a homely and harmless custom and an evidence of warm-hearted hospitality became an anachronism—something not quite decent or respectable, and at the same time a little ridiculous, as the many barbs of derision and ridicule that were hurled at it fully reveal.

BUNDLING IN OTHER LANDS.—The custom in England, Scotland and Northern Continental Europe, while much older than in its transplanted form in America—having been a social inheritance from feudal times—nevertheless passed out in much the same manner. It had outlived its usefulness and its time.

Not only has bundling been traced to numerous countries and provinces in the feudal ages—being distinctly a practice of rural people, of rude social status—but Professor William Graham Sumner states that the Christians in the third and fourth centuries practiced it, even without the limiting conditions which were set in the Middle Ages. Bundling was a means then used to test themselves by extreme temptation. It was a test or proof of the power of moral rule over natural impulse.

A number of sects in the Middle Ages, in renouncing marriage, introduced tests of great temptation. Individuals, too, believing they were practicing holiness by carrying on the battle between "the flesh" and "the spirit" subjected themselves to similar tests.

For centuries bundling, or analogous customs, prevailed in all sections of the British Isles. Even at the time of the Roman conquest the promiscuous sleeping together which prevailed there led Caesar to consider the Britons polyandrous polygamists. Other ancient writers offered similar comment. This was bundling in its crudest primordial form.

The social histories of England, Ireland, Scotland and Wales all abound in stories of courtship and marriage customs that come within the sociological order of bundling. Very often each section had its own peculiar variation, and with it there developed an ethic which they recognized and respected, although it may have been lost to an outside observer, who saw only the crudity of the practice. For instance, there was the so-called "island custom" of Portland, England, which lasted well into the nineteenth century.

According to the custom of this locality a woman before marriage lived with her lover until pregnant and then married him. She was always strictly faithful to him while they lived together, but if no pregnancy occurred the couple might decide that they were not meant for each other, and break off relations. As a result, for a long period of years no illegitimate children were born, and few marriages were childless.

With the development of the Portland stone industry, workmen were imported from London who promptly took advantage of the convenient "island custom", but refused to fulfil the obligation of marriage when pregnancy occurred. This outside trifling and playing false with what was a long established, seriously considered local custom caused the custom to fall into disuse.

The social conditions of primitive, rural Wales, like those of the other Celtic countries—Scotland and Ireland—are said to have been more rude in the sexual relationships than in England at a comparable period. Always, however, we find at the root of these problems that all-pervading nemesis of early humanity—poverty. Richard Twiss, in his *Travels,* described the custom in eighteenth-century Ireland.

B. B. Woodward, in his history of Wales, re-creates the following picture of the domestic habits of the people at an earlier period: At night a bed of rushes was laid down along one side of the hovel, covered with a coarse kind of cloth, made in the country, called *brychan*. All the household lay down on this bed in common, without changing their garments. The fire was kept burning through the night, and the sleepers kept warm by lying huddled closely. When, by the hardness of their bed, one side was wearied, they got up, sat by the fire for a while, and then lay down again on the other side.

It was this custom of promiscuous sleeping that accounted for what was considered by many observers at a much later date as a great moral laxness among the population, with an absence of feminine delicacy among the women. Out of this aboriginal practice, which influenced the amatory life of the

Welsh peasants, developed the bundling of courtship in its characteristic form.

The custom of *handfasting* among the old Scotch, which will be considered in a subsequent chapter, bore a close relationship to the sexual habits already described. Suffice to say at this point that a witness before the Royal Commission on the Marriage Laws in 1868 testified that "night visiting" (a form of bundling) was still common among the laboring classes in some parts of Scotland. In extenuation, the witness said they have no other means of intercourse. It was contrary to custom for a lover to visit his sweetheart by day—doubtless because he did not have the time, and the lass had no time for him either. The parents condoned the practice because "Their daughters must have husbands and there is no other way of courting."

The custom had considerable vogue and no little prestige in Holland under the name of *queesten*. It is said that parents encouraged it. A girl who had no *queester* was considered lacking in some desirable feminine qualities. The houses in the country were built for the convenience of the custom. We are told that in 1666–1667 every house on the island of Texel had an opening under the window where the lover could enter so as to sit on the bed and spend the night making love to the daughter of the house.

So stringent was the code of the folkway governing the practice that rarely did any harm occur. If it did, the man was mobbed and wounded or killed. The custom can be traced in North Holland down to the eighteenth century.

In Norway the practice was called *night-running,* on account of the long distance between the homesteads. The routine in that country was for the girl to put on several extra skirts and go to bed. In due time the young man entered by the door or window and took his place in bed alongside of her. They talked all night, or until overcome by weariness and fell asleep.

The custom existed among the peasants of Germany down to recent times, but in some sections it was restricted to one night in the month, or certain nights in the year.

Among all peoples who practiced bundling everywhere there seems to have been the common denominator of poverty, or at least the necessity of observing the utmost economy. It was essentially a rural custom among hard-working, frugal-living peasants who after their day's toil found an occasional evening free to answer the call of the mating instinct.

CHAPTER V

Primitive Marriage Practices

PROMISCUITY.—We have already observed Westermarck's theory that marriage in some form, however shadowy the outline may have been in many instances, has existed from the beginning of human society. We also have the testimony of other anthropologists that the sexual relationship at the earliest stages of mankind must inevitably have been promiscuous, a sort of indiscriminate sexual communism.

In support of the latter contention, we have a great deal of evidence from pioneer investigators of primitives within historic times, and also of sociologists, ethnologists and other professional observers of human nature in its most uninhibited state in modern times.

Primitive man, in whom the sexual impulse was still purely instinctive, of course, had no knowledge of marriage in anything approaching the modern sense. At the lowest level it is probable that the men in a horde or tribe or clan cohabited quite indiscriminately with the women of the group. If there were any distinctions made, or preferences shown, they were probably based on physical force. This, however, does not alter the fact of the promiscuous relationship. Under those conditions it was of course impossible to determine the paternity of children, so that the offspring belonged to their mothers or to the tribe.

GROUP MARRIAGE.—In the case of the smaller nomadic units, this promiscuous relationship within the group may well have resembled what Westermarck designated as a form of marriage. This would be considered an example of group marriage, a practice that has had considerable prevalence both in ancient and, among uncivilized races, in more recent times.

Group marriage is the marriage of one totem with another—that is, the men of one totem group marry the women of another, and *vice versa*. No individual man, however, has any particular wife. To illustrate, if twelve men of the first totem married twelve women of the second totem, then each one of the dozen men has an equal share of each of the dozen women, and *vice versa*.

This, of course, represents an advance over unrestricted sexual promiscuity, and is the basis of family life in many primitive societies. Group marriages have existed down to recent years—and perhaps even at the present time—among the Australian aborigines and certain other primitives.

The prevalence of group marriage among our own early ancestors is revealed in the following statement of Julius Caesar, in his description of the marital practices of ancient Britain: "The husbands possess their wives to the number of ten or twelve in common, and more especially brothers with brothers, or parents with children." This is a special form of group marriage, there being variations in the detailed arrangement according to the folkways that shaped the social life of the people.

Polyandry—the espousal of one woman and several men—is also regarded by some authorities as the vestige of a primitive form of group marriage, arising from a deficiency of women in a totem. Under this arrangement one woman was left as the representative of a totem married to several husbands.

Mythology, which arises from the beliefs and practices of the childhood of humanity, confirms the indiscriminate and unrestrained sexual relationships of prehistoric times. In the Indian myth Brama is wedded to his own daughter Saravasti. The same myth occurs among the Egyptians and in the Norse "Edda."

The Egyptian god, Ammon, was the husband of his mother, and boasted of the fact; and Odin, the Norse god, is referred to as the husband of one of his own daughters. The sexual relationship of certain of the Egyptian dynastic rulers in early historic times bears out the analogy of the myth to fact. If we were as well acquainted with the marital customs of India and the Norse countries at a corresponding period, it is likely that we should find similar practices, as we do indeed among certain savage tribes.

Writers of Greco-Latin antiquity have cited numerous graphic instances of promiscuity in actual practice. Strabo relates that "throughout the Troglodyte country the people lead a nomad life. Each tribe has its chief, or *tyrant*. The women and the children are possessed in common, with the exception of the wives and children of the chief, and whoever is guilty of adultery with one of the wives of the chief is punished by a fine consisting of the payment of a goat."

Herodotus described the Agathyrses (Scythians) as the most delicate of men, their ornaments being chiefly of gold. They have their women in common, he reported, in order that they may all be brothers, and that, being so nearly related, they may feel neither hatred nor envy toward each other.

In the Andaman Islands, the women were said to have been held in common until quite recently. Every woman belonged to all the men of the tribe, and resistance to any of them was a crime severely punished.

According to Major Ross King, some aboriginal tribes of India, notably the Kouroumbas and the Iroulas, have no idea of marriage, and live in promiscuity. The only prohibitory rule consisted in not having intimate relations with a person belonging to another class or caste.

Strabo affirmed a similar practice among the Celtic population of ancient Ierne (Ireland). The custom seems to have been prevalent in antiquity throughout the British Isles, which were then inhabited by various barbarous tribes or clans, as noted by explorers from the Mediterranean civilization.

Dr. Adolf Bastian, in describing his travels in the Orient, reports that in Swaganwara the daughters of the Rajah enjoyed the privilege of freely choosing their husbands. Four brothers who settled in Kapilapur made Priya, the eldest of their five sisters, queen-mother, and married the others.

THE CONSANGUINEOUS FAMILY.—Lewis H. Morgan, the American ethnologist, who did so much to interpret the form of family life and social organization of the Indian tribes, particularly the Iroquois, indicates the principles of the consanguineous family, which he assumes as a higher form of the sexual relation that gradually developed from the state of general promiscuity.

Under this form the marriage groups are arranged by generations. All the grandfathers and grandmothers within a certain family group are mutually husbands and wives. Their children constitute another cycle of husbands and wives. And, again, the children of these, when they have attained the proper age, are mutually married.

This may be described as a form of group marriage limited

to one generation. Brothers and sisters and cousins of the first, second and more remote grades are all acknowledged as brothers and sisters, and also as husbands and wives.

Morgan, through his long study of Indian life in particular and of ethnology in general, which included living for years with the existing tribes as a virtual member of the group, did more than any other authority to throw a revealing light upon their forms of social organization and government. He was the first to discover the identity existing between the totem groups of the North American Indian and the gentile organizations of the Romans.

The most famous cases of consanguineous marriage within historic times, of course, are those of the Egyptian dynastic ruling family, the Ptolemies, who habitually married their sisters, cousins and nieces.

CUSTOM OF EXCHANGING WIVES.—The custom of temporarily exchanging wives and lending wives to visitors has been observed in many parts of the world. Among the Banyankoles in Central Africa, when a man and his wife visited a friend, they invariably exchanged wives during the time of the visit. A similar custom prevailed among the natives of the Hawaiian Islands.

Marco Polo wrote that in Eastern Tibet no man considered it dishonorable if a foreigner had relations with his wife or daughter or sister or other woman of the family. On the contrary, it was deemed an act of good fortune. Such was their superstition that they considered it would bring the favor of their gods and idols, and presaged an increase in temporal prosperity.

Among others it was thought that the lending of their wives to foreigners would result in nobler offspring. This is an exogamous concept that has had wide prevalence in one form or another among many primitives, often forming part of their religious rites.

The exchanging of wives is still practiced among the Eskimos. It seems to be mutually agreeable to the man and his wife. Sometimes the exchange is made for what appears to be practical reasons. For instance, if a man who is going on a journey has a wife encumbered with a child that would add to the difficulties of traveling, he may exchange wives with some friend who remains in camp and has no such inconvenience. Or, a man will want a younger wife to travel with him, in which case an exchange can usually be effected.

It is not necessary to have any particular reason, however, as the custom is so thoroughly established in Eskimo folkways that among friends it is the usual thing to exchange wives for a week or two every few months. At the time of tribal gatherings or general festivities, it is one of the principal diversions.

Occasionally it turns out that the exchange reveals to both couples a more satisfactory or harmonious relation, in which case the exchange is made permanent.

There are also superstitions that govern the exchanging of wives. After the incantations of the *angakut* are performed in the evening among the Hudson Bay Eskimos, it is obligatory to exchange wives. The women must spend the night in the huts of the men to whom they are assigned. If any woman should refuse to go to the man to whom she is assigned, it is believed she would be sure to be taken sick. The only stipulation entering into this ceremonial exchange is that the man and the woman in question must not be near relatives. It is also believed that the practice is efficacious in averting some great trouble, such as pestilence or illness that may threaten them.

Among the Himalayan mountaineers, the exchange of wives

was a usual practice when two of the men became disgusted with their respective spouses and hoped thereby to effect an improved domestic arrangement.

MAGICAL SIGNIFICANCE OF RITES.—The relationship between marriage, with its normal sequence of offspring, and the productivity of fields has been dramatized by all primitive peoples. Marriage rites are used that are appropriate to and timely with the planting and harvesting of crops, and frequently at no other time of the year. Whether the rites are conceived to bring productiveness to the marriage, or whether the marriage is believed to favorably influence the crops, is a moot question. It is quite likely that the belief may embrace both concepts—a magic working both ways, stimulating alike the fertility of the marriage and of the fields.

In Morocco marriages are celebrated generally in the autumn, at the close of the harvest when the granaries are full of corn. In some sections of the country, a wedding is seldom known to be performed at any other time. The peasantry of many European countries have also favored the autumn, corresponding to the period of the agricultural festival.

This is notable in its departure from the traditional late spring preference, especially the month of June, so much favored by the peoples of the English-speaking world. Even this, it will be noted, is a seasonal selection of important significance, as it corresponds with the time when the planting season is normally completed.

Among the Brahmans of India there are but four months in the year—March, April, May and June—during which marriage may be celebrated. Only in this season is it considered a favorable time for marrying. The plebeians of ancient Rome celebrated their great festival, the *Cerealia,* in honor of Ceres, goddess of the grain, during the period April 12–19.

In China, too, the spring season is especially favored for promising marriages, although the last month of the year—corresponding with the completion of the harvest—is also considered desirable. The Votyak of Kasan still retain the ancient custom of marrying at a definite period of the year, which is before the hay harvest, about the end of June.

The celebration of May Day (the name popularly given to the first day of May) throughout Europe can be traced back to, and is a survival of, rites originally offered to the old Roman goddess *Maia,* who was worshiped as the principle and cause of fertility. One of the essential features of this celebration was a ritual marriage of the goddess to a partner who represented the male element of productive power, from which arose habitual acts of license which, however, were not repugnant to early moral sentiment.

The Roman *Floralia,* celebrated in honor of *Flora,* the goddess of flowers and of the spring, superseded the devotions to *Maia.* It was instituted in Rome in the year 238 B.C., on account of a bad harvest, the celebration taking place between April 28th and May 3rd. Among the observances of the *Floralia* are mentioned gay costumes, dramatic performances and dances described as frequently extremely sexual in character, but to the ancients merely emphasizing the procreative character of the rites.

The importance attributed by the ancients to their gods and goddesses of fertility, and the necessity of paying homage to them in order to benefit by the spell of their magic, is clearly indicated by the fact that the Romans had no less than three major divinities—*Ceres, Maia* and *Flora*—of this character. There were also other lesser and local divinities of fertility, who were propitiated by acts and suggestions of procreation.

In modern India the Holi festival is celebrated in March or

April with the singing of songs generally erotic in their implications. The naturalistic basis of the custom is joy at the creative impulses felt in the spring and manifested both in the vegetable and animal world.

Even now among the peasantry of various European countries, spring and midsummer festivals are celebrated with bonfires, music and dancing, always associated with love- and match-making.

So May Day has come down through the centuries with traditions bearing on the fruitfulness and productivity of nature, as revealed by man, and the flora and fauna upon which his welfare, even his very life, depends. It was all of magical beginnings. In civilized times, it has lost most of its grosser outward manifestations, although retaining the symbolic significance that gave it being, even to the May Pole, which is admittedly phallic in origin.

LICENTIOUSNESS AT CERTAIN FEASTS.—Among various peoples promiscuous sexual relations are indulged in at certain feasts. This is thought to be a survival of a more general ancient promiscuity, later limited to seasonal festivals. However, the later practice seems always to be of the character of a magical rite.

The Koko-nor Tibetans held a celebration known as *t'iao mao hui,* "the hat-choosing festival." During the two or three days the feast lasts a man may carry off the cap of any girl or woman he meets in the temple grounds who pleases him, and she is obliged to come at night and redeem the pledge.

In Madagascar orgies of great licentiousness formerly accompanied the birth of a child in the royal family. On such an occasion the streets and lanes of the capital were the scenes of unrestrained caprice, and the period during which the debauchery lasted was called *andro-tsi-maty,* meaning a time when the law could not condemn nor the penalty of death be inflicted.

TREE MARRIAGE.—Tree marriages, among other forms of mock nuptials, are widely prevalent in various parts of India. Among the Brahmans of southern India it is the established custom that a younger brother should not marry before an older one. To fulfil this requirement, when there is no satisfactory bride in sight for a senior brother, he is married to a tree, which leaves the younger one at liberty to take a wife.

According to the theory of animism—which is universal among primitive peoples—all animate and inanimate objects possess a spirit. The brother who is married to the tree is in reality married to the spirit which resides in the tree. This custom shows remarkable ingenuity in overcoming a convention prejudicial to the interests of certain individuals, and still satisfies the demands of the folkways.

In other cases tree marriages occur simultaneously with the regular marriage of the couple, the idea being to divert to the tree some evil influence which would otherwise attach to the newly wedded pair.

Mock marriages are also carried out among the Punjab of India in the case of a widower taking his third wife. It is celebrated with a certain tree or bush, and sometimes with a sheep, which is dressed up as a bride and is led by the groom around the sacrificial fire while the real bride rests near by.

This act is a precaution against a train of ill luck which has caused the death of two former wives, and in order to insure protection to the new wife. It is believed that the malicious jealousy of the first wife has been instrumental in causing the death of the second one, and the characteristic features of this ceremony are to divert such evil influences to the substitute in the mock marriage. We use the term "mock marriage," but it is all very serious with them. In the case of a widower taking a fourth wife, it is believed that the evil influence of the first wife has spent itself, and therefore no mock marriage is deemed necessary.

CIRCUMCISION AS A PREREQUISITE OF MARRIAGE.—The importance of circumcision in the limited culture of primitive peoples is attested by the fact that it is conceded to be the oldest surgical operation. Furthermore, it is still the most widely practiced form of surgery, and the only one having a mystical or religious significance.

Leaving aside the general practice among the Jews, Mohammedans and certain Christian sects, such as the Abyssinians, Bogos and Copts, we are here concerned only with it as a rite incident to marriage. Among the tribes that so consider it are most of the natives of the West Coast of Africa, the Kafirs, nearly all the peoples of Eastern and Central Africa, Madagascar, the aborigines of Australia, Melanesia, the Indian Archipelago, Polynesia and many of the Indian tribes of the Western Hemisphere.

There is undoubtedly magic significance attached to it among these peoples, as there was to its origin among the Jews, Mohammedans and those Christian sects who continued it as a religious rite. That it was originally considered the physical symbol of spiritual purification is indicated by several references in *Romans* ii, of which it is only necessary to quote the following: "and circumcision is that of the heart, in the spirit, not in the letter" (verse 29).

The importance of the rite among primitive peoples undoubtedly rests on the fact that it makes the boy a man, and gives him the appearance of sexual maturity. This in turn signifies he is capable of procreation, thus enabling him to fulfil his duties in marriage. If it results in this outward appearance, then, in the logic of the primitive mind, there must be some favorable connection between the practice and the benign spirits.

In those communities where circumcision is a prerequisite of marriage, eligible girls would not think of considering an uncircumcised youth as a prospective mate. The folkways with respect to this custom are so thoroughly established that it would be thought indecent and objectionable to show encouragement to a youth who had not been initiated by undergoing this tribal rite.

Among many peoples of Africa and certain natives of the Malay Archipelago and South America, the girls also undergo a ritual analogous to circumcision, which is also looked upon as a necessary preliminary to marriage. Whether the practice applies to one sex or both, it is always a serious obligation, one of the most sacred rites performed by the tribe.

SUTTEE.—A hideous practice which prevailed in India from legendary times down to the present century was *suttee,* the burning or immolation of the widow on the funeral pyre with the body of her husband; or, separately, if he died at a distance. The word is an English corruption from the Sanskrit *sati,* meaning "true wife" or "good woman." The custom was based on injunctions of the orthodox Hindus' religious teachings. It appears to have originated among the Indian royalty as a "wifely privilege", and afterwards became generalized and made legal under the native laws.

Akbar, the Mogul emperor, acting from his Mohammedan viewpoint, forbade the *suttee* about 1600. His rule had no effect whatever on the practice. In the year 1803 there were 275 women sacrificed on funeral pyres within a radius of thirty miles of Calcutta. In six months of the year 1804, in the same area, the number was 115.

The British Government outlawed the practice in 1829, but so strong was the custom that it continued in isolated parts of India as late as 1905, when several persons who had participated in a *suttee* in Behar were condemned to penal servitude.

When the rite was suppressed under British rule, the Hindu priesthood resisted to the utmost, appealing to the Veda, as sanctioning the ordinance, and demanding that the foreign rulers respect the native religious law. It was proven, however, that the priests had actually falsified their sacred Veda in support of the rite, which was based on long and inveterate practice, and not on the traditional standards of Hindu faith.

For a long time after *suttee* had been suppressed, it was said that the prohibitory law was not a kindness to widows, as their continued existence was so wretched that death would have been preferable. They were subjected to physical abuse and mental torture, and shunned as creatures of ill omen.

Usually the wife went willingly to the sacrifice, but force was used if she showed reluctance. Often one dead man took many wives with him. Some went eagerly, even gaily to the new life, many were driven by force of custom, by fear of disgrace, by family persuasion, by priestly threats and promises, or, if necessary, by sheer violence.

Widow sacrifice is found in various regions of the world under a state of low civilization. Tylor finds traces of a rite similar to *suttee* among ancient Aryan nations in Europe—Greece, Scandinavia, Germany, the Slavonic countries—and accounts for it by direct inheritance from the common antiquity of them all. Striking examples are found in both myth and early historical writings.

In Greek lore we learn of the Trojan captives laid with the horses and hounds on the funeral pyre of Patroklos, of Evadne throwing herself into the funeral pile of her husband, and

Pausanias's account of the suicide of the three Messenian widows. In Scandinavian myth Baldr is burned with his dwarf foot-page, his horse and saddle. Brynhild throws herself on the pyre of her beloved Sigurd, and men and maids follow after them to Valhalla.

The Gauls, in Caesar's time, burned at the dead man's elaborate funeral whatever he held dear. Old Slavonic legends describe the burning of the dead with clothing and weapons, horses and hounds, faithful servants, and, above all, wives. St. Boniface reported that the Wends kept matrimonial love with so great zeal that the wife might refuse to survive her husband, and she was held praiseworthy among women who slayed herself by her own hand, that she might be burned on one pyre with her lord.

The primitive theory of this seems to be that the departed husband shall enjoy the company of his wife, and others as the case may be, in the other world. There was also the belief that a widow is dangerous because the ghost of her husband clings to her after his departure. She is therefore taboo, and must be slain that his spirit may depart in peace with her.

Even in modern times the custom has been widely followed by savage tribes in many parts of the world. Among the Comanches it was the practice to kill the man's wife to accompany him on his journey. In various parts of Africa wives were sacrificed at the death of their husbands. This was also the case in the New Hebrides, New Guinea, Melanesia and the Fiji Islands. In Darien it was customary to inter with a chief all his concubines.

Similar customs, with slightly different ceremonial forms, prevailed among some of the Chinese and Japanese peoples; also among the Tartars, and a number of Indian tribes of the Western Hemisphere.

THE PURDAH.—Another custom working great hardship on women is the *purdah,* literally keeping them out of sight. The name originated from a curtain, which was supposed to shield all respectable women from the gaze of men, other than those of the immediate family. It was formerly quite universal in the Mohammedan countries, especially Turkey, Persia, and India. The woman who sits behind a curtain is termed a *purdah-nashim.*

The purdah supplemented the veil worn over the face of the Moslem women, before the dynamic Kemal Ataturk banished both from Turkey into which he introduced so many modern innovations during his brief but spectacular career. The custom, while declining, is still maintained by some traditional upper-class Mohammedans who have not been too drastically affected by the changes of the twentieth century, especially those brought about by the two World Wars.

In a broad sense the purdah is part and parcel of the oriental tendency to seclude or segregate women, to keep them apart from, and out of contact with, the normal activities of life, except those that revolved around the exclusive sphere of the husband. The term has been absorbed into the English vernacular in the phrase "to lift the purdah," meaning to divulge a secret.

FAMILY LIFE AMONG THE SIMIANS.—In a treatise on primitive marriage practices it will be pertinent to make brief mention of the family habits of man's closest subhuman relatives, the simians. We are considering, of course, the animals in their native habitat and wild state, as no particular significance can be placed upon the actions of those placed together in captivity, in an entirely artificial environment. It is therefore necessary to depend upon the reports of naturalists who have spent considerable time living and traveling in regions inhabited by the animals.

Max Moszkowski, writing on his travels in Sumatra, states that the higher monkeys or apes usually live in families consisting of father, mother and one or two young. C. de Crespigny, reporting on his sojourn in Borneo, gives the following description of the orang-utan: "They live in families—the male, female and a young one. On one occasion, I found a family in which were two young ones, one of them much larger than the other, which I took as proof that the family tie had existed for at least two seasons. They build commodious nests in the trees which form their feeding ground, and, so far as I could observe, the nests, which are well lined with dry leaves, are only occupied by the female and young, the male passing the night in a fork of the same or another tree in the vicinity. The nests are very numerous all over the forest, for they are not occupied above a few nights, the orang-utan leading a roving life."

Hornaday and Wallace found the orang generally quite solitary in his habits, the old males invariably being alone. They did find, however, adult females with a nursing infant, and sometimes a next oldest offspring, apparently from the previous year, who had not yet left his mother's side to shift for himself. Adult males were also less frequently seen accompanied by half-grown young ones.

The testimony regarding gorillas is more specific. They have been observed to live in small bands, usually with but one adult male in each group. It is said that when the male first realizes he is seen, he gives a terrific yell that resounds far and wide through the forest. At the first cry the females and young quickly disappear. He then approaches the enemy in great fury, giving vent to his dreadful cries in quick succession.

Winwood Read mentions that when a family of gorillas ascend a tree to eat a certain fruit, the old father remains seated at the foot of the tree on guard. When the female is pregnant he builds a rude nest, usually about fifteen or twenty feet from the ground. Here she is delivered and the nest is then abandoned. The male is said to spend the night crouching at the foot of the tree protecting the female and the young from the nocturnal attacks of leopards. An instance is mentioned where a band of gorillas was attacked by two Bulu men. The old gorilla of the band first got his family out of danger and then returned to the encounter.

The family life of the chimpanzee was found to be very similar. Georg Schweinfurth relates that this ape also is found either in pairs or even quite alone, only the young being seen usually in groups. T. S. Savage seldom observed more than one or two nests upon the same tree or in the same neighborhood. Unlike the monkey, they do not live in villages, and are more often seen in pairs than in groups. The same author says it is not unusual to see "the old folks" sitting under a tree regaling themselves with fruit and friendly chat, while their children are leaping around them and swinging from branch to branch in boisterous merriment.

It is not only the simians that live in a more or less durable union. This is also the case with the hippopotamus, with whales, seals, certain of the antelopes, reindeer, gazelles, and among the smaller animals, squirrels, moles, the ichneumon, and of course many species of birds.

Thus we see that the pairing instinct, coexistent with the parental care of offspring, is very extensive throughout nature, extending far into the subhuman world. It clearly indicates that mankind has by no means a monopoly of the impulse to mate and care for his young over a prolonged period of time.

Being necessary for the existence of certain species, the instinct has been fostered by the process of natural selection. So primitive marriage practices, or family life, have indeed a very long biological background. Mankind does not always seem to have made the most of his heritage.

CHAPTER VI

Primitive Religious Marital Ideas

MARRIAGE AND THE GREAT RELIGIONS.—The great religions of the world—Judaism, Hinduism, Buddhism, Christianity and Mohammedanism, to list them in the order of their seniority—have exercised vast influence upon marital ideas, and the ceremonies and ritual connected with the marriage relationship. The numerous subdivisions of these groups have made lesser contributions to the subject, as they have for the most part continued the general practices of the parent body, with certain variations, and all modified to some extent by the traditional influences of their own environment.

When it is stated that the great religions have exercised such influence, it is not to be inferred that the authority of religion over marriage began with the rise of these respective religious bodies. Considering religion in its broadest sense, i.e., belief in a supernatural power or spirit, there has been a religious jurisdiction over marriage since long before the dawn of history.

Ages before there existed the concept of a personal divinity, there was a belief in a multiplicity of gods, dominating all the unknown and mysterious phenomena that surrounded and bewildered primordial man.

There was animism—the association of a spirit with all sorts of animate and inanimate objects. There was magic, which exercised so powerful a hold upon the primitive mind, and still does, to a greater extent than the uninitiated appreciates. There was sun-worship—the most rational of all the early forms of adoration of a higher power. And there were various forms of mysticism, fetishism, shamanism, phallicism, and many other religious *isms* that might be mentioned.

Furthermore, the influence of any religious philosophy upon marriage does not mean primarily formulating a set of rules or regulations governing the marital relations. That is one of the end results, rather than a formative factor. The real influence of a religion of whatever kind upon such an institution as marriage is to be found in its attitude toward men and women as human beings. More especially is the attitude toward woman the decisive factor, as the biological handicaps of the female in human society have been exploited mercilessly for the most part by the dominating male.

Many of the marital practices prevalent under savage and barbarous social systems have been described in the previous chapters, and others will be considered under their proper classifications in subsequent sections of this book. We are here concerned with the primitive influence upon marriage by the great religions in their formative years.

It is true that each of the great religions took over from their pagan predecessors certain forms and rituals—which the people understood through ages of practice—and adapted them to their own ends. It is also true that there is some overlapping of ideas among the great religions themselves, which have had to a great extent a common heritage in Asiatic tradition.

Christianity, for instance, is an offshoot of Judaism, as the genealogy and chronology of the Old and New Testaments reveal. Jesus, of Jewish birth and heritage, is the Christian Saviour. Moses is still the major Prophet of Jew and Gentile, and the Mosaic law dominates the ethical code of Western civilization and its institutions. By the same token, the views of women and marriage held by Hebraic society at the beginning of the Christian era were those that prevailed in the formative years of Christianity.

The same telescoping of ideas will be found in many aspects of Hinduism and Buddhism, originating and evolving as they did in India. All the great religions came out of Asia. Mohammed, coming along at a later period, took what he liked of Judaism, Christianity, Hinduism and Buddhism, added the result to his own revelations, and gave to the world the creed of Islam (meaning "resignation" or acceptance of the divine will).

MARRIAGE AMONG THE ANCIENT HEBREWS.—The position of woman among the ancient Hebrews was an unenviable one, as it was among most primitive pastoral peoples. However, as our own ethical and religious system evolved from the Hebraic culture, we often overlook this fact, especially as many of the disabilities under which woman has labored through the centuries have been condoned by our Christian civilization.

Sumner reminds us that the Jewish idea of marriage was naïve and primitive. The purpose was procreation. There seemed to have been little ceremony about marriage, beyond the fact that the suitor induced the father to surrender the daughter in return for gifts. The bride had no choice in the matter whatever, and as this was the custom of her time, she did not expect to be consulted. In a word, it was marriage by purchase, and sexual union, as indicated in *Genesis* xxix, was the only principal marriage rite.

No priestly function was necessary. The arrangements having been completed, the man took the woman as wife by repeating the formula: "Be thou consecrated to me", which was later extended to: "Be thou consecrated to me by the law of Moses and Israel." In the rabbinical period the betrothal and wedding were united.

Afterwards the bride was led or carried to the house of the groom, in a procession, with dancing and rejoicing. Ten guests (adult males) must be present in the groom's house, as witnesses, where prayers were recited and a feast enjoyed. At one period, two bridesmen led the couple to the nuptial chamber where they watched over them until after the conjugal union. The purpose of this was that there might be witnesses to the consummation of the marriage—which was held all important—and not merely to the wedding ceremony.

When the custom of the presence of witnesses in the bridal chamber became objectionable in later times, a tent was substituted for the chamber. Later a scarf, ceremoniously spread over the heads of the pair, took the place of the tent.

The low status of woman in ancient Hebrew society is further evidenced by the fact that the Ten Commandments of the Old Testament are addressed exclusively to man. In the Tenth Commandment the woman is mentioned together with the domestic servants and domestic animals. The man is warned not to covet his neighbor's wife, nor his man-servant, nor his maid-servant, nor his ox, nor his ass, nor anything that is his neighbor's. Woman, then, is treated rather as an impersonal object, a piece of property, that man should not covet if in someone else's possession.

The Genesiac admonition, "Be fruitful and multiply," exercised an immense influence over the ancient Jews. The sexual function is therefore emphasized as the fulfilment of the first divine command to mankind. It is the realization of God's will for a peopled world. The pious Jew still reads in his book of prayer:

"And so our Creator and Maker ordered us to be fruitful and multiply, and whoever does not engage in reproducing the race is likened unto one who is shedding blood, thus diminishing the essence of the deity, and he is the cause that the holy spirit shall depart from Israel; his sin is great indeed."

Just as it was sinful to abstain from marriage, so it was unlawful to live childless in the marital estate. One was not permitted to marry a woman too old or too young to bear children. If, after a period of years, the wife bore no children, the husband was obliged to divorce her and marry another who would bring him offspring.

The man who destroyed the powers of procreation was twice a murderer. Even he who was born sterile had no place in the religious communal life. A Jew was forbidden to castrate even an animal.

But with this preoccupation with sex, the ancient Jews held to the almost universal primitive taboo that stigmatized woman as unclean, and the biological processes of menstruation and childbirth necessitated purification and penance. There was thus the inescapable paradox—sex was both right and wrong; righteous and sinful. The burden of the dilemma could only be made bearable by the most precise laws governing the situation.

In Talmudic lore the conduct of the married couple during the woman's menstruation is elaborately formulated. As the punishment for sexual relations during the menstrual periods is untimely death for both husband and wife, means were devised to guard them from temptations that might lead them to commit this horrible sin.

Consequently it was prescribed that the two must not show an affection toward each other during this time. The husband must be careful not to touch his wife, even without any desire.

He must not even hand her anything so small that it may cause their fingers to meet. He may not eat out of the same dishes with her, nor drink from her cup; but she may eat and drink out of the dishes he has used. He may not sit upon her bed, even in her absence, and she is not permitted to make his bed in his presence. He must not even see any part of her body that is customarily covered.

Leviticus xii dwells on the problem of purification after childbirth in the following manner: "And Jehovah spake unto Moses, saying, Speak unto the children of Israel, saying, If a woman conceive seed, and bear a manchild, then she shall be unclean seven days; as in the days of the impurity of her sickness (menstruation) shall she be unclean. . . . And she shall continue in the blood of her purifying three and thirty days; she shall touch no hallowed things, nor come into the sanctuary until the days of her purifying be fulfilled. But if she bear a maidchild, then she shall be unclean two weeks, as in her impurity; and she shall continue in the blood of her purifying three score and six days."

The low status of woman is here shown, not only by the curse of her uncleanliness in itself, but in the statement that the impurity is twice as great in the birth of a female child as in that of a male child. Manhood and fatherhood are joyfully exempt from these penalized disabilities.

Furthermore, the newly married woman was obliged to be able to prove, clothes in hand, that she was a virgin at the moment of her marriage, and if the charge of not being a maiden was sustained, she was subject to stoning to death by the men of her city, as described in *Deuteronomy* xxii, 13-21.

It may well be said that in citing these extreme instances of discrimination against and hardness toward women, we are going a long way back in the social calendar. This is naturally true, because our subject in this chapter is Primitive Religious Marital Ideas. The cases cited have been taken from unimpeachable authorities, the holy books of the people in question. Furthermore, the influence of these early teachings remained for centuries to color the thought and ideas of both Jew and Christian in their attitude toward women and marriage. Unfortunately, traces of the taboos and prejudices still remain.

MARRIAGE AMONG THE HINDU CULTS.—In India, because of the peculiar relation of the household to the social structure, marriage may be said to be almost compulsory—like conscription in time of war. According to the Hindu lawgivers, anyone making gifts to, or taking gifts from, a Brahman who remains a householder, but does not marry, goes to hell. The unmarried householder is a person to be shunned, and it is sinful to accept hospitality from him.

The performance of the duties of a householder is looked upon as a spiritual discipline, for in its true idealistic sense, the household is not primarily a means of insuring the comfort and security of the individual, but is one of self-abnegation, having its manifold obligations to gods and men—meaning devotion to religion and charity.

To the Hindu, expenditure by the householder for the welfare of those in need is not a matter of generosity, but a primary duty in the interests of his own fulfilment. This duty is not only that of the rich, but also of the poor, according to their means. Manu says: "The *rishis,* the forefathers, the gods, the guests, and all living creatures, expect to be maintained by the householder."

Because of these injunctions, it has been said that the Hindu ideal of marriage has no regard for individual preference or inclination; it is, indeed, rather afraid of them.

With the orthodox Hindus, marriage is a religious sacrament

which cannot be revoked. A woman convicted of adultery may be deprived of her status and turned out of her caste, but even in this case divorce in the ordinary sense is an impossibility. She cannot form a new marital tie, and often remains in the husband's house on the footing of a slave.

Other reasons for marriage than renunciation are recognized, as survivals of earlier and more material concepts, or due to weakness of the human will, but they are frowned upon. Manu classifies these as the *Gandharva* (by mutual choice), *Rakshasa* (by conquest), *Asur* (by purchase), *Paishacha* (by taking advantage of helplessness). It will be seen that in none of these is the social will manifest, but only the desire of the individual.

The marriage of mutual choice, or *Gandharva,* is stigmatized by the ancient sage because it is "born of desire", and has not as its goal the welfare of society. Accordingly, it is considered best that the bride should be given to a man who has not solicited her.

According to the Brahman idea, motherhood, insofar as it is concerned with the physical nurture of offspring, is not essentially different in man and the lower animals, being a function of biological, not of sociological life, governed by instincts which are of Nature, not by man's own creative power. However, where the mother undergoes voluntary penance for the elevation of the human race, keeping her natural instincts vigorously in subordination to the dictates of mind and soul, there she finds a field for her own creative effort.

Kalidasa, the great dramatic and lyric poet of India, in his *Sakuntala* and other works, looked upon marriage as a state of discipline, not intended for gaining individual happiness.

Now, according to the Indian ideal, even the home must be given up in the course of time, in quest of the Infinite. The household, in fact, is set up only as an important stage in this quest. Even at the present time, it is not uncommon for householders, when their children are grown up, to leave their home and spend their remaining days in some place of pilgrimage.

Thus far, we have presented the Hindu ideal of the marriage relation, of the sex factor and of the position of woman as set forth in the Code of Manu. Countless numbers of Hindus have lived up to and carried out this ideal, at least as consistently as the Christians of the Western World have practiced their ethical precepts. However, in its practical aspects the picture of the Hindu marriage system and of the national attitude toward woman, leaves a great deal to be desired, if the Western mind is at all capable of grasping the situation.

In the preceding chapter, we have discussed *suttee,* the burning or immolation of widows, and of the cruelty visited upon those who were spared this fate after the practice had been prohibited by the British government. In a subsequent chapter some of the evils involved in child marriage will be taken up—a custom that the religious leaders of the Hindus have tried to perpetuate in the face of strong outside opposition.

TEMPLE PROSTITUTION.—Modern India has much in common with ancient Greece with respect to the position of its women. The wife is carefully isolated from social life, and as a consequence is not an educated, cultured person, but rather a disciplined cog in the household menage. There is a class of courtesans, however, well educated and respected, who furnish intellectual diversion and companionship for those who adhere not too strictly to Manu. It is said to be the custom for the Hindus in the large towns and cities to frequent the society of courtesans for the charm of their wit and their conversational ability.

There are or were prostitutes attached to the temples, but

in our Western lights we probably should not be too hasty in passing judgment upon a time-honored institution which we do not understand. These temple attendants learn to read, sing and dance.

Many years ago, J. A. Dubois wrote that in Southern India every temple, according to its size, entertains a band of so-called *deva-dasi,* that is, "servants or slaves of the gods," to the number of eight, twelve or more. They perform religious duties, consisting of dancing and singing, twice a day, morning and evening. They are also obliged to assist at all the public ceremonies, which they enliven with their dance and merry song. But as soon as their religious activities are over, "they open their cells of infamy, and frequently convert the temple itself into a stew."

These dancing girls are bred to this profligate life from infancy. They are taken from any caste, and are frequently of respectable birth. It is said not to be uncommon to hear of pregnant women, in the belief that it will tend to their happy delivery, making a vow, with the consent of their husbands, to devote the unborn child, if it should be a girl, to the service of Pagoda. In doing so, they imagine they are performing a meritorious duty. Among the Kurubas when there are no sons in the family, the eldest girl is occasionally so dedicated. Among the Voddas, if an adult female remains unmarried, she may be dedicated to a free life in the name of Yellamma, who is their patron deity.

The ceremony of dedication frequently resembles that of a formal marriage, and the woman is actually regarded as the wife of the god to whom she is devoted. Thus the dancing girls who serve in the pagodas of Kartikeya, the Hindu God of War, are betrothed and married to him, after which they may prostitute themselves.

THE LEVIRATE.—The custom demanding that a dead man's brother must inevitably, under certain circumstances, marry his widow has been widespread. It is known as the *levirate* (from the Latin *levir,* brother-in-law). Among the Hindus and some others, the obligation arises if the dead man left no children. The *levirate* often encouraged polygamy, for the duty of marrying a dead brother's widow may exist even when the living brother is already married.

The Bible prescribes the *levirate* law in *Deuteronomy* xxv, 5-6: "If brethren dwell together, and one of them die, and have no son, the wife of the dead shall not be married unto a stranger: her husband's brother shall go in unto her, and take her to him to wife, and perform the duty of a husband's brother unto her. And it shall be, that the first-born that she beareth shall succeed in the name of his brother that is dead, that his name be not blotted out of Israel."

A contrary ruling is given in *Leviticus,* but the custom may have changed after the earlier injunction. The fact that the brother-in-law who failed to marry as directed in *Deuteronomy* was exposed to shame for his delinquency indicates the social force behind the law. Furthermore, while the practice ultimately fell into disuse, a symbolic rite relating to it is still practiced among orthodox Jews. In a formal ceremony the widow loosens her brother-in-law's shoe (this and his foot must be clean, according to rabbinical law), and spits on the ground before him. This symbolism closely adheres to the ritual set forth in *Deuteronomy,* following the verses quoted, when the living brother fails to marry his widowed sister-in-law.

In India, the principal object of the *levirate,* with respect to the widowed fiancée, was to furnish the deceased man with a fictitious son, who could perform for him the sacrifices to the *manes,* a duty of the highest importance in the religion of Brahma. The law of Manu imposes the *levirate* even on the brother of a betrothed man who dies, viz.: "When the husband of a young girl happens to die after the betrothal, let the brother of the husband take her for wife." (It will be noted that the state of betrothal is considered equivalent to marriage.)

The *levirate* has been practiced among many peoples besides the Hindus and the Hebrews, among whom may be mentioned the New Caledonians, the Mongols, the Afghans, the Abyssinians and certain of the American Indian tribes. It is believed that an important factor in the prevalence of the custom is the fact that the wife was considered a piece of property, bought and paid for, and was inherited as such by the nearest of kin—the brother.

Among some of the African Negro tribes, the eldest son inherits and marries all his father's wives with the exception of his own mother.

PRIMITIVE CHRISTIAN VIEW OF MARRIAGE.—Christianity introduced a concept of marriage—taken over from the Hebrews—which differed greatly from that generally held by the principal contemporaneous peoples of culture, the Greeks and Romans.

St. Paul, who did more than any other of the founders of Christianity to mold the traditional Western attitude with respect to woman and marriage, considered celibacy preferable to the married state. "It is good for a man not to touch a woman. Nevertheless, to avoid fornication, let each man have his own wife, and let each woman have her own husband" (*I Corinthians,* vii, 1-2). If the unmarried and widows cannot contain, let them marry, "for it is better to marry than to burn." He was true to his own views and refrained from marriage.

Marriage, according to the doctrine of Paul, is therefore at best a compromise between indulgence and renunciation of sexual passion. Celibacy was proclaimed as the Christian ideal because the unmarried, being free from domestic obligations, can care for the things of the Lord.

The early fathers of the Church, Tertullian and Jerome (in anticipation of the end of the world) considered virginity an end in itself. They thought it pious and noble to renounce the function on which procreation depends; first, because matters of the spirit were infinitely more important; secondly, because in view of the imminence of the approaching end of the world, it was futile to pay attention to such a thing as propagating the race.

Commenting on the utterances of the Apostle Paul, Tertullian emphasizes that the better of two alternatives is not necessarily good. It is better to lose one eye than two, but neither is good. So, also, though it is better to marry than to burn, it is far better neither to marry nor to burn. Marriage "consists of that which is the essence of fornication," whereas continence "is a means whereby a man will traffic in a mighty substance of sanctity."

Gregory of Nyssa and John of Damascus lamented that if Adam had preserved his obedience to the Creator he would have lived forever in a state of virgin purity, and some harmless mode of vegetation would have peopled paradise with a race of innocent and immortal beings.

Eusebius and Hieronymus agreed that the teaching of the Old Testament, "Be fruitful and multiply," was no longer suited to the times, and did not concern Christians. Origen declared: "Matrimony is impure and unholy; a means of sensual passion." To escape temptation he emasculated himself.

Toward the end of the fourth century, a Council of the Church excommunicated the monk Jovinian because he denied that virginity was more meritorious than marriage.

In brief, during the first centuries of Christianity marriage was tolerated only as a necessary expedient for the continuance of the human race, and as a restraint, however imperfect, on what was considered the natural licentiousness of man.

Many of the early Christians, especially the Montanists and Novatians, strongly disapproved of second marriages by persons of either sex. Such a marriage was described as a "kind of fornication," or as "specious adultery." There was also involved in this premise the belief that when husband and wife were united in the hereafter, the presence of an extra spouse would prove an embarrassing or unchristian-like triangle.

These doctrines, of course, were not characteristic of Christianity only, but were largely a social heritage directly from Judaism and Greek philosophy, and, indirectly, from the more ancient civilizations of Babylon, Egypt and India, among all of which women were held in low esteem.

In the laws of Manu, for instance, we find the warning: "The cause of dishonor is woman; the cause of hostility is woman; the cause of worldly things is woman; therefore woman should be shunned." Besides the belief in the degradation of woman, the fear of woman is repeatedly naïvely implied. These are the same thoughts, if not in the same words, as expressed by the Christian fathers.

Christianity's early contribution toward this concept of woman and marriage was therefore not a new one, but rather a fresh and vigorous re-emphasis of the subject by a new and zealous organization imbued with the missionary spirit.

THE MOHAMMEDAN REACTION TO ASCETICISM.—It seems quite likely that no small part of the success of the prophet Mohammed in gaining converts to his new religious doctrine in the early part of the seventh century A.D. was due to the emphasis placed on sensual joys, in contrast to the early Christian asceticism.

Mohammedanism is a man's religion; sex is an integral part of it—not only in this world, but even more so in the next, where sensual delights without limit and without end are promised to the faithful.

The position of women in the creed of Islam is decidedly one of subjection. They are excluded from participation in the religious rites in the mosque; they must carry out their liturgical exercises in the privacy of their homes. They are to remain hidden from the strangers' eyes, but must remain ever accessible to the husband, their master.

Mohammed exhorted his followers to give full and free expression to the sexual impulse: "Your wives are your tillage; go in therefore unto your tillage in what manner soever ye will." Even the fast need not interfere with the connubial duties. "It is lawful for you on the night of the fast to go to your wives; they are a garment unto you and you are a garment unto them." In short, the function of woman was to satisfy the Moslem's passion and to raise his children.

Polygamy is allowed, but not without restriction. Four wives is the legal limit for a Moslem, although he may cohabit with any number of concubine slaves.

The Prophet, however, was allowed as many wives as he wished. As polygamy is recognized as the cause of much marital strife and unhappiness in Mohammedan countries, as well as elsewhere, monogamy is the rule of the great majority of Moslems.

A Moslem may marry a Christian woman or a Jewess, but a Mohammedan woman is not under any circumstances permitted to marry an unbeliever. In all cases, however, the child born of a Moslem, whatever the mother's faith, is required to be raised as a Mohammedan.

Incestuous marriages, in contrast with the early Hebrew practices, are strictly forbidden, as is that to a woman who is related to the faithful "by milk in the degrees which would preclude his marriage with her if she were similarly related to him by blood."

This proscription refers to in-law connections; that is, a marriage to a mother-in-law, or a step-mother, a step-daughter, a son's widow, a brother's widow, etc. Marrying two sisters at the same time is also forbidden, as is marriage with two women who stand to each other in the relation of aunt and niece; or with unemancipated slaves, if he already has a free wife.

The Moslem rite has less formality than that of Christianity or any other of the great religions. It does correspond somewhat, however, with the simple marriage rite of the early Christians, before the Council of Trent. A simple declaration of a man and woman who have arrived at the age of puberty, before two witnesses, of their intention to marry each other, and the payment of part of the dowry—which is indispensable, and must amount to at least ten dirhems (about one dollar)—is sufficient for a legal marriage.

A girl under age is given away by her natural or appointed guardian, with or without her consent. It is strictly forbidden to the believer to see the face of any woman who is neither his wife nor his concubine, nor belongs to any of the forbidden degrees.

As was the case with all early religions, Mohammedanism

considered woman unclean. If a man touched a woman, he was required to purify himself before going to pray. The mere act of touching a woman was looked upon as something of an offensive nature. "O true believers, when you prepare yourself to pray . . . if you have touched a woman, and yet find no water, take fine clean sand and rub your faces and hands therewith."

This attitude toward woman—part of the great universal taboo among all peoples in the pre-scientific age—was predicated upon the biological fact of menstruation and the universal belief in evil spirits. It is said that even to the present day many of the Mohammedans have a fear that malignant spirits may enter the woman during the sexual relations. In Morocco it is always considered necessary for the husband before having intercourse with his wife to say *"bismillah"*—a supplication meaning "in the name of Allah", lest the devil should enter the woman and make the child a villain. This belief has the support of Mohammedan tradition.

In pointing out many of the crude beliefs and primitive ideas inherent in Mohammedanism, it would be grossly unfair not to make at least passing reference to an intellectual and cultural side of its history which is often overlooked.

During several centuries of the Christian era, especially that bleak period commonly referred to as the "Dark Ages", the educated Moslems did much to keep both the spirit and letter of civilization from perishing from the earth. From the ninth to the thirteenth centuries, they were admittedly the teachers of barbarous Europe.

The real renaissance of Greek culture took place under the patronage of the Abbasides, the most celebrated Moslem dynasty, and classical literature would have been lost irretrievably had it not been for the home it had found in the schools of Islam.

Arabic philosophy, medicine, natural history, geography, history, mathematics, grammar and rhetoric flourished and left many invaluable legacies to the culture and knowledge of the Western World when it finally took them up.

CHAPTER VII

Marriage Taboos

MEANING OF THE SEX TABOO.—Taboo, meaning "forbidden", is a word adopted from the Polynesian (*tabu*). The practice of taboo is found under various names all over the world, but nowhere has it been so systematized as in Polynesia. It is an important—an almost all-important—factor in the lives of all known savage and barbarian tribes. It is an integral part of all primitive religions. It was almost equally momentous in the lives and religious observances of the ancient Hebrews, the Hindus, the early Christians and the Mohammedans.

Taboo is something forbidden because the tabooed object is regarded as potent to injure, owing to its *mana,* or mysterious (spiritual) power, which may be either holy, as a priest's or king's possessions, or evil and unclean. The fear of malignant spirits is the basis of taboo; so we can readily see how extensive and universal has been this fear.

Fear of the unknown, fear of the unseen, fear of strange phenomena, all are bound up with taboos. Certain persons (priests and members of the ruling family), certain animals (the tribe's totem), and certain objects, are held to be imbued to an unusual degree with this *mana,* and hence are regarded as holy. They are held in awe, and ordinary man must not have personal contact with them.

Taboos are held on other things because it is considered that they bode ill. The list of such tabooed persons and objects is almost limitless, taking into consideration the vagaries of different peoples, but the taboos on injurious or destructive influences seem principally concerned with such things as a dead body, a new-born child, blood—particularly a woman's blood, and therefore women in general, because of the menstrual cycle, its association with the loss of virginity and the phenomenon of childbirth; the sick, outcasts, sometimes foreigners, criminals (the primitive idea of crime often being much different from ours), animals, even words and names, and many other things at one time or another. Taboos may be permanent or temporary, private or public.

A river is tabooed by a king until the fishing season is over; a forest until the game is caught, a field until the crop is harvested. A public taboo is where a whole community is made taboo while gathering the crop. This renders it impossible for any member of the tribe to do anything else until the taboo is removed and prevents any stranger from approaching the tabooed ground. The removal of the public taboo is made by a priest, who repeats a spell and performs certain rites over the tabooed people.

What is not taboo is *noa* (common). There may be a taboo on knots, locks, crossed arms and legs—in brief, on all things that suggest an impediment.

The most rigorous taboos, however, are concerned with sex, which is not to be wondered at, considering its vast importance both in individual and social life. The sex taboo is essentially a set of inhibitions which control and restrain the intercourse of the sexes with each other in ordinary life.

Taboo on Women.—The belief that a woman's blood is fatal to a man leads at stated periods to a temporary taboo of women, even among civilized Hindus. For the same reason in many countries men may not eat with women. At menstruation women are forbidden to touch men's food or utensils.

It is only by an understanding of the *mana* principle, with the belief in sympathetic magic that is bound up in the concept, that we can obtain an insight into the almost universal custom of the *woman shunned* under certain conditions, and the sex taboo among primitive peoples. The transmission of *mana* through contact is inherent in the notion of sympathetic magic, which is the belief that the qualities of one thing can be mysteriously transferred to another, especially through touch.

The avoidance of the menstruating woman, so widespread throughout the primitive world, was undoubtedly due to the belief that this function was a demonic possession. A woman during this period was held to be unclean and possessed by a demon. Primordial man could not be expected to know that the phenomenon of menstruation was in any way associated with reproduction. When the association was ultimately discovered, the taboos had become a fixed practice in social life, and such established customs are not dropped merely because the reason for their origin has become known. Furthermore, by this time the reason for their origin had long since been forgotten, so the practice remained valid for the all-sufficient reason that it was a custom.

Among the Maoris, if a man ate food cooked by a menstruous woman, he would be "tabu an inch thick." An Australian native who discovered that his wife had lain on his blanket at her menstrual period, killed her for violating the taboo and died of terror himself within a fortnight. Death is indeed the penalty dealt a menstruating woman who dares to touch anything that the men use, or even to walk on a path that is frequented by men.

The primitive man's fear of women at the time of her sexual

crises—menstruation, pregnancy and childbirth—is really but an intensification of his attitude toward her at all times. If she is possessed by demons on these occasions, how can he be sure that she is entirely free of evil influences at any other time?

Notwithstanding all the precautions that are taken to purify her and drive out the malignant spirits, he is not entirely reassured, so woman remains suspect. No small part of the elements involved in the belief in witchcraft and in the horrors of witch-burning in civilized countries of the Western World as recently as within the past two or three centuries was due to this latent feeling.

TABOO OF CHILDBED.—Restrictions are imposed on women in childbed apparently for similar reasons. At such periods women are considered to be in a dangerous condition, and may infect any person or thing they might touch. They are to all intents and purposes kept in quarantine until, with the recovery of their health and strength, it is evident that the danger has passed away.

In Tahiti it was customary to seclude a woman after childbirth for two or three weeks in a temporary hut erected on sacred ground. During the period of her seclusion she was forbidden to touch food and had to be fed by another woman assigned for that purpose. If anyone else touched the child at this period, thus exposing himself to the curse, he was subjected to the same restrictions as the mother until the purification rites had been performed.

Likewise, among the Alaskan Kadiaks, when a woman is about to be delivered, she retires to a low hovel built of reeds, regardless of the season, and is considered so unclean that no one will touch her, and she is fed with food at the end of a stick.

EVIL OMEN OF THE STILLBORN.—Some primitives regard the danger as still worse, and the pollution more deadly, if the woman has had a miscarriage or has been delivered of a stillborn child. In such case she may not go near any living being. The slightest contact with her or with anything she has used is extremely dangerous. She receives her food at the end of a long rod. After three weeks, she may return to her home, subject only to the restrictions of an ordinary confinement.

The evils inherent in a *concealed* miscarriage are still more terrible. In this case not only the husband and family are in jeopardy, but the whole country; even the sky may become troubled. To quote a medicine man of the Ba-Pedi tribe: "When a woman has had a miscarriage, when she has allowed her blood to flow, and has hidden the child, it is enough to cause the burning winds to blow and to parch the country with heat. The rain no longer falls, for the country is no longer in order. When the rain approaches the place where the blood is, it will not dare come further. It will fear and remain at a distance. That woman has committed a great fault. She has spoiled the country of the chief, for she has hidden her blood which had not yet been well congealed to fashion a man. That blood is taboo."

In a case of this kind they go and arrest the woman. They compel her to show where she has hidden the result of her unsuccessful attempt at childbirth. They dig at the spot, then sprinkle the hole with a decoction of two sorts of roots prepared in a special pot. A little of the earth is taken from the grave and thrown into the river. Water is then brought back from the river and sprinkled where she shed her blood. She herself must wash every day with the medicine. Then the country will be moistened again by rain. The country is purified!

THE TABOO OF INCEST.—The widespread feeling of revulsion toward incest, or sexual congress with very close blood relatives, has been the subject of exhaustive commentary. That it is anti-social is generally conceded, and therefore immoral, because too close inbreeding tends to degeneration of the offspring.

There have been some notable exceptions to this rule, but they may be explained by the fact that the parents in question, as individuals, were quite exceptionally gifted, and therefore passed on these gifts or desirable characteristics to their children. Such fortunate background, however, cannot be assured when inbreeding takes place at random and on a more considerable scale, so the practice is justly considered detrimental to the race. Even the primitive savages appear to have discovered this.

Some authorities find evidence of a close connection between sexual modesty and the aversion to incest, or, perhaps, more strictly a sexual aversion which prevails among members of the same small domestic circle.

Bentham stated as a psychological fact that individuals accustomed to see each other and to know each other from an age which is neither capable of conceiving desire nor of inspiring it, will see each other with the same eyes to the end of life.

In primitive society the incest prohibition applies primarily to relations between brothers and sisters, or more especially between brothers and younger sisters. Everywhere in primitive society there is a sharp distinction drawn between elder and younger sisters. The two belong to different classes of kinship, and the relation bears a different name. In most tribes the elder sister stands much in the same position as the mother.

The Nayars of the Malabar coast, for instance, have an extraordinary respect for their mother. The primitive attitude toward the mother is probably not so much that of affection, as we know it, as it is of awe toward one whose magical properties were responsible for the existence of the son. The mother was held in esteem if for no other reason than to propitiate the good *mana* with which she was imbued, and to keep in her good graces. The curse of a mother was the most terrible imprecation that could descend upon the human head. The primitives regarded it as the only curse the effects of which could never be avoided.

As they honored their mothers, in like manner these savages regarded their elder sisters. But with the younger sisters, they never stay together in the same room, and they observe toward them the utmost reserve. They say that dangerous situations might else arise, the younger sisters being thoughtless. Their respect for their elder sisters, being of a maternal sort, precludes any thought of sexual intimacy, and therefore it is unnecessary to guard against it.

In Tonga the elder sisters are likewise treated with remarkable deference. A chief will show his respect by not even daring to enter the house of his elder sisters. Among the natives of central Australia, a man may not speak to his younger sisters, but there is no restriction as to his speaking to his elder sisters. These views represent the attitude of many primitive societies.

Marriage between mother and son has been particularly abhorrent to almost all primitive tribes. The exceptions to this rule are so slight as to be negligible. Unions between father and daughter, however, are much more prevalent, but tend to come under the tribal ban with a higher degree of civilization. The mother-in-law taboo is very widespread, and usually begins with betrothal. In some tribes a man may not touch or speak to his mother-in-law, nor the latter have any contact with her son-in-law. They are forbidden to pronounce each other's names. This prohibition with respect to names is a common feature of all taboos between persons. To mention a name is a form of contact; it calls forth the spirit of the other person, and is to be avoided.

The basis of this taboo is unquestionably the prevention of incest with a new kinswoman. Other reasons have been ascribed for the prohibition put upon all social contact between the principals of this relationship. It has been called a natural sequence of marriage by capture through which the people had passed. Thus, when the capture was a reality, the indignation of the girl's mother would be real, and the groom would shy away from one whom he had so cruelly offended by stealing her daughter. With the passing of marriage by capture, the maternal anger and the groom's embarrassment became symbolized. These symbols continued long after the origin of the practice had been forgotten.

EXOGAMY.—We know that exogamy—the law prohibiting marriage between persons of the same blood as a prevention of incest—has had wide application in primitive society. Among the natives of New Britain it was believed that marriage within the totem (tribe) would result in the death of the woman. If this taboo were violated her parents or relatives usually killed her for shame, so that the belief became a reality. The groom's life was likewise in jeopardy, unless he fled.

The exogamous principle works as an obstacle to matrimony in many instances where there are natural difficulties to its fulfilment. It has been found, for example, that unmarried men are more frequently met with among the Tungus than among the Chukchee, not only on account of the considerable price to be paid for the bride, but more so because marriages are strictly exogamous, and a bride may be taken only from another clan than that of the bridegroom, which added to the difficulties of marrying.

The same observation has been made with reference to the natives of Pentecost, where all marriages between near relatives are prohibited, and the chance to marry at all is considerably diminished. As a result, with the decreased population, a man very often could not find a wife, even though in the midst of numerous women.

Marriages between cousins are disapproved by the Eskimos, and also by the Mahlemuts and the Chippewas, as well as many other American Indian tribes. The Algonquins put to death those who violated this rule. The Greenlanders do not marry near relatives, even to the third degree. They consider such unions unnatural and contrary to the wishes of the gods.

In Polynesia marriage with blood relatives is taboo and rarely occurs. The natives of Andaman do not permit marriage with those even distantly related. The Dyaks are specific in prohibiting a man from marrying a cousin, aunt or niece. Marriages in Samoa are carefully guarded against incest.

ENDOGAMY.—Correlative with exogamy is endogamy, which enforces marriage within a social or political group. These two principles are not necessarily contradictory, as they may refer to different groups of persons. Hence endogamy and exogamy may and often do occur side by side with each other among the same people. It has been well stated that there is everywhere an outer circle out of which marriage is definitely prohibited or considered improper, and an inner circle within which no marriage is allowed. Both the terms *endogamy* and *exogamy* were coined by J. F. McLennan, the Scottish sociologist and anthropologist.

We have only to look about us to find this principle in operation. For instance, in our present-day society it is not customary to marry outside our race (referring to color). It is true this is sometimes done, but the penalty is heavy in social disapproval and ostracism, when, indeed, the law itself is not violated by so doing, as would be the case in many states. This is an example of endogamy.

On the other hand, it is not customary for marriage to take place between very close blood relatives, such as brother marrying sister, niece marrying uncle, nephew marrying aunt, and so forth. Not only are the laws and mores generally set against this practice, but it is repugnant to all normal individuals. Here we have an example of exogamy.

In primitive society where social life is not stabilized by education, formal training and ethical precepts, as we know these influences, where the individuals are thrown together more promiscuously, and cohabitation is apt to take place from the time of puberty—when the mind is still immature and undiscriminating—experience has taught the necessity of formulating stringent taboos to control the primary impulses. These taboos, as we have seen, are associated with sacred rites and backed by the belief in sympathetic magic which is inherent in primitive psychology.

While civilized man has quite rational ideas regarding the prevention of inbreeding, and generally has an abhorrence of incest, the primitive concept of the whole subject is often more vague and involved. For instance, very distant cousins and even persons whose blood ties are imaginary—kinfolk by virtue of some tribal rite—may be forbidden to marry under the exogamous principle.

Endogamy is the essence of the caste system as it exists among the Hindus. Their religion forbids the intermarriage of persons belonging to different castes. Not only must a Hindu refrain from marrying outside the limits of his caste, but where, as is usually the case, the caste is divided into sub-castes, he must not ordinarily marry outside his sub-caste. In some instances he may marry in certain sub-castes but not in others.

The tendency in civilized society against mating members of different social strata is an analogous example of class endogamy, which has had wide application in both the ancient and modern world.

In Rome patricians and plebeians were not permitted to intermarry until the year 445 B.C. In most countries in medieval times a freeman could not contract a lawful marriage with a serf. When nobility finally emerged from the class of freemen as a distinct order, marriages between persons of noble birth and persons who, although free, were not noble were considered misalliances.

No one holds that endogamy represents a stage in the evolution of marriage through which all tribes once passed, and strictly endogamous communities are not nearly so common as those practicing exogamy. It should be noted that endogamous rule applies only to what might be called legal marriage, and does not usually exclude concubinage. Pride in blood is not always the motivating principle of endogamy; it may represent the desire to keep certain highly prized traditions the exclusive property of a clan or community.

There are dangers in inbreeding which the primitive mind seems to have perceived in giving direction to the exogamous principle. Inbreeding preserves a type, but weakens the stock. Outbreeding strengthens the stock, but enfeebles the type.

The taboo having been established very early in primitive society, the holy men and chiefs, who generally were the supervisors of the procedure, soon came to realize how great was the power that came to them through the associated superstitions.

As the hereditary beneficiaries therefore, they did their utmost to carry on the traditions and to prevent any outside influence from weakening them. One of the advantages seen in endogamy by these hereditary beneficiaries was that it tended to conserve the tribal traditions.

As human nature in an environment steeped in superstition is inevitably conservative and resists change, it was not difficult to perpetuate practices, once they became established, that worked to the interests of the privileged class.

Food Taboos.—Malevolent spirits being omnipresent, according to primitive notions, it was believed that evil could enter the body with the food. Undoubtedly the occurrence of stomach ache and other alimentary disorders confirmed this impression. Therefore, very stringent taboos were practiced applying to food and drink, and their consumption.

Furthermore, at the time of eating the soul might escape through the mouth, or be extracted by the magic arts of an enemy present. There was a belief among some savages that the indwelling spirit leaves the body and returns to it through the mouth. Hence there was a double jeopardy; first, that the individual's spirit may leave the mouth and venture too far to return safely; secondly, that in the absence of one's own spirit, a homeless or evil spirit may enter the mouth and take its place.

Precautions were therefore adopted to guard against these dangers. As an example, it is only possible to prevent the soul from straying when one is in the house. At feasts the whole house may be shut up so that the soul may stay and enjoy the good things set on the festal board.

The members of a Madagascar tribe bar their doors when they eat, and will not knowingly permit anyone to see them eating or drinking. They are doubly particular that a person of the opposite sex shall not see them doing so. A traveler had to bribe a native to see him drink; but not even a bribe was sufficient inducement for the man to let a woman see him drink, so powerful was the influence of this taboo.

The primitive was therefore exceedingly careful with whom he ate or drank, and once having made his decision to do so with a stranger, after having made the proper magic signs as a protection, the partaking of food together was a pledge of friendship, or even a symbol of newly formed kinship.

The Atiu Islanders, to this day, refuse to eat with the missionaries, and the Papuans will not eat food that has been touched by a white man. Among certain Eskimo tribes, the woman is forbidden to eat with her husband. In many African tribes it is a capital offense to eat with a woman. The belief is that the man who eats with a woman runs the risk of sudden and mysterious death. It is therefore strictly taboo.

In view of these ordinary precautions taken by the common people, it will readily be understood that the precautions taken by the king and priests are extraordinary. If any man or beast saw the King of Loango eat, that man or beast was instantly put to death. A favorite dog, having run into the room when the king was dining, was ordered to be killed on the spot. It is said that the king's own son, a boy of twelve, once inadvertently saw his father drink. Immediately the king ordered his own son's death. It is believed that great evil—even death—shall come to the king if anyone sees him eat or drink, and consequently the one unfortunate enough to witness this act is sacrificed to save the monarch.

Taboos such as this, and there are many others that set the king apart from all his subjects, result in traditions that enhance the royal prerogative. One cannot envy the monarch these dubious privileges, but it is part of a system of which he is a hereditary victim, and he would be the last, seemingly, to want a change. This has been the attitude generally of all victims, high or low, of superstitions and shackling traditions throughout the ages.

TABOO OF WIDOW MARRIAGE.—Even in the modern world, according to convention, it is not general for widows to remarry until after the lapse of a certain period, which used to be known as the widow's "mourning year."

In most primitive societies this custom amounts to a set prohibition for periods ranging from a few months to several years, or even permanently. In the savage mind, the widow is a bearer of ill-luck, and the taboo on remarriage is a safeguard for the males of the tribe against death infection, of which her late husband was a victim.

In addition to the prescribed lapse of time that must ensue between the decease of her husband and the widow's remarriage, certain purificatory rites are performed to dissipate the corpse lien or taint that is upon her. Until this result is satisfactorily accomplished marriage would be a great risk alike for the widow and for the second husband.

All sorts of misfortune may befall the man who consorts with an unpurified widow. The foolhardy man is doomed to be drowned, to die in battle or to fail in whatever he undertakes.

There is also the prospect of the deceased husband's ghost bullying her into lasting widowhood, unless by the performance of suitable rites the intimidating spirit can permanently be banished. Jealous ghosts are said to be particularly the bane of Hindu widow-brides.

A widow married by the more ceremonial of the two Creek forms of marriage was considered an adulteress if she spoke or made free with any man within four years of her bereavement. In Borneo widows may not remarry before the annual spirit feast. If they do so, they are fined by the relatives of the deceased. The amount of the fine is significantly the same as that for adultery, and the new husband is also fined as if for seduction.

Among the Igorots if a widow (or widower) should remarry within the year of mourning, she (or he) would be killed by a ghost "whose business it is to punish such sacrilege." Here we have an example of affronted ghosts apparently delegating their power of vengeance to a special agent of the spirit world.

In the southeastern district of the Chinese province of Fuhkein match-makers are reluctant to arrange a marriage between a young bachelor and a widow. It would bring ill luck to the second husband and his clan because the vindictive spirit of the first husband, peevish over the infringement upon his ownership, would "hover over them all."

In some communities those widows who remained unmarried and loyal to their husband's memory were accorded especially considerate treatment for their constancy. Rich Chinese families were glad to have a chaste widow living with them. She reflected honor upon them, and was treated with unusual respect, so that she might remain true to her ideals. To the poor, on the other hand, the chaste widow was a prohibitive luxury. They could not afford to support a drone or to refuse the bride price which her second marriage would bring them.

Widow marriage is still strictly forbidden among the Brahmans and almost all the higher castes of India. The Manu disqualifies the son of any remarried woman as an heir. A chaste widow is promised the highest renown in this life, and a place in heaven near her husband. To make the accomplishment more certain she is expected never even to mention the name of another man after her husband's death.

Where compulsory widowhood is found limited to the chieftain class and their class is known to have once practiced widow immolation, the present practice is regarded as an immolation symbol.

The Koran prohibited the remarriage of Mohammed's widows. "It is not right for you to wed his wives after him ever; verily that is with Allah a serious thing."

DEIFICATION OF WOMAN.—We have examined a great deal of the evidence of the low estate in which woman was held throughout the course of history and, inferentially, during a considerable prehistoric period, as revealed by myth and legend.

Man's attitude toward woman has been predicated on an ambivalent emotionalism, i.e., on the opposite feelings co-existing of fear and desire. Woman and her biological functions were different—therefore not understood. Anything not understood was suspect.

She has been deified in the abstract sense by pagan peoples in the form of numerous goddesses, especially those associated with fertility and sexual allurement. At the same time, in actual life, she has been subjected to all sorts of individual imposition and social subjugation.

She has been deified, too, by many religions, whose followers have treated her, in reality, with outrageous inhumanity.

Woman's psychic and intuitive qualities, no less than the physical, have baffled man, and these uncanny attributes have caused her to be castigated universally for sorcery, black magic and witchcraft down to modern times. Even today in isolated, backward communities, there is a latent reservoir of this feeling toward woman that sometimes flares up in direct accusation of some eccentric female.

Woman's seeming prophetic powers were widely recognized by the ancients. The oracles at Delphi, Argos, Epirus, Thrace and Arcadia were feminine. There was a cult of Sibylline prophetesses whose influence was felt throughout the ancient world, and Greek and Roman philosophers attested to the validity of their powers. Magic and medicine were interrelated arts, and women were the principal custodians of the hereditary formulas for making potent charms and cures from herbs and other substances.

Woman was both weak and strong. She was weak with the disabilities incident to menstruation, pregnancy and childbirth. She did not fight alongside the warriors of the tribe, nor did she join them in the hunt and chase, except in some unusual instances. On the other hand she was bafflingly strong in natural resources which enabled her to withstand the shock of injury, the waste of disease and the disintegration of old age better than her mate. Such a paradoxical being was one to be feared, no less than desired.

It is small wonder that primitive man considered that woman was in possession of, or in league with, supernatural powers, sometimes for good, often for evil purposes. It was therefore to protect man that elaborate systems of taboos were devised, the relics of some of which have come down to us to the present time.

DEDICATION OF VIRGINS TO DIVINITIES.—The ancient world viewed generation as something supernatural, a process that involved traffic with the mysterious realm of the spirits, and to be approached and safeguarded by magic rites.

Among peoples practicing nature worship, phallic ceremonials were performed as a magic charm to insure the fertility of the fields and abundant harvests.

The act of generation was deified by cults such as Astarte in Phoenicia, Aphrodite and Adonis in Syria, Ishtar and Mylitta in Babylon, Isis and Osiris in Egypt, Mithra in Persia, among many others. Greece and Thrace had their analogous cults of Demeter and Dionysus, and there were the Roman deities of Flora, Ceres and Maia. The Romans had the institution of the Vestal Virgins, and India had its numerous temples in which virgins were dedicated to various deities.

So-called temple prostitution and the custom of the sacrifice of virginity to the gods indicate the supernatural relation ascribed to the sex act by ancient peoples within historic times.

Herodotus has transmitted to us a striking account of the Babylonian custom known as *hetairism,* which demanded that every native woman, once in her lifetime, sit in the temple of Mylitta, or Venus, and have intercourse with some stranger. He wrote that many, disdaining to sit with the rest, being proud on account of their wealth, came in covered carriages, and took up their station at the temple with a retinue of servants attending them. Many sat down in the temple, wearing a crown of cord around their heads. There was a continuous line of those coming and going. Passages were marked out along which strangers passed and made their choice.

When a woman had once seated herself, she must not return home till some stranger had thrown a piece of silver into her lap and cohabited with her outside the temple. He who threw the silver must say: "I beseech the goddess Mylitta to favor thee." The silver may have been ever so small, for she would not reject it, as it was not lawful for her to do so; such silver was accounted sacred. The woman followed the first man that performed the rite of throwing the silver, and refused no one.

Those who were beautiful and shapely were soon chosen, and set free; but the homely and deformed often waited a long time, even for a period of several years before their obligation was fulfilled. After having completed the rite that was her sacred obligation, the woman returned to her home, and henceforth lived a virtuous and dutiful life.

It is believed that this custom, and similar rites practiced in Phoenicia, Cyprus and elsewhere, were survivals of exogamous practices of great antiquity, designed to secure an infusion of foreign blood into the native strain. The sacredness in which the procedure was held is indicated by the religious formalities surrounding it.

The practice probably combined what was considered an exogamous necessity, through fear of too intensive inbreeding, and a sacrament to the principle of fertility and fruitfulness. It is well established that both of these customs existed in many ancient societies, often side by side, and their final mergence into a single sacrament would have been a natural culmination toward the end of their long course.

CHAPTER VIII

Chastity

CHASTITY A WIDELY ESTEEMED CONCEPT.—The concept of chastity has occupied the mind and evoked the admiration of peoples of both the ancient and modern worlds, but for widely different reasons. Civilized people esteem chastity as a desirable virtue because it is in accord with the accepted code of morality. But ideas of morality are not universal and changeless. They differ greatly in various parts of the world, and have changed from time to time in those parts from which we derive our social and ethical heritage.

Primitive man esteemed chastity, when he considered it at all, because to him it represented a magical value. Always in primitive society we come back to the association of magic with some human characteristics or biological phenomenon. It may be a beneficent or a malignant manifestation of magical charm, a portent for good or of evil, but it is an influence that attains contact with the spirits, and therefore is one to command attention.

With the advent of marriage by purchase, and the stabilization of the principle of property rights, chastity acquired a value that it had not attained under prior social systems. Woman as salable property had an added value if chaste, which would not have received a second thought under the more primitive system of marriage by capture. Consequently, the mores soon made premarital chastity a virtue, which at first gained recognition in governing and property-owning circles, and finally became the accepted social code.

Elaborate precautions for the preservation of chastity both before and after marriage were evolved among many peoples. In some instances a woman was considered as defiled if she were accidentally touched by any man other than her husband. This is an example of sympathetic magic, where the slightest personal contact results in contamination. In modern Korea women have been put to death when strange men have accidentally touched their hands. It is not even proper for a friend or acquaintance to inquire after the women of the family.

Man in the primitive state did not and still does not think of chastity at all as an abstract moral consideration, as we understand the term. To him it is a concrete matter that hinges on some definite problem, such as the well-being of the tribe, the acquisition of adequate food, triumph over one's enemies in battle, overcoming pestilence or catastrophes of nature.

What have these material problems to do with the question of chastity, you may ask. It is all bound up with the ever-present influence of magic, as we shall see in a moment. In the meantime, let us take up the associated phenomenon of modesty.

MODESTY CONSIDERED A CONSEQUENCE OF FEAR.—As woman in primitive times was a form of booty, a prey of the conqueror in wars and raids, and the prize of the successful rival in single combat, she early developed a psychological armor against the male in sexual matters. It may have been frail, and undoubtedly at times ineffective, but by and large it became a factor to be reckoned with.

Just as primitive man subconsciously feared the female—not physically, but because of her unique biological functions that have already been pointed out, woman, for her part, acquired a dread of the male, in general, that came to dominate her life. The individual man had to overcome this dread by various attentions in the form of wooing or courtship, if he wished to gain her interest and confidence.

It thus became second nature in woman to conceal from the masculine gaze those parts of her body which are most apt to stimulate man's sexual desire and leave her open to sexual aggression.

Modesty has been described as "the timidity of the body". The classical example of womanly modesty has been admirably presented in the Medicean Venus, who withdraws the pelvis, at the same time holding one hand to guard the pubes, and the other to protect the breasts. The whole inference of this artistic expression is feminine defense of the sexual centers against the undesired advances of the male.

The sentiment of modesty is therefore fundamentally based on fear, which in a more civilized age and a more refined environment has become perhaps a subconscious fear. Nevertheless, the latent fear is there ready to assert itself when need be, as no society has yet evolved under which woman has been entirely free from the danger of sexual aggression.

Fear is a natural, instinctive defensive emotion that causes man or woman to react automatically when in danger, or when there seems to be danger. Associated with reasonable judgment and poise, it is a valuable defensive measure without which one could not go very far along the hazardous paths of life without falling a victim to unrecognized dangers.

Notwithstanding its prehistoric background, the sentiment of modesty is a quality which has to be inculcated by education, fortified by experience and freshly acquired in each generation. Unlike the instinct of fear, it is not an inborn trait that expresses itself automatically in the new-born infant. The young child knows nothing of shame, until it is taught to react by precept and experience in the characteristic manner, which is part of the process of socialization.

Modesty is largely contingent upon the sense of vision. For this reason darkness greatly facilitates sexual indiscretion, often without a full realization of any change in attitude, or without causing offense to the sense of modesty. In the dark, nakedness seems less naked, because the condition is no longer apparent to sight, but only to touch.

The cynical Casanova, whose experience in profligacy was inordinate—unless he boasted more shamefully than he philandered—remarked that the easiest way to overcome the modesty of a woman is to suppose it non-existent. He supplemented this by quoting an ancient maxim to the effect that modesty, which seems so deeply rooted in women, only resides in the linen that covers them, and vanishes when it vanishes.

It has been remarked that modesty seems at times to be entirely concentrated in the blush, which has been called the *sanction of modesty*. Consequently, shame becomes less intense when the observer is unable to see one's face and eyes and cheeks. The defensive mechanism of modesty tends to lose its effectiveness under the spell of darkness.

Modesty and the sense of shame are manifested in different ways by peoples of different social culture. There is no single part of the human body which has not been regarded as the very center of modesty by some people somewhere. Women of the Moslem world cover the face, and would feel ashamed beyond words if a man other than the husband should see the exposed face. Arab women are even more ashamed to expose the back of the head than to unveil the face.

Thus we see that modesty is a highly conventionalized sentiment. The standards vary greatly among different peoples. The Japanese regard nudity with indifference, and the sexes bathe together nude in natural hot pools. They nevertheless wear loose garments to conceal the contour of the figure; whereas people of the Western World, who regard naked association between the sexes as horrifying, wear clothing to emphasize the contour of the figure, including the secondary sexual characters, such as the breasts. In civilized life clothing tends to accentuate rather than to conceal the difference between the sexes.

When missionaries try to impose their ideas of proper clothing and standards of modesty upon primitives, they often succeed only in bewildering the barbarous mind, which has its own traditions of what is modest. We are told that an African Negro, struggling to harmonize these two ideas, wore a tall silk hat and a pair of slippers as his only garments when he tried to obey Livingstone's admonition to clothe himself in the presence of white women.

Lombroso reports that in the African tribe of the Dinka both the men and the women have a highly developed sense of shame. It was absolutely impossible to persuade the men to allow a medical examination of their genital organs, or the women of their breasts.

The complete development of modesty only takes place at the advent of puberty, although it may appear earlier in the case of sexual precocity. It is not to be inferred, however, that modesty is purely a sexual phenomenon. The sexual factor is the simplest and most primitive element of modesty, but it is by no means the only one. The social and idealistic impulses also develop about puberty, and the sentiment of modesty is related to these as well as to the sexual impulse.

Theologians have concerned themselves very much with the

question of modest dress, even speculating on the raiment, or lack of it, most suitable for appearance in Heaven. Swedenborg, among others, taught that in Heaven all would be naked, for clothing was a punishment for the sin of man. Another school of thought, represented by Erasmus, contended that "angels abhor nakedness," and that in Heaven men and women both would wear clothes of great richness and beauty.

MODESTY AS ALLUREMENT.—It is believed that the sexual modesty of the female is founded in the fluctuation of her sexual periodicity. It is an involuntary expression of the organic fact that the time for love is not the present.

It is characteristic of the male to desire the woman who is not too readily attained—the obstacles of amorous pursuit stimulating the ardor of the lover. Modesty and reluctance therefore become an asset to woman as the love object. This attribute has been described as a secondary sexual character, a trait that arouses sexual interest and stimulates desire. Modesty is at once a potent sexual charm, and an expression of the erotic impulse, however subconscious the motive may be. It has been noted that women who are sexually cold are notably lacking in those traits that are characteristic of feminine modesty.

The incident of the pursuer and the pursued is an essential element in courtship. The coyness of the female is a phenomenon noted throughout nature, and in the human sphere it is cultivated with all the arts of feminine ingenuity. It is the substance out of which the coquette concocts her endless schemes.

Montaigne, the great French essayist and moralist, pertinently asks: "What is the object of that virginal shame, that sedate coldness, that severe countenance, that pretense of not knowing things, which they understand better than we can teach them, except to increase in us the desire to conquer and curb . . . ?"

The ingrained modesty of women toward men in courtship is reflected in the marriage customs and magic rites of even the most primitive peoples, and many of these practices have been preserved in current usages.

Even the woman of easy virtue may assume the defensive mantle of modesty, and indeed may do so quite naturally and legitimately, as modesty is a valid expression of the feminine erotic impulse. The spontaneous modesty of the young, unsophisticated girl, however, has a quality of its own, a charm that her more worldly-wise sister can hardly affect convincingly.

THE MAGICAL VIRTUE OF CHASTITY.—Belief in the magical potency of chastity and asceticism is very widespread, from ancient times down to modern times.

Influential chiefs in the Congo keep in their service a virgin to care for the arrows, shields, rugs and other war equipment. They are hung up in her room or on trees near it. It is believed that the girl's virginity imbues these things with some extraordinary virtue which their user in turn "catches." If the girl custodian loses her virginity, the articles are destroyed as tainted and dangerous to those who might use them.

Unless medicine-women of certain Guarani tribes in Paraguay observed the laws of chastity, they were considered to have lost their effectiveness. Magical power was ascribed to the Virgin Sun-brides of Peru, who received a message from Prince Uiraccocha, after his great victory over the Chancas, announcing the triumph "which had been granted in return for their prayers and *merits.*"

The Vestal Virgins of **Rome were** similarly esteemed for

their supernatural powers. When Cornelia was being led to execution by the questionable order of Domitian, she exclaimed: "Is it possible Caesar can think me polluted, under the influence of whose sacred functions he has conquered and triumphed?"

Pliny relates the legend that in refutation of a charge of incest, the Vestal Tucca proceeded to carry water in a sieve from the Tiber to the temple of Vesta. On an occasion when the sacred fire went out and the responsible Vestal was suspected of unchastity rather than carelessness, she tore off a piece of her linen garment and threw it upon the altar. Straightway a great flame shot out from the dead ashes in proof of her innocence.

As late as the first century, A.D., it was generally believed that the Vestals had the power by a certain prayer to rivet runaway slaves where they stood, if they were still within the city. A similar power was attributed to one of the *gangas* of Doango.

The Vestals were compelled to remain unmarried during the thirty years they were engaged in offering sacrifices and performing other rites ordained by the law. If they permitted themselves to be violated they were delivered up to the most miserable death.

After the expiration of the term of thirty years they might marry on leaving the ensigns of their priesthood, but it is said that very few did this, as those who did suffered calamities which were regarded as ominous by the rest, and induced them to remain virgins in the temple of the goddess till their death.

One of Ovid's narratives gives a colorful account of how the magic spell of chastity worked a miracle. A vessel bearing a statue of Cybele from Pessinus to Rome stuck fast on a shallow at the mouth of the Tiber. In this crisis one Claudia, a woman under suspicion of unchastity, saw a chance to vindicate herself. Stepping forth from among the matrons who had gone to Ostia to welcome the statue that by divine decree was to be received by a chaste hand, she called upon the goddess to prove her innocence. "Chaste thyself, thou wilt follow my chaste hand," she cried. Pulling slightly at the rope, she forthwith dislodged the vessel.

Besides the virgins who professed perpetual virginity in the monasteries, there were other women, of the blood royal, who led the same life in their own houses, having taken a vow of continence. These women were held in great veneration for their chastity and purity, and as a mark of worship and respect they were called *Ocllo,* a name sacred in their idolatry. However, if they lost their virtue, they were burned alive or cast into the "lake of lions."

There is venerated in Tunis the tomb of a holy Moslem woman who, we are told by the faithful, adroitly transformed her would-be ravisher into a woman. Lella Inma Tifelleut, a Moslem saint of some renown, was abducted by a lawless and passionate suitor. When he opened the curtains of the litter to embrace his prize, she had been magically restored to her home, leaving behind her a dove to fly in the face of the amazed lover.

Not only in the early period of Christianity, but throughout the Christian era, there is evidence of some supernatural quality attached to chastity in the lore, legends and practices of the Church. Even in secular literature, we find tributes paid to its magic charm. Milton has written:

> 'Tis chastity, my brother, chastity;
> She that has that is clad in complete steel.

. . . .

Some say no evil thing that walks by night,
In fog or fire, by lake or moorish fen,
Blue meagre hag, or stubborn unlaid ghost
That breaks his magic chains at curfew time,
No goblin or swart fairy of the mine
Hath hurtful power o'er true virginity.

SUBMITTING PROOF OF VIRGINITY.—Until comparatively recent times, public exhibition of "proof of virginity" was demanded by custom among the peasantry in most countries of southern and eastern Europe. In Little Russia the proofs were paraded at the end of a pole through the streets of the village. In Greece the bride's nightgown was left hanging for some days in the window. The same custom prevailed in Sicily. Even to the present time it is considered necessary that the bridal couch be inspected by the respective mothers of bride and groom, or other female representatives of the families.

Among the Bedawi, also, it used to be the rule to hang the appropriate garments bearing the proofs of the bride's virginity on a lance in the middle of the camp or village, and to leave them there for several days. In southern Celebes the proofs are exhibited to the guests on a silver salver. In Baluchistan, among the Brahui, the proofs of virginity are examined by a jury of matrons. The Kulngo Negroes of the French Sudan exhibited in public the customary proofs.

The custom was one of the ceremonials observed at royal weddings in Spain. When the Emperor Charles V married Isabella of Braganza the "proofs" were solemnly exhibited for the inspection of the assembled grandees. The fact that this formality prevailed in the exalted royal circles of Spain indicates the practice was implicit in the customs of the country.

MASCULINE CHASTITY.—Male chastity, especially as related to the clergy, has been a question which has received much attention in the history of ecclesiastical procedure, and it took many centuries for the Church to formulate its present definite laws on the subject.

Savages as a rule do not lay much emphasis upon masculine chastity, other than in connection with magic rites. There have, however, been some exceptions noted in which this quality has been highly esteemed for itself.

Writing of some North American Indian tribes, Chateaubriand tells us that the highest praise they can give to a girl is to say, "She is worthy to be a man's first love." Masculine chastity is thus esteemed a recompense for chastity in woman, rather than a reward for her beauty.

A practical form of chastity flourishes among almost all savages. Not, however, the asceticism of permanent abstinence from sexual relationships as having any special merit, which is a denial of the laws of nature as revealed to the eyes of primitive man. The higher type of savage does esteem chastity for its values, magical or real, as a method of self-control which contributes to the attainment of important ends.

Restraint and the ability to bear pain are invariably emphasized in the initiation of youths at puberty. The practice of refraining from sexual intercourse before expeditions of war and hunting, and other serious endeavors, calling for great muscular and nervous strain, regardless of the reason given, is a shrewd method of economizing energy.

With respect to chastity, either male or female, among primitive peoples, we must take into consideration the important fact that marriage among them usually takes place upon the advent of puberty, or shortly thereafter; in any event, much earlier than among civilized peoples. This has a direct bearing on the problems incident to premarital continence, if the tribe makes any effort to preserve sexual virtue. Many, perhaps most, savage tribes do not seem to do so, at least in the case of both sexes, and among some a qualified condition of promiscuity prevails.

Continence for various periods, to commemorate some special event, or achieve some object, is well known in various parts of the world. The Tahitians, for instance, held to the belief that if a man abstained from sexual intercourse for some months before death, his lot was improved in the hereafter. This belief would tend to foster continence among men with any kind of sickness, even a slight illness, as the anticipation of death occupies an important place in the primitive mind.

The priestess of the Whydah Snake would prescribe abstinence from certain foods and from conjugal relations for those consulting her.

Among numerous tribes continence for certain periods is a mourning observance. In mourning a New Caledonian chief, conjugal abstinence lasted from fifteen days to one month. In Sierra Leone sexual intercourse is taboo for ten days in mourning a commoner, and thirty days for a person of prominence. In Whydah it is taboo for one year, and among the Baganda during the whole mourning period.

A young widower of the Stlatlum tribe, an inland division of the Salish of British Columbia, was required to forego sexual relations for a year, particularly if he possessed "mystery powers." It was not unusual for him to exile himself into the forest during this mourning year to purify himself and seek "mystery powers."

Women are taboo to a Naga for one year from the time he puts up a memorial stone to his ancestors. Conjugal continence is observed in China during the three years' mourning. It is observed by the Hindus during their ten days of mourning. In Egypt continence was required during the seventy-two days of mourning for a king.

The prescription of continence is sometimes demanded in connection with fertility rites (although the opposite practice more often prevails); also as a weather charm and a charm to make fish and game plentiful. During the rain-making ceremonies and until the rain comes, the men of the Karamundi tribes of Southwest Australia are tabooed from their wives, or the charm is spoiled. At Panai in the Torres Straits during the four weeks' Mawa ceremony to ensure a good crop, no one is permitted to cohabit, "as it will bring bad luck." In Nicaragua continence was observed during the sowing season.

Among the Behring Strait Eskimos during the Bladder Festival—a propitiation of game animals which lasts about ten days—the men keep absolutely apart from the women. The Indians of Nootka Sound follow the same custom during the week preceding an expedition. Bangala trappers on land or water must abstain from sexual intercourse from the time of making or setting up a trap until the quarry is caught and eaten.

Similar rules apply to women who work in primitive agriculture. Women in New Caledonia engaged in planting are forbidden sexual intercourse for a stated time before and after their work. The Thompson River women of British Columbia are required to live chastely while digging and cooking the sunflower root.

In ancient Mexico, for five days before the feast to the divinity Mixcoatl, the god of the tornado, and for four days before that to Tlaloc, the god of rain, conjugal abstinence was observed. A similar rule prevailed in Peru in preparing for the annual sun festival of *Raymi*.

Pliny reported that the three thousand families of the Sabaei who had the sacred hereditary right of cultivating the famed Arabian incense tree were not allowed while pruning or harvesting to receive "pollution" from intercourse with women or from contact with the dead. He added, "It is by these religious observances that the price of the commodity is so considerably enhanced."

The vow of continence was the fifth of the five major vows of the Buddhist *bhikkhu*. Breaking it involved excommunication. Less serious offenses were coming "into bodily contact with a woman, by taking hold of her hand, or by taking hold of her hair, or by touching any part of her body," addressing "a woman with wicked words, exciting passion as those of a young man to a maid," sitting with a woman in a secluded spot, or, unchaperoned, preaching the Dhamma "in more than five or six words," to a woman.

The coming into intimacy with sacred things in the primitive world commonly requires continence; the same condition applying in the practice of Christianity and other great religions. Paul held that conjugal intimacy was incompatible with prayer (*I Corinthians*, vii, 5). St. Jerome prescribed continence to the communicants of the early Church on Saturday and Sunday, the communion days.

Certain Christian ecclesiastics held to the theory of the magical danger of unchastity. In ancient Welch law a married priest is enumerated among the thirteen things "corrupting the world, and which will ever remain in it; and it can never be delivered of them."

Mosheim, an ecclesiastical historian of the eighteenth century, states that although marriage was permissible for the clergy in the third century, yet the unmarried obtained a higher reputation for sanctity than the married priest, *"owing to an almost general persuasion that they, who took wives, were of all others the most subject to the influence of malignant demons."*

Under English ecclesiastical law, "at feast-tides and fast-tides laymen were not to have connexion with women," and the married were required to abstain three nights before and one night after communion. The Scotch Covenanters and the New England Puritans even tabooed kissing on Sunday.

The sixteenth-century Russian household rule, the *Domostroi,* prescribes continence on Sunday, Wednesday and Friday; also during the fasts of the Saviour, Lent, and that of the Mother of God.

There were constant disputes and controversy in the early centuries of Christianity between those who advocated complete continence and celibacy of the priesthood, and those who disagreed with this extreme course. Jovinian, the fourth-century Italian Churchman, vigorously opposed monachism and celibacy, but himself remained unmarried. Even long after his time, the followers of Jovinian within the Church continued to advocate the principles he set forth.

St. Jerome, the leading contemporary anti-Jovinian, declared that a priest who has "always to offer sacrifice for the people must pray, and therefore always abstain from marriage." The Church Councils and pontifical authority became more and more decided in favor of celibacy, and strict enforcement of this ecclesiastical law may be said to have begun with Gregory VII (Pope, 1073–85).

Gregory from the first attacked the evil of clerical marriage and incontinence. To further his cause he stirred up the people to refuse to accept the sacraments from any other than a celibate and pure priest.

The opponents of Gregory condemned his action as an innovation upon ancient discipline. Others defended it as but the application of the ancient discipline with renewed vigor. As late as the twelfth century, synods declared the marriage of persons in holy orders to be not only unlawful but invalid.

According to St. Jerome the only justification for marriage was that it might result in the birth of virgins. He went as far as to say that the end and purpose of the man of God was "to cut down with the axe of Virginity the wood of Marriage."

GIRDLES OF CHASTITY.—These strange devices have been contrived by the zealous male to preserve the purity of his sexual property—wives or concubines, as may have been the case.

Somewhere around the twelfth century, if not earlier, the ingenuity of man produced mechanical contrivances which have come to be known as *girdles of chastity,* or *padlocks of chastity*. It has been suggested that they were the vulgar materialization of an earlier symbol—the Herculean knot, which was used to fasten the woolen sash of the Grecian maiden, which the husband alone was to untie on his nuptial night.

The resemblance, however, is more marked by its dissimilarity than its likeness. The girdle of virginity, worn by the Hellenic maiden, was put on at puberty, and removed after marriage. The medieval girdle of chastity was presented to the wife by the husband after the marriage consummation as a token of mutual understanding, namely, that the wife would be faithful and the husband might not be consumed by jealous fears, particularly in his absences from home.

It seems likely that the device was introduced into Italy from the East, and later adopted by other countries. One of the earliest incidents relating to its use is that concerning Francisco Carrara, the Frances II of that family, well known as the Tyrant of Padua. His cruelties and infamies were so notorious that when he was captured by the Venetians he was forthwith executed.

The girdle of chastity associated with Carrara, and with

which, according to tradition, he locked up his mistresses, has reposed in the Ducal Palace in Venice for centuries among other relics of the Tyrant.

That the practice seems to have been especially prevalent in the Bergamask section of Italy is indicated by the words which Rabelais puts into the mouth of *Panurge:* "The deuce, he that has no white in his eye, take me then with him, if I don't buckle my wife in the Bergamask fashion, when I go out from my seraglio."

The folly of setting external restrictions on women in matters of love has always been recognized by minds keen enough to sense the fact that forbidden fruit is invariably deemed the sweetest. Æneas Sylvius, who afterwards became Pope Pius II, is quoted as having remarked, "Those jealous Italians do very ill to lock up their wives; for women are of such a disposition they will mostly covet that which is denied most, and offend least when they have free liberty to trespass."

The account of the introduction of the chastity belt into France has been given by Brantome in his *Les Vies des Dames galantes.* One day at the fair at St. Germain a dealer offered a dozen belts for sale. Five or six jealous husbands purchased them and proceeded to affix them to their wives, but legend has it that locksmiths were soon requisitioned to make duplicate keys, which resulted in threats to the dealer by some of the gentlemen of the court who had been taken in by the false security for which he had paid.

In the later part of the seventeenth century, Jean Buvat makes reference to a girdle of chastity which had been forced upon Charlotte Aglae d'Orléans who married the Prince of Modena. We are told that it was a belt of velvet, which surrounded both the loins and thighs of the wearer and apparently contained a metal plate, with a small orifice, which was tightly pressed against the pudenda. From what Buvat says, these devices were well known to him and were often used in Italian society.

The literature of Germany and Austria of the sixteenth century also refers to the use of the belt. In this connection Fischart, in his edition of *Gargantua,* has a passage in which he mentions the wiles and cunning of females against which steel plates and padlocks are of no avail.

In 1889 a skeleton was discovered in a church yard in Upper Austria, in which the bones of a female were still encircled by a chastity girdle. According to the account of the antiquarian who was present and able to obtain the girdle, excavations were made with the view to the restoration of parts of the church, when an ancient leaden coffin was unearthed. Around the pelvis region of the skeleton was a kind of hoop, joined in a number of places, and fitted with both an anterior and a posterior plate, the latter being riveted to the hip-band and the former being secured by locks.

The Musée de Cluny in Paris, and other museums in Europe have well-known examples of these devices. One in the Farnham Museum in Blandford, Dorset, England, is a steel belt with engraved designs on both frontal and posterior plate. The ornamentation is open work, cut out of the metal, and the hip-band is equipped with two alternative clasps for securing it around the body. There are small holes around the edges of the plates for the purpose of sewing on a lining of velvet or other soft material.

Traces of the practice of using chastity belts have been found even in our own country. H. W. Shoemaker, in *Publications of the Pennsylvania Folk Lore Society* (Altoona, 1930, xii), and other authorities on the folk lore of that state, refer to the use of chastity belts among the pioneer Pennsylvania women, and to a lesser extent Indian girls during the early history of that colony. These belts were made of heavy leather, studded with rivets. A strap passed between the legs and joined at the back other straps which were passed around the body, the contraption being secured by a padlock.

Dingwall states that there were two names by which these belts were known: one a Pennsylvania Dutch colloquialism, *Eiholder,* probably being a corruption of the Dutch "een houder" (restrainer); the other was *Futsashdupper,* meaning, according to local interpretation, "private organ shield."

We are told that mothers used to fit their daughters with these devices when the girls went on picnics or excursions, and that these "Day Belts", as they were later called, continued in use until comparatively recent times among the mountaineers of Central Pennsylvania. The saying, "I'll clap a belt on her", is still heard in this section when some unruly girl proves to be too fond of boys' company.

There is a record of the use of external means to protect the chastity of young girls in some barbarous tribes. Among the Yakut virginity was protected by an intricate arrangement of leather trousers secured with straps, which a girl was not allowed to remove even at night.

The traditions of this unique practice, however, are bound up chiefly with Italy and France, where examples of the original belts have long reposed as museum pieces, and allusion to them in literature is quite extensive. Thus we cull from the sharp-witted Voltaire:

> Since that time, in Venice and in Rome
> There is no pedant, cit or gentleman
> But, to guard the virtue of his house,
> Lays up a stock of girdles and padlocks.
> There, every jealous man, without fear of blame,
> Holds under lock and key the virtue of his dame.

INFIBULATION TO INSURE VIRGINITY.—A more primitive method than the use of chastity belts or girdles, and a more prevalent one, is known as *infibulation*. The practice involves the use of a clasp, fibula or buckle, or other means to achieve the same results. The custom is of very ancient origin, and still survives in many parts of the world, including Siam, Burma, Java, certain parts of India, and many sections of Africa. Strabo refers to the practice as having been common among the Ethiopians.

WHITE FOR PURITY.—Modern civilized people, too, have their penchant for stressing purity in connection with the wedding rites and for other ceremonial purposes. The tradition of a white ensemble for the bride is a very old one, and in accord with the almost universal practice of using white as the symbol of purity.

Among many peoples white is regarded as a sacred color, as well as denoting purity. White animals have been worshiped in certain parts of the world, notably the white elephant in Asia and Africa. A white dog was used by the Iroquois Indians as a sacrifice in their ceremonials.

The early Romans were accustomed to wearing white on joyous occasions, such as feast days and other celebrations. The Greeks esteemed the white rose as a symbol of joy.

It is said that the ancient Patagonians made a practice of painting their bodies white on all occasions of rejoicing. On the eve of a wedding celebration, the whole body was covered with an application of white substance.

The pure white diamond, above all other precious gems, is most esteemed and desired by the prospective bride as the ideal stone for the engagement ring.

CHAPTER IX

Child Marriage

INFANT BETROTHAL.—The practice of arranging the marriage while the parties concerned are still infants is very extensive in primitive societies. It should be borne in mind, however, that infant betrothal does not necessarily imply marriage in very early childhood.

Child marriage does take place in many parts of the world at a tender age, an age that is all too young to fulfill the responsibilities and obligations of matrimony, as there is abundant evidence to show. Probably a contributing factor to the incident of child marriage is climate, as this custom prevails mostly in tropical or semi-tropical lands, in which both girls and boys reach sexual maturity at an earlier age than in the cold or temperate zones.

There are exceptions in this respect, however, as the marriage of very young girls, and boys little older, is known in the more northern latitudes, even among the Eskimos. With respect to these latter cases, it is only fair to say that the practice does not appear to have reached the point of shameful abuses to undeveloped children, as it has in some instances elsewhere—in India, for example.

There are two general types of infant betrothal. The first concerns the arrangement for the marriage in infancy, or even before birth, of boys and girls of similar age. The second practice is to betroth female infants to grown men who may be old enough to be their father, or even their grandfather. This latter form of infant betrothal is indicative of a low stage of civilization, and especially a society in which women are kept in a state of extreme subjection. The betrothal of infants or marriage of children to each other, with all its objections, is at least not a matter of sex discrimination.

The principle of marriage by purchase has in modern times reached its greatest peak in Africa, where that purchasing power is used extensively to secure girls in infancy as future wives. The practice is especially prevalent in the slave-mongering regions of Western Africa.

An illustration of the anomalous result of betrothing an infant with a mature man is given by a medical resident in Old Calabar, who states: "I have seen a strapping man, in the prime and vigor of life, dandling on his knees and kissing a baby two or three weeks old that he expects to become his wife and the mother of his children some fifteen or twenty years later. Pointing to her, he says, 'You see my new wife?' "

The child usually remains in the charge of her mother until the age of puberty, though she often may join the household of her future husband when very young and be brought up as one of the family. The mother of a betrothed child is considered as acting for the future husband, and the latter accordingly often pays her for her services and expenses while the immature child is in her care.

He thus actually considers that he has the same claim on his child-wife as he would were she mature and living with him. In West Africa this extreme view is taken and no man except the husband dares touch or come near a betrothed or married woman, not even to shake hands.

The alloting of girls at birth, or before, is the general rule among the Australian natives. As soon as a female child is born, or even before, on the presumption that it will be a girl, she is promised to some one of the tribe, without reference to the age of the intended husband, which may exceed that of the father. This practice is also quite prevalent throughout Melanesia, and was especially common in the case of chiefs and men of distinction among the Polynesians.

It has been supposed that the difficulties experienced by the men in procuring wives, especially young wives, may be a principal cause of infant betrothal, which is widespread among uncivilized races. Its great prevalence among the Australian aborigines is undoubtedly due to the demand for women in their tribes.

It is the custom in Eastern Victoria to affiance more than one girl to the same youth, on the principle that the girl may die. On the other hand, one girl may be betrothed to several men; if the man to whom she was first betrothed dies before she is old enough to be claimed as his wife, then she is married to one of the other men.

In New Guinea, the betrothal of infants to one another is the common practice, and it is said the children are formally married when scarcely able to walk. This latter, however, seems to be quite exceptional, as among a great many tribes in which infant betrothal is the custom, the marriage either does not take place, or is not consummated, until puberty.

This practice is very common among all the peoples of Northern Asia, and is well-nigh universal among the Turkic population of Central Asia. It also prevails among some of the Eskimo and Alaskan tribes.

There is related the story of a Tasmanian native who, being concerned about the attention which a young man was paying his wife, hit upon the plan of betrothing his newly born daughter to the suspected rival. From that moment it became impossible for the latter even to look at his future mother-in-law. In a previous chapter we have noted the effect of the mother-in-law taboo, here exemplified.

It was a custom among the Ainu to betroth children, but the young man and his fiancée were not absolutely bound to marry. This is unusual in connection with child betrothal, as generally the carrying out of the arrangement sooner or later is a sacred obligation.

Economy is a factor that sometimes enters into the matter of infant or child betrothal. Among some of the Congo tribes the youth selects by preference a girl-child of six or seven years because she can be bought more cheaply at that age than when she is older. There is also the desire on the part of the girl to come into early possession of the things which are paid for her.

In areas where elopement or the abduction of girls is a recognized custom, parents are desirous of marrying their daughters as early as possible so as to prevent an undesirable runaway match. Child betrothal may also be a means of preserving the virginity of the girl, which is a quality highly regarded in the bride among many primitive peoples who practice marriage by purchase.

Malinowski reports that in the Trobriand Islands infant betrothal is regarded at least in name as equivalent to actual marriage. The betrothed are spoken of as husband and wife, and thus address each other. Although this status is called a marriage by the natives, and ceremonial rites are performed and gifts exchanged, there is the recognition of a difference between betrothal and the actual marriage, for when the two grow up they have to marry again.

During the period prior to actual marriage, while it is not seriously expected that the couple shall be chaste and faithful to each other, there has to be a pretense to that effect to conform to the proprieties. A flagrant transgression on either side would be resented by the offended party, and might even be called "adultery." In brief, both parties to the betrothal must carry on their amours with discretion, and due regard for appearances. This is an interesting aspect of sexual practices in a primitive society, and shows a close analogy to the regard for appearances that is called for in civilized communities when irregularities occur in the sexual relations.

In the Dutch East Indies also, where infant betrothal is the rule, the girls have complete liberty of action until the time of marriage. Often the future husband wants to put a stop to this by hastening the nuptials.

CHILD MARRIAGE IN INDIA.—Child marriage in India is based on the belief that celibacy is an impiety and a misfortune: an impiety, because one who did not marry put the happiness of the males of the family in peril; a misfortune, because he himself would receive no worship after his death.

A man's happiness in the next world was dependent upon his having a continuous line of male descendants, whose duty it would be to make the periodical offerings for the repose of his soul. The adoption of a son to fulfil this requirement is a doubtful expedient, as the Rig-Veda regards that procedure as unsatisfactory.

The ancient notion still survives in India "that a Hindu man must marry and beget children to perform his funeral rites, lest his spirit wander uneasily in the waste places of the earth." The very name of son, *Putra,* means one who saves his father's soul from the hell, called *Puta.*

Furthermore, marriage completes, for the man, the regenerating ceremonies, expiatory, as is believed, of the sinful taint which every child is supposed to contact in the mother's

womb; and being, for sudras and for women, the only ceremony for the purpose which is allowed. This is one of the
ordinances of the Veda.

A high-caste Hindu can be subject to no greater reproach
than to have an unmarried daughter at the age of puberty. A
family with such a daughter is believed to be under the dis-
pleasure of the gods. In a strict interpretation of certain texts
of Hindu religious law, her unmarried status entails retrospec-
tive damnation on three generations of ancestors.

The sacred writings of ancient India treat the subject with
poetic imagery, as will be noted in the following passages:

> So many seasons of menstruation as overtake a maiden feeling
> the passion of love and sought in marriage by persons of suitable
> rank, even so many are the beings destroyed by both her father
> and mother.
> A damsel should be given in marriage before her breasts swell.
> But if she have menstruated before marriage, both the giver and
> the taker fall into the abyss of hell; and her father, grandfather and
> great-grandfather are born insects in ordure.
> There is no atonement for a man who has intercourse with a
> "Vrishali", *i.e.,* a woman who has her courses before marriage, and
> even contact through inadvertence with the husband of such a
> woman has to be atoned by ablution of both person and dress.
> The father, mother and elder brother who tolerate a girl in her
> courses before marriage go to hell. A Brahman who will marry
> such a girl is not to be spoken of or admitted into society.

Early marriage in India therefore solves two problems explicit in the customs and mores of the land: It insures the
marriage of somebody's daughter at a satisfactory age (prior
to puberty), and it starts somebody's son on the way to ful-
filling his ordained mission of continuing the line of unbroken
descendants. The souls of ancestors cannot remain in heaven
unless there are male descendants to keep up the sacrifices.
Male descendants, therefore, cannot be provided too soon.

Under the laws of Manu a man may give his daughter in marriage before she is eight years old to a man of twenty-four, or a girl of twelve to a man of thirty, and he loses his dominion over her if a husband is not provided for her by the time of puberty. Intercourse before puberty is expressly forbidden by the Hindu law.

Observers have reported that in some parts of the country cohabitation often takes place before the child-wife has reached the age of puberty, and it does so, at the latest, immediately after her first menstruation. Incidentally, puberty occurs among the girls of India at an earlier age—generally between twelve and thirteen—than in our temperate zone.

India is a country of marriage brokers and professional marriage-makers. Competition between these gentlemen for husbands is so keen that it is no uncommon thing for a desirable husband to be approached and overtures of marriage made to him (or to his guardian, if he be a minor) while his present child-wife is breathing her last, and certainly before her body has been cremated.

The Mohammedans of India, as well as the Hindus, practice child-marriage and tenaciously cling to it, notwithstanding the efforts of the British government and of the more enlightened native leaders to dissuade them from the custom, which has many harmful consequences.

Mahatma Gandhi has declared: "I loathe and detest child marriages." Furthermore, he maintains that the Hindu scriptures give no sanction to this custom, and that even if they do so, they are wrong.

Of the unmarried girls in India in general only one in every fourteen has turned her fifteenth year. Among the Hindus marriage is contracted at an earlier age than among the population as a whole. At the higher ages practically no girl or woman is left unmarried except those suffering from some infirmity or disfigurement, concubines, prostitutes, beggars, religious devotees and a few members of certain hypergamous groups.

Hypergamy requires girls to marry into a higher sub-caste than their own, or at least forbids them to marry into a lower sub-caste. By this arbitrary narrowing of the field of prospective bridegrooms, some potential brides are forced into undesired spinsterhood, unless they become religious devotees or otherwise order their lives.

The practice of hypergamy is especially apt to lead to the postponement of marriage in the case of poor families. A poor man with several daughters finds it extremely difficult to pay the bridegroom price, or dowry, and as a consequence his girls remain unmarried long after the age of puberty. This is so frequently the case that in various castes the hypergamous sections no longer penalize a man for failing to marry his daughters at the age of pubescence.

The Zoroastrian books, like the sacred writings of India, stress the fact that a man should marry and beget progeny. Ahura Mazda said to Zoroaster: "The man who has a wife is far above him who lives in continence; he who keeps a house is far above him who has none; he who has children is far above the childless man."

No greater misfortune could befall an ancient Persian than to be childless. The bridge of Paradise was barred to him who had no child. The first question the angels there will ask him is whether he has left in this world a substitute for himself; and if the answer be "No," they will pass by and he will stay at the head of the bridge, full of grief. The implication of this is that the man without a son cannot enter Paradise because there is nobody to pay him the family devotions.

The goddess Ashi Vanguhi, the impersonification of piety, and the source of all the good and riches that are connected with piety, rejects the offerings of barren people—old men, courtesans and children.

ANTIQUITY OF CHILD MARRIAGE.—There has been considerable controversy as to whether the custom of child marriage in India is of great antiquity or of comparatively modern origin. Some writers, inclined to the latter theory, believe the practice originated in the first millennium of the Christian era. Others maintain it goes back to prehistoric times.

The evidence seems to favor the latter. We have it on the authority of Megasthenes that in his time (306–298 B. C.) early marriages prevailed in India in the case of girls, who might be wedded when seven years of age.

Now what are some of the results of this age-old custom upon child-life in particular, and the life of women in general in that country? A recent census showed that there were sixty million girls in India under the age of fifteen and of these eight and a half million were married. Among infants *under five years of age,* fifteen in a thousand were married or widowed. There were nearly four hundred thousand girl widows under fifteen years of age, who under the existing code must never remarry.

There were also a million and a half widows between the ages of fifteen and twenty-five. The great number of widows among children and young women is due, not only to the fact of early marriage, often with the disparity in the ages of the husbands and wives, but chiefly to the prejudice against the remarriage of widows.

The prohibition of widow marriage is held in the most strict regard by the higher caste Hindus as a mark of respectability. As is the case in almost all societies, the lower castes ape the practices of their superiors in order that they may raise their own social status. Those castes lowest in the social system are most apt to violate this traditional custom, as the bride price that may be offered the family is a strong temptation in their poverty.

As a means of protecting immature child-wives from physical injury by the husband, the Indian Penal Code, as amended, stipulates that a man who has sexual relations with his wife before she reaches the age of thirteen years is guilty of rape, and is punished by imprisonment which may extend to ten years. He is also subject to a fine.

Obviously, a law of this kind is very difficult to enforce, as only in the most extreme cases and under great provocation will the victim make complaint to the authorities. Equally difficult is the problem of obtaining corroborating witnesses, as members of neither the man's family nor the girl's can be induced to testify against a husband who, according to their sacred beliefs, is acting entirely within his rights.

Among the various factors that may be mentioned as primarily responsible for the maintenance and encouragement of child marriages are the following:

1. *Religious tradition.*—The custom is one of the sacred injunctions of Brahmanism, the most orthodox and influential Hindu religion, and therefore has the sanctions of religious authority. On the basis of this authority, it carries great weight among the followers of Indian religions outside of Brahmanism.

2. *Low estimate of woman.*—The deeply ingrained belief in India that women are by nature utterly depraved makes a very early marriage necessary, as that alone can insure the bride reaching her husband in a state of physical purity. Furthermore, the fact that the girl is never consulted in a

marriage arrangement (as an infant she would be too young to understand the consequences anyway) makes it easier to conclude the transaction. It is very often a "transaction" in a business sense, with a price paid to seal the bargain.

3. *The rigid caste system.*—The hide-bound caste system, and the ever-increasing sub-divisions of the castes, requiring that marriage take place between principals of the same caste, or the approved sub-castes, greatly narrow the field of choice for marriage, and stimulates the competition of parents seeking suitable alliances for girls, who must be provided with husbands *before attaining puberty.*

4. *Poverty.*—In the lower, impoverished castes where the fathers or guardians receive purchase money for the bride from the bridegroom's family, the need or desire for this money is a strong inducement for an early wedding. Moreover, girls being an economic burden, it is all the more reason to leave no stone unturned to espouse them as early in life as possible.

5. *The marriage brokers.*—Professional match-makers whose business it is to find suitable husbands for girls exert all their persuasive powers to effect early marriages in order to collect their fees. Life at best being uncertain, the sooner the ceremonies are performed the more sure are the brokers to receive their percentage of the dowry as a fee.

6. *Social tradition.*—Social custom having put the seal of its approval on child marriage, having decreed that early marriage is the *proper* thing, few will risk the verdict of social ostracism and disgrace by defying the custom. It must be remembered that postponement of the wedding of a daughter beyond the age of puberty is *orthodoxly impossible,* and as difficulty in obtaining a bridegroom reflects upon the social

and religious status of the girl's family, an early marriage is desired to avoid any chance of failure later on.

7. *Feminine intrigue in the household.*—Mothers-in-law, aunts-in-law, and sisters-in-law dwelling in a joint-family home are all equally desirous that the brides who are to come and share the home with them shall be children, indeed young children, amenable to discipline and motherly handling.

The girl-wife, too, in many cases looks forward to what she believes to be the glamour of the elaborate Hindu marriage ceremonies, which often last for not one, but many days, even weeks in wealthier circles, and offer a welcome change from the dull routine of her normal secluded life. To the immature, subordinated girl it is a colorful pageant in which she shines as the central figure—a Cinderella story come to life in which she is the heroine.

8. *Masculine advantages.*—Not the least important of the powerful influences which foster the tradition of child-marriage is the advantageous sexual position accorded to men under the religious law which sustains it. It should be remembered that the Hindu widower may remarry over and over again, and at *any* age he can have a child-bride. Moreover, if one wife fails to bring him offspring he may marry a second one, while the joint-family system relieves him of the inconveniences which might have been his lot under other circumstances, inasmuch as the young wife is not necessarily called upon to run the household. The elder women of the establishment do that and also help the inexperienced child-wife to rear her children.

9.—*Suppression of infanticide.*—Even the humane program to root out infanticide has had the effect of increasing the incentive to child-marriage. The fairly successful suppression by the British government of the once common practice of infanticide is by no means a negligible factor in the urge for early marriages. It means that the number of girls in the matrimonial market has been increased, and as a husband has to be found for *every* girl, if the family is to remain respected and in good social standing, the competition for desirable bridegrooms has become more brisk, with the tendency to lowering the age of matrimony.

CHILD MARRIAGE IN EUROPE.—The Roman law stipulated the minimum age limits of fourteen and twelve years for the male and female, respectively. This law was adopted by the Church and still remains in force in many Christian countries. A number of other Christian nations and states have revised the minimum age limit upwards from a year or two, to several years, in response to agitation resulting from a more enlightened social consciousness.

In many countries, however, in which the canonic age limit has not been preserved, the obstacle to marrying at an earlier age than that which the law permits may be removed by dispensation.

Not only has the general tendency of modern legislation been to raise the age limit, but modern civilization has generally proved unfavorable to the frequency of marriage. In the industrial countries of Europe, more than a third of the male and female population beyond the age of fifteen live in a state of voluntary or involuntary celibacy. An important cause of the decline of the marriage rate and the rise of the age of marriage in Europe, as well as in modern society generally, is the increasing difficulty in supporting a family under existing economic conditions.

The latest available United States census figures show a condition in this country no more favorable to marriage, as the proportion of unmarried males and females over the age of fifteen, including the widowed and divorced, is considerably over one-third of the total population within the same age limit.

It may be argued that it is unfair for statistical purposes to include the widowed and divorced among the unmarried, as these persons had once been married. It should be borne in mind, however, that as presently unmarried they are now in direct competition with the single persons, not only in the marriage market, but generally in the labor field as well.

The present tendency for young married women to continue gainful employment after marriage also makes them competitors in the labor market with the single workers. This seems inevitable and in accord with the evolution of our present industrial civilization. Often it is only by the joint earning capacity of both husband and wife that married life would be possible for a great many young couples, and this arrangement tends to promote marriages that would otherwise be impossible, thus reducing the celibate percentage of the adult population.

During medieval times child marriages were very common in nearly all European countries. In England from the end of the thirteenth to late in the seventeenth century, child marriages were prevalent, at first in the higher classes; later among all classes of society. In Scotland premature marriages reached such proportions that in the year 1600 they were forbidden; the age limits being set at fourteen and twelve years for males and females respectively. The reason, as is so often the case in eradicating a harmful social condition, was economic. The principal motive was to avoid feudal dues on the part of tenants to the crown, if the father should die and leave infants who would thus became their wards.

Marriages, too, in Italy and France at the time of the Renaissance occurred at a very early age. In distinguished families betrothal was by no means unusual at the age of two or three years. At this tender age Vittoria Colonna was affianced to the Marquis of Pescara.

Consummation usually took place at the age of twelve. La Claviere, writing of the times, said "that was a favorite age with the husbands; though, according to the best judges, fifteen was the age when the physical charms were at their best, and the soul was most malleable—a view dating as far back as Hesiod and Aristotle."

In vain the French physicians implored the men to wait at least until the fourteenth year. But they demurred, for it was humiliating for a father to have a fifteen-year-old daughter on his hands. At sixteen they would have called it a catastrophe.

Champier, one of the most serious of the contemporary writers, proposed that after the age of sixteen young women should be provided with husbands by the State, on the lines of Plato's system. It is said that some parents betrayed such haste to get their girls off their hands that they anticipated the ceremony, handing them over to their husbands-elect on the strength of a mere promise of fidelity.

Looking at the subject from its various angles, child marriage in general appears to be due to several factors, prominent among them being: religious superstitions, especially with respect to the interests of the dead in the other world; the ignorance and rapacity of parents, and their utter disregard for the rights and well-being of the children; abuse of parental authority through personal vanity and social ambition; and, in some instances, attempts to promote the interests of the children, in a given society, by avoiding alternative evils inherent in the prevailing system.

THE TRAGEDY OF INFANTICIDE.—The hideous practice of kill-
ing infants—usually females—has prevailed among savages
from primitive times. It is believed to have originated in the
early struggles for food and security. As long as men were
few in number, enemies scarce and game plentiful, there was
little temptation to eliminate the female infant. In fact, there
were some things in savage economy which women could
do better than men—occupations which his pride or laziness
induced him to leave to the women.

However, with even a slight increase in population in any
given area, with neighboring tribes encroaching upon each
other's game preserves, leading to wars and reprisals, female
children became a definite handicap. They ate, and did not
hunt or fight. They were a drain on their mothers when
young, and, when grown up, were a temptation to rival tribes.

As fighters and hunters were required and valued, it was to
the interest of every tribe to rear, if possible, healthy male
children. By the same token, it was less to their interest to rear
females, as they were less capable of self-support and less valuable to the defense of the community. Infanticide, therefore,
grew out of this predicament.

It is said that in Africa, where the hot climate and the
abundance of tropical fruits make the conditions of existence
easy, there are no well-authenticated cases of the custom of
destroying new-born children.

The practice has survived down to modern times in many
parts of the world, in most cases obviously for the reasons
already cited. Other motives have been ascribed as the cause,
including primitive religious observances, but it appears that
these are merely attempted rationalizations of causes that
had their origin in the struggle for existence.

As a result of this cruel custom, the tribes were often left with a deficiency of young women of their own, thus seriously disturbing the natural balance of the sexes within the hordes, and forcing them to prey on one another for wives.

One of the interesting theories of the origin of exogamy, as set forth by J. F. McLennan, is that this practice, induced by necessity, in time established a prejudice among the tribes observing it against marrying women of their own stock. The objection to this hypothesis, as Herbert Spencer has pointed out, is that if each tribe had fewer women than men, how could the tribes get wived by taking one another's women?

Where infanticide is practiced as a human sacrifice to the gods, it is often the male child that is preferred for the purpose of the sacrifice. It has been suggested that tribes of matriarchal character, in which women were dominant, used the male child as its sacrificial offering; the gender of the child being the opposite of the dominating sex in a given order in which infanticide is practiced.

Infanticide is not regarded in the lower stages of culture as a criminal act, but as a matter of expediency in tribal life and economy, and parents are not condemned for refusing to rear a child when it is not propitious to do so. The Australian aborigines, among the lowest type of surviving savages, destroyed many of their offspring simply because the infants were "too much trouble to look after."

In seasons of drought the tribes near Adelaide killed all new-born children. Thus mass infanticide was prompted, no doubt, not only through want induced by the drought, but by a belief that there was some evil magic which connected this misfortune inflicted by nature with the newly born infants. New-born infants are always suspect among savages and they have many taboos to protect themselves against malevolent influences from this source.

Among the Veddahs of Ceylon a family is not allowed more than three children; all above that number are killed. Likewise in the Marshall Islands no child after the third was allowed to live. Failure to exercise such moderation with respect to progeny is commonly regarded in primitive societies as a manifestation of unpardonable improvidence.

Among the natives of Ling-Chow, in Cochin-China, the improvident rearing of offspring was regarded as disreputable. Consequently all children born during the first three years of marriage were regularly done away with, and in any case all families were limited by infanticide to a maximum of one female and two male children.

In certain instances, for economic reasons, the boy is sacrificed rather than the girl. This was customary among the Abipones, because when a son grew up, it was necessary to buy a wife for him, whereas a price could always be obtained for a grown-up daughter. Perhaps this is a relic from the time when the tribe was matriarchal in character.

The natives of two-thirds of the South Sea Islands practiced infanticide more extensively than any other peoples known to history. The reason obviously is that the islands are of very limited extent and are as thickly populated as they could be and support life by the natural products of the soil.

Probably the best known instances of infanticide are those which existed in various forms throughout India, but which are now almost completely suppressed through a system of reporting births and deaths, and of police supervision in districts suspected of the practice.

In some parts of India it was the custom to cast the child into the Ganges (whence the reverence paid to the crocodile, which fed upon the children), or to poison it with opium or datura spread upon the mother's breast. Still other methods were used in making infanticide a sacrifice to some god.

Although forbidden both by the Vedas and the Koran, infanticide in India was practiced principally by certain tribes of lower caste, as well as among the Rajputs. The persistence of the custom among the latter was due to the fact that it was considered dishonorable for a girl to remain unmarried, and the necessary expenses of her marriage were a ruinous burden upon the parents.

When infanticide has become established as a custom among a savage race, its practice, like all usages connected with birth or marriage, frequently assumes a sacrificial or religious import, and by some authorities this is considered to be the explanation of the origin of the custom of sacrificing children to the gods.

CHAPTER X

Matriarchy, or the Mother-Family

THE MATRIARCHATE.—The hypothesis of a *matriarchate,* or
a social group, clan or tribe, ruled or dominated by women is
a controversial one, based largely on the findings presented in
the early 1860's by J. J. Bachofen, the scholarly Swiss ethnologist.

It was Bachofen's contention that since in all races there exist survivals of a period when children took the mother's
name, instead of the father's name, when property descended
in the female line instead of the male, and women held certain
exclusive economic privileges, these facts among other data,
including legends and myths, indicate that at an early period
in human society, women were generally the dominating element in family and tribal life.

In brief, Bachofen explained mother-right as a consequence
of the supremacy of women, economically and politically, in
the early stages of primitive society.

A Scottish contemporary, J. F. McLennan, quite independently also arrived at the theory of mother-right, but on other
grounds. He regarded what he called kinship through females
only, as due to uncertain paternity resulting from early promiscuity, or polyandry.

McLennan's hypothesis has been supported by later ethnologists, at least in those instances where it has been known to

prevail. Not all authorities agree that mother-right, or matri-
lineal reckoning, has everywhere preceded father-right as a
form of primitive family organization, but the preponderance
of evidence seems to favor this supposition. It is inconceivable, McLennan maintains, that anything but the want of
paternal certainty could have long prevented the acknowledg-
ment of kinship through males.

Morgan has shown in his comprehensive treatises on the
North American Indians, especially the Iroquois, not only that
reckoning of descent took place through the female line, but
that women did enjoy many rights and privileges not granted
them in patriarchal savage society. They were generally on a
plane with men politically, and economically they held superior influence and power. In every way the women were the
equals of the men, and in certain respects had decided advantages.

The maternal family system has existed in modern times not
only among the tribes of the Iroquois Confederation and other
American Indians, but also among certain African, Asiatic and
Polynesian groups, notably the Kamchadales, the Chamorros,
the Balondas, the Dyaks, the Garos, the Khasi, the Trobriand
Islanders, the Tahitians and Tongans, and the Hovas of Madagascar.

Blood kinship, or the identity of blood and body, is recognized only in the mother line by many of these peoples. There
is often a complete ignorance of the role of the paternal element in procreation. As Malinowski points out with respect
to the natives of the Trobriand Islands—who are utterly
ignorant of physiological paternity—they believe the whole
process of generation lies between the spirit world and the
female organism. Their belief in this respect is so firmly established that there is simply no room for physical paternity.

It is now generally conceded that Bachofen and his school of thought were not correct in assuming, because of the maternal line of descent, that the position of woman was necessarily a dominant one economically and politically, although there have been instances, and notable ones, where women have held such supremacy. These cases are well worth studying.

Morgan points out that in the Iroquois Long House the matron maintained a vigorous control of domestic affairs, and that in general women were accorded a position of importance and respect in the affairs of the tribe. They voted in the council of the tribe on equal terms with the men, and in economic matters they held a superior position.

It has been found to be the rule among many tribes that while descent is reckoned through the female line, it is not the mother or wife who exercises an authority over the children and affairs, which the husband does not possess, but the woman's nearest male kinsman, *i.e.,* her brother or maternal uncle. These male kinsmen even exercise authority over the husbands who come to live with the wife's family, which is the usual custom in these societies.

THE MATERNAL FAMILY—MATRILOCAL MARRIAGE.—The arrangement whereby the husband immediately after marriage goes to live with his wife's relatives and in a sense becomes subordinated to the members of her family, is known as matrilocal marriage.

Under this system the young man regards his father-in-law's house as his own, and often becomes the chief support of the household. He does not become his own master until after the death of the father-in-law. Even then, in many cases, he continues to be subordinated to some male member of his wife's family, and in some cases to the wife.

The Bering Strait Eskimo, who goes to live with his wife's family, transfers filial duty of every kind from his own people to those of his wife. Among the Aleuts of Kadiak Island the husband always lives with the parents of his wife, although occasionally he may visit his own relatives. It is the practice for the husband to discard his own name, and to take that of his wife's family.

Among the Vancouver aborigines one of the great inducements to marriage was that the new husband thereby acquired hunting and fishing rights over his wife's property. If the marriage terminated, the property reverted to the woman's sole use, and became a dowry for her next matrimonial venture. This is an interesting phase of the wife's ownership and control of property, and the economic power implied in the arrangement necessarily gives her a favorable, if not a dominant, position in the community.

The Kwakiutl of British Columbia had a modified form of the matrilocal system. The husband took up his abode in the home of the bride, but on making a special payment could remove her after three months. The idea of marriage by purchase is bound up in this procedure, which indicates that the wife is essentially the property of her family, but that after the lapse of a suitable time—probably in the nature of a trial marriage—the wife may be removed from the family domicile upon payment of a stipulated bride price.

The domestic life of the Zunis, one of the Pueblo tribes, has been described as almost ideal and one that might well serve as an example for civilized races. The house belongs to the women born of the family. There they come into the world, pass their lives and die within the maternal family walls. The brothers leave as they grow up to make their home with their respective wives.

The idyllic customs of the Zunis have been thus described by an observer: When the native girl takes a fancy to a young man, she makes him a present of hewe-bread as a token, and becomes affianced. He sews clothes and moccasins for her, and combs her hair out on the terrace in the sun. The security of the marriage tie rests with the woman. To her great honor, it is said she rarely abuses the privilege; that is, never sends her husband "to the home of his fathers" unless he well deserves it.

Among some of the Caribbean tribes of the West Indies, the women never quit their father's house after the marriage. Polygamy is sometimes practiced, and in this case the husband visits and lives with his several wives in turn at the homes of their respective parents.

In Caracas, if a native takes a fancy to a girl, he tells her so and then goes to her home. If she gives him a basin of water to wash himself and something to eat, this gesture indicates acceptance of his proposal. There are no other formalities, and the marriage is consummated. The continuance of the marriage is entirely dependent upon the wishes or whims of the young woman. If she becomes dissatisfied with him for any reason, or for no reason, she dismisses him and takes another. He, in turn, takes another wife.

Among some of the American Indian tribes the husband and wife never quit their own families and their own homes to make one family and one home for themselves. Each remained in his or her own home, and the children born of these marriages belonged to the women who bore them. The marriage did not establish anything in common between husband and wife except the bed, for each dwelt during the day with his or her parents.

It was the custom among the Sioux for the young man, as soon as he became a husband, to forsake his father's tent and live with his wife's people. These women were said to have had great ascendency over their husbands. Among the Crees the young husband likewise went to live with his wife's family who, however, treated him as a stranger until after the birth of his first child. He was then finally accepted into the family and felt closer to them than to his own parents.

In some of the American Indian tribes among whom the husband went to live with the wife's parents, if his contribution to the family larder through hunting and fishing was not satisfactory, or if for any reason his wife's people got tired of him, he was dismissed.

Upon the marriage of the eldest daughter, among the Kansas, Osage and allied tribes, she became the mistress of the maternal home and her parents were subordinate to her. Her sisters, as they grew up, became the wives of the same husband. A great chief was usually attended by one or two wives who looked after his establishment, but the majority of his spouses remained with their own relatives, and the husband visited them as he pleased.

Among the Khasi of Assam, the women hold a singularly favorable position in the tribal political economy. Real estate, houses and private property are transmitted in the maternal line, descending from mother to daughter. In one locality the position of pontiff is held by a woman, her successor being selected from a group of her female kin.

The matrilocal custom of marriage prevails among the various tribes of the Orinoco. From the moment of marriage, the husband leaves his own home and dwells in the abode of his wife's family. He hunts and fishes for his father-in-law, and is entirely dependent upon him. As is the practice in most cases of this kind, if the wife tires of her husband, she turns him out of doors and the marriage is terminated.

As in the case of so many tribes of the American aborigines, it was the custom also, and still is, for women throughout most of Africa to remain after marriage with their own families. This rule applies from the most primitive and backward to the most advanced African races.

A typical example, exogamous in character, is that of the Bushmen of South Africa, who led a nomadic life in small groups. With the consent of one of the matrons, a man might attach himself to a wandering band and become the husband of one or more of the women, contributing his share of the products of the chase to the group. If he proved unsatisfactory, the association was dissolved, and he joined another troop, where he found new wives. A most important requirement is that a man may on no account marry into a group connected with his own family. He must find wives in a group outside his kin (exogamy), and upon marriage he severs all ties with the family to which he belonged, and becomes a member of his wives' clan.

One of the African tribes has a proverb expressive of this situation: "Happy is she who has borne a daughter; a boy is the son of his mother-in-law."

David Livingstone thus describes the marital arrangement of the Banyai of the Zambesi region: "When a young man marries he is obliged to come and live at their village. He has to perform certain services for the mother-in-law, such as keeping her well supplied with firewood; and when he comes into her presence he is obliged to sit with his knees in a bent position, as putting his feet towards the old lady would give her great offense. If he becomes tired of living in this state of vassalage and wishes to return to his own family, he is obliged to leave all his children behind; they belong to the wife."

The Malay family is definitely matrilocal, with some characteristics of its own. It has been described as a "Motherhood," consisting of the old house, with the mother and her descendants in the female line, unmarried sons and daughters, daughters' children, and so on. The father forms no part in the arrangement.

The Malayan father remains much closer in family bonds to his brothers and sisters than he does to his wife and children. Both the husband and wife continue after marriage to live in their respective households. The husband is not even charged with the obligation to feed and maintain his wife and children; that responsibility rests upon the maternal family to whom the wife and children belong.

The actual head of the family is usually the brother of the wife (or of the mother) called "mamak." He has administrative authority over the property, but according to custom, it is his sister who keeps the family valuables and money in her room. The family property rests entirely within the Motherhood. When a Malay dies, his personal belongings pass to his maternal family—first to his brothers and sisters, then to the children of his sisters, but never to his wife or her children.

THE IROQUOIS MATRIARCHATE.—The Iroquois form of family and political organization has been cited as a conspicuous example of mother-right with resultant privileges and powers to the women of the clans. The tribes originally constituting the Iroquois Confederation of northwestern New York and southeastern Canada were the Mohawks, Oneida, Onondaga, Cayuga and Seneca. At the beginning of the eighteenth century the Tuscarora tribe became affiliated with the league, but not quite on equal terms with the five great tribes.

In addition to hunting and fishing the Iroquois tribes showed considerable knowledge of agriculture. They lived in villages consisting of a limited number of Long Houses, covered with bark over wooden frames. The size of the houses may be deduced from the fact that they were often capable of domiciling one hundred or more individuals. The Long Houses were not only the family homes, but also had ceremonial significance.

The ceremonial life of the Iroquois was centered about several great feasts, associated with their tribal economy. The Strawberry Festival took place in early spring, coinciding with the ripening of these berries; followed by the Bean and Raspberry Festivals. In the fall the great Corn Festival was celebrated with the ripening of the maize, and in late January or early February there was the Mid-Winter Festival, a feature of which was the sacrifice of a white dog by strangulation.

The Corn, Bean and Squash were personified in the "Three Sisters"—*Our Mothers*—of Iroquois mythology. The women played the leading part in the agricultural and handicraft activities of the tribe. The work in the fields, planting, hoeing, harvesting and storing the produce, as well as preparing the food for consumption, was almost exclusively done by the women.

A considerable degree of communism was characteristic of early Iroquois tribal life. Certain fields, not associated with the individual households, were shared by the community as a whole. Moreover, the excess produce of the more fortunate families was divided among the less favored members of the village. The supplies from the communal fields were likewise partly utilized in this way, as well as for the preparation of the large amounts of food required at the periodic tribal festivals.

As has been noted, woman had her obligations and responsibilities no less than her rights and privileges. This is characteristic of all savage tribes that are matriarchal in function. The family organization was maternal in character, consisting of a head woman, or matron, her immediate male and female descendants, the male and female descendants of her *female* descendants, and so on. The maternal families, consisting of the individuals of three or four generations living at one time often numbered from fifty to as many as one hundred and fifty or even two hundred members.

Each family, or clan, was closely associated with one or more Long Houses. The type of marriage was exogamous—no member of a clan being permitted to marry a woman of the same clan. The family names were totemic, taken from the names of animals and birds, and marriage was prohibited between persons of the same totem.

Thus a Mohawk Bear man was not only forbidden to marry a Mohawk Bear woman, but the same prohibition prevented him from marrying a Bear woman of any of the affiliated tribes. He must therefore marry a Hawk, Wolf or woman of some other totem outside his own clan.

Upon the death of a chief, the matron of the maternal family to which the chief had belonged chose his successor, usually a maternal nephew or younger brother of the deceased chief, but in any event a member of the same maternal family. Having reached her decision, the matron would call a meeting of the members of her maternal family for the ratification and approval of her choice.

The matron in question was then constituted a delegate to the chiefs of the Brother clans, Cousin clans and Council of the Chiefs, to obtain their concurrence in the action, which was usually given. It is equally interesting to know that after the election of the new chief, the matron of the maternal family continued to watch and supervise his activities.

If the new chief proved neglectful of his duties, showed a

tendency to intemperance or dishonesty, or proved lacking in patriotism in his behavior toward the tribes of traditional enemies, such as the Sioux or Algonquins, the matron forcefully brought the delinquencies to his attention. If he persisted in his offensive ways, the matron could divest the chief of his office. When necessary she issued an ultimatum to him in the following formal language:

"I will now admonish you for the last time and if you continue to resist to accede to and obey this request, then your duties as chief of our family and clan will cease, and I shall take the deer's horns from off your head, and with a broadedged stone axe I shall cut the tree down." This last phrase symbolized his deposition as chief, and the matron received back the deer's horns—the symbol of his chiefly office. In this manner was an unworthy chief deposed by the representative woman of his clan.

It is thus seen that although the women were not hereditary rulers, the office was essentially in their control, and they had unusual political, economic and social power and influence.

In certain instances when a woman performed extraordinary acts of heroism or patriotism, for which the tribe wished to show grateful recognition, she was made an honorary chieftain. This was termed a Pine Tree chieftainship—the recipient of the honor being conceived as straight as a pine. The office, however, was purely an individual honor and not transmissible by inheritance.

As women constituted public opinion, and the chief was responsible to them for his actions, very naturally no attempts were made to subjugate women in the manner of so many savage and barbarous tribes. It is an ironic reflection on the evolution of our own democratic way of life when we recall that among the Iroquois Indians, all adults, both male and female, were admitted to the council or democratic assembly where they enjoyed equal suffrage; whereas, it took decades of education and agitation and, in the end expensive, concentrated campaigns on the part of the white women in approximately the same area to secure like rights and privileges, which were finally achieved as late as the year 1919.

The economic supremacy of the women is best illustrated by the fact that ownership of the land among the Iroquois, as in practically all the American Indian tribes, was vested in the women. When the Indians conveyed land to the United States Government, the signatures and authority of the women had to be obtained in order to make these transactions legally valid. The signatures of the men were of no account.

The matron of the maternal family in whose power it was to make and unmake chiefs, often knew in advance who the new chief was likely to be, a fact of which the prospective new chief was of course aware. This knowledge naturally influenced the behavior of the young man. He realized he was under the scrutiny of one who held supreme power, upon which the future of his career depended.

The Iroquois women were not only fully equal to the men in their political, economic and social status, and in some respects superior, but also took a prominent part in the ceremonial affairs, which are always important in tribal life. Of the six ceremonial officials which it was customary for each clan to elect for the purposes of preparing and supervising ceremonial procedure, three were women and three were men. These officials made the decision as to the period when the great tribal festivals were to be held, selected the number and personnel of the men and women who were expected to officiate at the festival, supervised the preparation of the huge quantities of food required, and looked after the appropriate overhauling of the ceremonial Long House.

Morgan states that all the members of an Iroquois *gens* (synonymous with "clan") were personally free, and they were bound to defend each other's freedom. They were equal in privileges and in personal rights. Even the sachem and chiefs could claim no superiority. They were a brotherhood bound together by the ties of kinship, and this kinship streamed through the female line. "Liberty, equality and fraternity, though never expressly formulated, were cardinal principles of the gens."

The *gens* was the simplest and lowest form of council in the tribe, and was thoroughly democratic, as every adult male and female member had a voice upon all questions brought before it. A social structure so democratically constituted from the ground up must inevitably leave the impress of its character upon the individuals. It helps to explain the quality of independence and personal integrity associated with Indian character in its native state. In every sense of the word the history of the Iroquois tribes furnishes a splendid lesson in the democratic way of life. Especially commendable is the just and equitable treatment, perhaps unparalleled in primitive societies within modern times, which they accorded to the members of the female sex, treating them with the respect, consideration and dignity due to the mothers of the race.

OTHER EXAMPLES OF THE MATRIARCHATE.—Bachofen has shown us evidence of the ancient existence of mother-right, which in his terminology is synonymous with the dominance of women, in Lycia, Athens (before the heroic age), Egypt, the Italic tribes before the founding of Rome, parts of India and Central Asia, Lesbos, Mantinea, and among the Cantabic. This by no means exhausts the list.

Plutarch expressly stated that in Sparta women were the sole property owners, which in itself would be an incentive to dominance, or would indicate economic supremacy.

A comparative study of feminine dominance as it has existed among the most diverse peoples, shows in the possession of the female sex those privileges and advantages that are the prerogatives of the male in masculine dominated society. Where women rule, woman is the wooer. The man furnishes the dowry.

The woman has the sole right of disposal over the common possessions. Often she alone is entitled to divorce her mate, if he is no longer agreeable to her. The husband adopts the name and nationality of the wife's family. The children are named after the mother and inherit from the mother. The parental duty of providing for the children is imposed on the dominant sex—the woman. Where the primitive custom of infanticide prevails under female supremacy, boys and not girls are the victims.

The gods, or at least the leading divinities, are for the most part feminine. Should it be stated in refutation that feminine divinities are also exalted in patriarchal societies, it may be pointed out that in all cases these tribal goddesses are of very ancient inception, and may well have originated under a previous or matriarchal system. They would thus quite naturally be carried over, as all peoples are reluctant to discard customs that bear the sanctions of religious authority, even when their original meaning has been lost.

Matriarchy therefore implies a reversal of the sexual privileges and prerogatives that obtain in a patriarchy or male dominated society. It is a well-known axiom that economic power is the source of social and political prestige and supremacy, and women certainly have held economic dominance among many ancient and primitive peoples. In numerous examples of mother-right, some of which have been cited in this chapter, women have held the social advantages inherent in their economic control.

It is evident from the research of Max Müller, the famous philologist, that the women of ancient Egypt were sexually the aggressors, in much the same manner that man is in modern society. Without a due regard for the natural behavioristic consequences of a feminine dominated society, he expressed surprise that "Egyptian women had been over-ready to play the man's part." He continued: "At least it seemed perfectly natural to the ancient Egyptian poets that an invitation to an assignation, in a poem packed with allusions, should proceed from a woman. To crown it all, the Egyptian man took delight in representing his inamorata as playing the seducer's part, as not content simply to run after him, but as plying him with wine and other intoxicants."

As Müller, like many otherwise able ethnologists, was not cognizant of the implications of matriarchal rule, he failed to grasp the real significance of his observations, and therefore expressed amazement and surprise that women could act in so forthright a manner. Other Egyptologists have commented on the fact, from their study of the ancient literature of the country, that in Egypt women were the wooers, and took the initiative in matters of love.

In the wooing of Joseph by Potiphar's wife, the onus of the episode is thrown upon the woman because of her aggressiveness. Joseph indignantly rejects the attempt to seduce him, and as a final resort runs away to preserve his chastity. The narrative is related with a solemn commendation of his masculine virtue, and contempt for the female seducer (*Genesis*, xxxix, 1–16). Here, too, we have the influence of the ancient

Egyptian mores, as Potiphar and his wife were Egyptians, imbued with the customs of their native land. Joseph, on the other hand, was bred in the patriarchal traditions of the Hebrews, who held to a sexual code that acted quite the reverse of the Egyptian.

Diodorus, who lived at the time of Caesar, was quite indignant over the position of women in Egypt. He resented the fact that in Egypt not the sons, but the daughters supported their aged parents. He therefore spoke disparagingly of the hen-pecked men of the Nile, who granted rights and privileges to the weaker sex that seemed outrageous to a Roman or Greek.

The wife in ancient Egypt exacted a promise of obedience from the husband, much the same as the traditional promise in western marriage which men receive from their wives to "Love, honor and obey." Diodorus remarked that among the people the wife had authority over the husband, and in the marriage contract the husband had expressly to "pledge himself to obey his wife."

Herodotus noted that among the Lydians the women not only sought out their mates, but assumed the role in the economic life of the community that is generally held by men. Wooing by the women plays an important part in the ancient sagas of Hindustan. By the Laws of Manu, a girl is permitted the free choice of her husband—a law long since nullified by the perverted customs of succeeding patriarchal dominance.

Among the Balonda, a rugged Negro tribe at the Zambesi in Africa, the women held a position economically superior to that of the men, as reported by Livingstone and other missionaries and explorers. Women are members of the tribal council. When a young Balonda marries, he must migrate from his village to the one in which his wife resides. He must at the same

time pledge himself to provide his mother-in-law with kin-
dling wood for her lifetime. The husband was so completely
subject to his wife that he could do nothing whatever without
her approval. No agreement was binding without her consent,
and even the performance of some trifling service called for
her concurrence. The woman, in turn, must provide her husband's food. Here we have the woman responsible for the family's maintenance, just the reverse of the status that obtains in
the patriarchal family system.

Jaeckel, referring to the Khasi tribe of Assam, stated that the
girls are the wooers. The courted male "has to make a vigorous
resistance, culminating in flight. He is finally captured and led
back to the nuptial residence amid the lamentations of the
parents." Here we have a relic of marriage by capture in reverse, the bridegroom being the object of the chase.

Similarly, among the Kamchadales, where the female sex
appeared in many respects to have been dominant, the women
were the wooers. We are told that the women positively
fought for the possession of eligible men. The men were so
subordinate to their wives that a husband never secured anything from his wife by force, but achieved his ends only by the
humblest and most persistent petitions and caresses.

The Chamorro men, of the northwestern Pacific Ocean
islands, who were famous for their physical strength, were
kept in complete subjection by their wives. The legal status
of the women was higher than that of the men, which is the
best indication of matriarchic rule, as the tendency of any ruling group is to keep a monopoly of power by legal sanction.
If a man for any cause gave his wife dissatisfaction, she did not
hesitate to chastise him by physical means.

Women, too, had a freedom in sexual matters not possessed
by the men. Conjugal infidelity was severely punished in hus-

bands, even when the offense was merely suspected, not proved. The accused husband was taken in hand by the women of the community. If the wife proved unfaithful, however, the husband had no redress. Under the circumstances, it was only the women who were privileged libertines.

A parallel situation prevailed among the Kamchadales. The married men had to conceal their illicit love affairs with the utmost care. The wives on the other hand openly indulged in amours, not considering it necessary to hide their infidelities from their husbands.

Winwood Read remarked that among savages generally it is the male seducer who suffers, not the unfaithful wife. This is the reverse of what happens in a patriarchal society. He wrote at a period when little attention was paid to matriarchal influences, and so he failed to note the connection among many of the savage tribes of which his remark was true. Among patriarchal groups the unfaithful wife is most severely dealt with, not infrequently killed, or sold into slavery.

SUPREMACY OF THE HEMITIC WOMEN.—Matriarchal institutions are still very much in evidence among the Hemitic people who occupy extensive territory in North Africa. Among them the woman owns the property, which she bequeaths in the female line; the man being entirely without property. Her name and social status are handed down to her female heirs. Descent from the woman determines the caste. The man may be a slave or a bondsman, but if the woman belongs to a high caste, the children will be high-born.

Again her economic superiority is evidenced not only in the ownership of property, but in the fact that the woman does and has charge of all the work. She makes the skins into leather and prepares the leather clothing and tents. She milks the cows, makes the butter, mends and weaves. The erection of the dwelling tents, or their removal, is her work. The man hunts, tends the cattle and engages in the wars.

It should be emphasized, in connection with the great amount of hard physical work that falls upon the woman's shoulders in matriarchal society, that this is neither a hardship nor a social drawback. We have seen this also in the case of the Iroquois society. The woman in the matriarchal order accepts her responsibilities, including hard toil, with her privileges. This training gives her the physical strength and self-discipline necessary to maintain her rights and dominating position.

Briffault points out that as workers, primitive women are generally more muscular and better developed, and sometimes larger, than the men. In several uncultivated races, the average height of the women is greater than that of the men.

Among these Hemitic people the woman characteristically chooses the husband, usually making her selection from among various rivals. Later, if a more attractive, daring or acceptable man appears on the scene, she may woo him with the same insistence. The husband, being subordinate, can do nothing in particular about it, and if he becomes objectionable, he is simply dismissed altogether.

In the true matriarchal society, while the wife has the right to divorce her husband, the latter does not enjoy a similar privilege. This, again, is a reversal of the divorce status in the primitive patriarchal way of life.

As a matter of fact, in the matriarchal order, the woman not infrequently showers her affections on her brother, to the neglect of her husband, subjects the latter to tyrannical tempers, and has no hesitancy in letting him feel her antipathy.

Polyandry seems to be a custom more prevalent in matriarchal than in patriarchal societies—polygamy being characteristic of the latter in their primitive forms. Strabo noted the existence of polyandry among the Arabs at a period when women exercised a dominant role.

Among the peoples of matriarchal character who practiced polyandry were the Garos, the Nayars, the Tlingits, the Sakai, and tribes of like tradition in Tibet and in Burma.

THE PASSING OF THE AGE OF MOTHER-RIGHT.—The numerous instances in savage communities in which we find fragments or recognizable traces of the maternal family suggest the last remaining remnants of a definite matriarchal society. They connote the evidence of a passing order—the original mother-family, with its privileges and prerogatives, in process of final disintegration or transition into paternal patterns.

Unfortunately, the origins of these customs are lost irretrievably, and only the shadowy, nebulous forms of legends and myths remain, in some instances, to account for the existence of female rulership in family and tribal life. Stories such as the Amazonian legends survive to remind us of the exploits of women who rebelled *en masse* against the tyrannous restrictions of the rising patriarchy.

We do know that the structure of society and the form of family life have gone through drastic changes in their evolutionary development. There is logic in the assumption, and at least circumstantial evidence to indicate, that the lowest stage of family organization in some sections of the world was hetairism, in which all the women of the group were wives in common. Matriarchy, the supremacy of woman over man in the family and clan, accounted for the middle stage. The third stage was patriarchy, the prerogative of man, which has been the prevalent system within historic times. Our present marital arrangement is the pairing system, with patriarchal influences predominating.

Considering the differences of the races, the diversity of social cultures in their unlike environments, and the isolation of many of them in a world with only rudimentary means of communication, there could have been no uniform change in their development. There must have been an overlapping of two, and sometimes of all three, of these forms of family and tribal systems over a great period of time. A study of the social life of many diverse races in modern times reveals remnants and vestiges of previous forms of family and tribal structure in the midst of a current form of quite different, even reverse, character.

Under matriarchal law comparatively peaceful conditions prevailed. Woman is biologically the conservator. Social relations were simple and the mode of life was a primitive one. The various tribes generally respected each other's domain. If one tribe was attacked by another the men took up arms for defense, and were ably supported by the women. The women generally were not inferior to the men in physical strength and skill, and could when necessary give a good account of themselves in combat with men.

CHAPTER XI

Patriarchy, or the Father-Family

THE RISE OF PATRIARCHAL RULE.—What are the factors that induced a gradual change from matriarchy, or female dominance, to patriarchy, which has been the source of our characteristic western family and social traditions? Change in living conditions due to greater emphasis on landed property and its transmission, the rise of the industrial arts, wars, resulting from the new social stimuli and frictions, pressure of population, etc., seem to furnish the answer. All of these factors tended to increase masculine influence, as the male is biologically the more active and aggressive of the sexes.

The change in mode of life from primitive agriculture to pastoral pursuits seems to have been the primary decisive influence in the transition. With the domestication of cattle and the growth of flocks, there appears a change in the social relationship of men and women. The possession of herds and flocks forced the herdsmen to range more widely, so that the men became more out of touch with, and out of authority in, their wives' kinship clan.

Where pastoral society had not come into existence, the patriarchal order had not developed. Confirmation of this is found on the American continent, where no domestication of cattle had taken place prior to the settlement by Europeans and the social order everywhere remained primarily matriarchal, whereas it had disappeared in the pastoral life of Europe and most of Asia.

Egypt, on the other hand, which derived its wealth primarily from agriculture and had never experienced pastoral life on a large scale, remained singularly exceptional as a country of matriarchal traditions in a high stage of cultural development and prosperity.

Professor Sumner has suggested that the change and transfer of dominance from the mother-family to the father-family may well be considered the greatest and most revolutionary in the history of civilization.

In the primitive economy of matriarchal society, women not only owned and held title to the land and other property, but performed most of the labor in agriculture and craftsmanship, as well as the domestic work. One of the fundamental differences between matriarchal and patriarchal ideology is that in the former society, hard work is implicit in ownership, while in the latter manual labor is, wherever possible, shunted upon an underprivileged class. In the earliest forms of patriarchy, it became the custom to enslave the men of vanquished enemy tribes, whereas formerly they had been killed.

The point has been made by Briffault that the enormous amount of labor performed by the women and the comparative leisure enjoyed by the men served to convey the erroneous impression that women in uncultivated society are in a condition of abject slavery, and that the degree of civilization may be measured by the idle status of women. This he labels as a patriarchal fallacy and misinterpretation, and the exact opposite of the truth.

The activity of the men and the idleness of the women—i.e., upper-class women—in patriarchal civilization is the measure of women's economic subjection.

The reverse state of things in primitive societies is the most firm guarantee against the possibility of female subjugation in those societies. The patriarchal subjection of women was only established when they became idle, or, more accurately, when they were separated from the labor and activities of clan economy, other than the domestic. They lost power and control when their hands were removed from the implements of labor. The use of implements of labor in primitive society is synonymous with ownership and control, and the latter position indicates economic dominance. Exceptions become evident only with the development of a slave class.

With the production of the necessities of life at a low stage of development, and capable of satisfying only the simplest demands, there was a minimum of rivalry between neighboring tribes. However, with the expansion of pastoral pursuits and the increase in population, resulting in rivalry for land and for the marketing of products, conflicts became increasingly frequent and intensified. The male, who played a secondary role in primitive economic life, hunting, fishing and occasionally fighting, became a more important figure with the demands upon him as a militant herdsman and professional warrior.

Furthermore, with the greater diversity of possessions, there ensued an increased division and specialization of labor. Agriculture and cattle-breeding increased beyond their former simple scope of family and clan activities. Tools and implements were required which necessitated special knowledge, and the making of these, too, became the province of men. Thus new sources of wealth and power came into possession of man, and he became the owner and master.

We know that among the peoples who practice mother-right, it is the custom for the married man to live and become identified with the wife's family, which contributes to his inferior status. The ancient patriarchal family was founded upon the marriage of one man and several wives, and, if the man was so inclined, the right of maintaining as many concubines as his means permitted.

With the rise of the patriarchal family, the husband began to take the woman away from her parents into his family abode. The practice of paying the bride's family for this privilege resulted in the traditional custom of marriage by purchase, or later by contract. Thus the relation of a wife to her husband became analogous to property. The same is true of the relation of children to the father. It is the father's right and privilege to sell his daughters and otherwise exercise tyrannical control over them, as well as over the sons.

Patriarchal authority having in time become established, there came with it the change from matrilinear to patrilinear descent, both with respect to name and property rights. The father, or patriarch, used the influence of his ownership of property—which often included flocks and slaves, weapons and produce—as means to exact obedience from his sons, especially the eldest, who generally inherited the property or the major part of it.

The genealogies and stories of family customs and conduct in the Old Testament offer a typical example of the patriarchal way of life. Patriarchy was already well established among the ancient Hebrews, a pastoral people, at that early period.

Among the contemporary inhabitants of a neighboring country, Egypt, mother-right was still the prevalent system, and the economic and social practices of the two peoples illustrate the contrasting characteristics of the two types of society.

Among the ancient Hebrews, as among all patriarchal peoples, women were utterly deprived of rights. Marriage was arranged by purchase or contract. Unqualified chastity was demanded of the woman, but not so of the man. Polygamy was permitted, and the man might not only have several wives, but concubines as well, if his means permitted the luxury.

If the man had reason to believe his wife had lost her virginity before their marriage, he was not only entitled to cast her off, but she might be stoned to death. The same punishment was accorded to the adulteress, but a man was subject to the same punishment only when he committed adultery with a Jewish matron.

The patriarchal family was belligerent and strongly militaristic, in contrast to the more passive and tranquil tendencies of the matriarchy. It was well adapted to serve the purposes of alien adventurers in their conquests over more peaceful agricultural peoples.

Patriarchy was thus fostered and became firmly entrenched by the Roman conquests of northern and middle Europe. The last remnants of any matriarchal practices or traditions that may have remained were rooted out as the countries of Europe became more and more an operating field for predatory hordes, mercenaries and armies.

The system fitted in with the institutions of slavery and serfdom on one hand, and ruling castes and militaristic authority on the other. In the patriarchal family wives and children were not only regarded to all practical purposes as property—as much so as slaves, serfs and cattle—but were even so in a legal sense. The father's authority was absolute over his children, even to life and death, and the legal status of the wife was very much the same as that of the child.

OLD RUSSIA THE LAST PATRIARCHY.—With the passing of patriarchy in its pristine form as a result of the decline of feudalism and the French and industrial revolutions, the last remaining evidence of the patriarchal family in anything like its real character was to be found in old Russia of the early and middle nineteenth century. Czarist Russia was too firmly rooted in the past to make anything but a slow transition.

LePlay, the reactionary French sociologist, wrote in evident admiration of this flourishing social anachronism as follows: "The old parents, finding ample means of subsistence in the nature of their locality, are able to gather around them four generations of their own blood. The father of the family, whose power is justified by his long experience, possesses the necessary ascendancy to hold both youth and ripe age in submission to the Decalogue and to custom." Later in this chapter we shall discuss the practice known as *jus primae noctis,* or "right of first night", which was a privilege of the patriarchal master, and survived in many places throughout the feudal period. This custom, with other sexual anomalies, continued in Russia down into the nineteenth century, long after it had become outmoded in western Europe. The marriage of children was in the absolute control of the father. When a youth reached the age of eighteen he was married without delay. Westermarck and others have related how the father was often anxious to marry his son at an earlier age in order to secure an additional female laborer, and then cohabited himself with the young wife during the son's minority. It was a common practice of the father to marry his young sons to grown-up women.

Baron von Haxthausen wrote before the Emancipation in 1861, "the patriarchal government, feelings and organization are in full activity in the life, manners and customs of the Great Russians." The adult son was subject to his father's authority until he himself had children and became the head of a family.

Marriages were so arbitrarily arranged by parents in the upper classes that the bride and bridegroom frequently never saw each other before the wedding. Among the peasantry and lower classes, they saw each other but never dared to speak about marriage because that was a thing which did not depend upon themselves.

While patriarchy has long since passed on as the dominant family system in modern society, traces of it still linger, as do remnants of even older systems. In fact many of our prevalent ideas and concepts with respect to sexual practices and relations between the sexes are heritages from the patriarchal age.

The double code of morality—a loose one for men and a restrictive one for women—is a survival of the patriarchal mores. The present tendency in our transitional period is toward a single moral code, the adjustment being made by a relatively more monogamous practice on the part of the male sex, and relatively greater freedom than in the past on the part of the female gender.

Strict paternal authority and arranged marriage are traditions which have survived and come down almost to the present day in many places, and still find existence in some localities and instances.

The traditional attitude toward illegitimacy, which has found cruel expression in the laws and mores of most European countries and America, definitely of patriarchal origin. Heartless severity in dealing with the offending woman and the illegitimate child was characteristically the patriarch's firm attempt to transmit his possessions and the family name only through legitimate heirs.

The faithless woman commits the worst deception possible in the patriarchal mind. She brings another man's children into his house to become the heirs of his property and name.

For this reason adultery, when committed by a woman, was punishable by death or slavery among all ancient peoples of masculine dominance. And the laws were formulated so that illegitimate children were deprived of name, family and rights.

The humanitarian maxim that there are no illegitimate children, only illegitimate parents, is a definite break with the ancient code. This enlightened concept is finding increasing expression in the laws of many states and countries.

The patriarchal principle which separated woman from ownership, resulting in upper-class circles in making a virtue of female idleness, has brought a train of untold neurotic disturbances to woman's life. The more prosperous middle class, ever ready to ape the ideology of its superiors, has adopted the practice, so that girls by training frequently become neurotic misfits, and only too often "gold-diggers" or "alimony-hunters", unfit to be useful, contented wives under any circumstances.

PATRIARCHY IN ANCIENT GREECE.—That a matriarchal system once existed in prehistoric Greece seems evident from some of its customs and legends. The annual celebration of the Thermophoria clearly exhibits all the evidences of such a regime. It was customary in Greece for women to appeal for advice and help to the goddesses only. Even at a later period Hellenic women celebrated the old festival in honor of Demeter, which lasted for five days, and in which no man was allowed to participate.

Religious customs are always the last of traditions to give way before a new epoch, and the Hellenic religion inevitably reflected the dominating character of ancient society. Among the ancient Hebrews we see patriarchy indicated in the character of the personalities and the manner of worship portrayed in the Old Testament.

In ancient Egypt we find the matriarchy just as clearly evidenced in the worship of the beneficent Sun gods Re and Osiris, and of the wise goddess Isis, whose magic powers typified the aspirations of Egyptian womanhood and reflected its dignity in the social life of the country.

The decline of the matriarchy in Greece forms the theme of the native myths, legends and drama. The tragedy *Agamemnon* by Aeschylus relates a deadly intra-family feud between Agamemnon, King of Mycenae and his wife Clytemnestra, that in the conflict of personalities dramatizes the struggle between the sexes for power and dominance. Some of the representative tragedies of Sophocles and Euripides likewise give dramatic expression to the jealousies and craving for power that typified the rivalries of the sexes in the transitional period from matriarchy to patriarchy.

In the patriarchal period of Athens married women and their daughters were restricted to the home and isolated in special rooms called *gynacontis,* wherein they dwelled and performed their domestic duties. They were denied social intercourse with men who visited the home. Even widows were under the domination of their nearest male relative, and were not at liberty to choose a husband. In Homer's *Odyssey,* we find Telemachus, in the following language, forbidding his mother to be present among her suitors:

"But go now to the home, and attend to thy household affairs;
 To the spinning wheel and the loom, and bid thy maids be assiduous
 At the tasks that to them were allotted. To speak is the privilege of
   men.
 And mine is especially this privilege, for I am the lord of the house."

It would have been unthinkable for an Iroquois matron to have been spoken to in that manner by any male member of the clan. Neither a common brave nor an exalted chief would have dared to dictate to a clanswoman as to the course of her personal or domestic affairs.

Upon leaving the house the Athenian matron was required to veil her face, so as not to arouse the desires of other men. The wife did not address her husband by name, but called him master—for such he was. She shared the husband's bed, but not his table. If she were known to commit adultery, the penalty for her sin was the forfeiture of life or liberty. Her husband might mercifully sell her as a slave.

The position of the man in his patriarchal glory was something entirely different. He enjoyed the utmost freedom in matters of sex. Courtesanship was developed on a scale as classic as other Greek arts. Women of beauty and intellect, usually foreigners, chose a free life in the closest association with men rather than accept the thraldom of marriage. The status of these women was far removed from a degrading prostitution, as the free living courtesans were in fact intellectual companions no less than sexual paramours.

The names and fame of these courtesans who consorted with the illustrious men of Greece, and particularly their intellectual discussions at the great banquets, are recorded in the pages of history, while the names of the wives are lost and unknown. One of the most famous of these women was Aspasia—noted for her genius, beauty and political influence—intimate of the great Pericles, who finally made her his wife, but she achieved her undying fame while still his mistress.

The wit of Phryne made her an intimate of Hyperides, and her beauty caused her to be selected by Praxiteles, one of the principal sculptors of Greece, as a model for his statue of Venus. Archænassa was the mistress of Plato, and Danæ supplied intellectual companionship and amorous diversion for Epicure. Lais of Corinth, Gnethanea, and other courtesans of equal fame afforded mental stimulus and erotic solace to the famous Athenian men of their period.

Demosthenes in his oration against Neæra pictured the attitude of the Greek men with respect to the sexual relations, as follows: "We marry women to have legitimate children and to have faithful guardians of our homes. We maintain concubines for our daily service and comfort, and courtesans for the enjoyment of love."

Prostitution developed to cater to the younger men, as would be expected in a society of the patriarchal type. Solon, who formulated the new laws of Athens, upon which his fame rests, introduced the public brothel under the administration of the local authorities. He decreed a one-price rate to all visitors, amounting to one obolus, which is estimated to be about six cents in American money.

The double standard of morality, and the class basis of prostitution—both fostered by the patriarchal mores—are evident in the following tribute to Solon by one of his contemporaries: "Solon, be praised! For thou didst purchase public women for the welfare of the city, to preserve the morals of the city that is full of strong, young men, who, without thy wise institution, would indulge in the annoying pursuit of better-class women."

THE ROMAN PATRIARCHY.—The most typical of all forms of patriarchy is that associated with Rome. The law of male descent was very dear to the Romans of rank, so much so that the name *patrician* was given to those who could point to their definite line of fathers and forefathers, indicating purity of blood and consequent political and social standing.

The very name *patrician* means "of the rank and dignity of the fathers." All power was centered in the father, or elder male of the family. Their foremost jurists boasted that scarcely any other race of men had the same power over their sons as the Romans.

One theory of the origin of the patrician class is that it was a Sabine race which conquered a Ligurian people established on the site of primitive Rome. The survivors of the conquered Ligurians become the plebeians, or common people of Rome. Briffault submits evidence to show that the social constitution of these aboriginal Romans (later the subservient class) was matriarchal, and that the clan organization consisted of "Motherhoods." All matriarchal influences and tendencies were promptly rooted out by the patricians.

The patricians were an aristocracy of birth and the hereditary ruling class. The family or community of kinship was designated by the term *gens*. The Roman *gens* included all those who could trace their descent, through males, from a common ancestor. It therefore consisted of many families allied by blood ties.

The hostility between the plebeians and the patricians was deep-seated and long-lasting. The two hostile classes represented not only a clash between the poor and the rich, between the influential and the disfranchised, but originally it was also a conflict between two forms of social organizations—the primitive matriarchal order and the rising patriarchal order. The latter won out because it was riding the tide of a far-reaching social ascendancy, the character of which has already been described. In the course of time the patricians and the plebeians became merged into one political class of Roman citizens, along patriarchal lines, with equal rights, at least theoretically.

The Romans held careful control over the marriage laws. Marriage was permitted only between Roman citizens, or between Romans and such foreigners as had by treaty the right of intermarrying with Romans. The legal contract which was enacted by the marriage ceremony was to all intents and purposes a deed of transfer or conveyance of the wife from her family to the husband.

The authority of the father as head of the clan was formulated as early as 450 B.C. in the Laws of the Twelve Tables. Paternal authority, or *patria potestas,* which presently will be more fully defined, was set forth in detail. The authority exercised by the father over his wife was known as "manus", *i.e.,* "in or under the hand" of the head of the house.

True marriage, or *matrimonium justum,* was permissible only between persons of equal social rank, but it involved various types of ceremonies differing in character and prevailing on different social levels.

Marriage could thus be performed with or without "manus" —subordination of the wife to the husband. If this condition was accepted, the marriage was known as *cum manu,* indicating that the wife was to pass under the tutelage of her husband. This status was accepted by the majority of marriages in the early period.

Marriage without "manus" indicated that the wife remained under the tutelage of her father. This status, while it also kept the woman under strict patriarchal supervision, had a certain strategic advantage for the wife, as there were sentimental ties with her father and his family which did not obtain with respect to the husband and his family.

Premarital love, or the opportunity for the couple to make their own choice, was not the order of the day. Marriages were arranged by the families, the principal thought being social prestige in the upper classes; among the lower classes, it was little more than barter or sale.

The marriage rite used among the highest and most aristo-cratic class was known as *confarreatio,* appropriate only to patricians and extremely elaborate in ceremonial and religious formality. Certain offices of the priesthood and that of vestal virgins were open only to children begotten of this type of marriage. One aspect of the Roman marriage contrasts strongly with that of the Greek, namely, in the former case the bridal veil is not white, but a flaming red.

A middle-class ceremony was that known as *coemptio,* simi-lar to the preceding one in that it was a true marriage, but civil rather than religious in character, and involving a sym-bolic sale of the woman to the man. A coin of nominal value—but significantly of high importance as an evidence of woman's status—was used for the purpose.

There was a third form of marriage, or a common-law equiv-alent, termed *usus,* by means of which a woman was brought under the authority of her husband. This was without any special ceremony and indicated a relationship where a man and woman had lived in marital association for one year. This mode of marriage prevailed as a rule among the plebeians. It had legal status—Roman law was seemingly all-embracing and explicit, and appeared to cover everything. The wife's consent must have been secured, and she must not have absented her-self from home three days.

In contrast to these legitimate forms of marriage, there ex-isted a legalized type of concubinage under the name of *matrimonium non justum,* or a union of a citizen with a woman of inferior rank. This was a form of morganatic union, as the offspring of such association were not allowed to inherit property, nor were they considered as members of their father's family.

Woman's inferior position is best illustrated with respect to the Roman view of adultery, a strictly double standard concept, characteristic of all patriarchal societies. If a wife committed adultery—with its menace to the purity of the male lineage—the husband was free to take her life without intervention even of the family council. Cato, the Censor, summed up the early Roman attitude toward marital infidelity in the following words:

"If you catch your wife in adultery, you would kill her with impunity without a trial; but if she were to catch you, she would not dare lay a finger upon you, and indeed she has no right."

Under ancient Roman law a woman was perpetually a minor. She could not own or transmit property, or enter into any business transaction. Even her children were not legally hers; she had no rights over them.

THE PATERNAL POWER.—The absolute and unconditional power of the Roman father over his children was expressed in the Latin phrase, *patria potestas*. A peculiar characteristic of this paternal authority is that, in the case of sons, it continued until the father's death, irrespective of their age or position, even after their marriage. Daughters passed out of the paternal power after marriage, to become subject to the husband, unless they were married without "manus", in which case they continued under the father's authority.

The son had no *potestas* over his own children until after his father's death. *Patria potestas* was thus not merely the authority of the father over his own children, but that of the oldest paternal ancestor over all descendants in the male line —son's children, son's son's children, and so on.

Under early Roman law the father had an unlimited right to expose to death all infant daughters except the first-born.

Sons and first-born daughters might also be exposed if they were deformed. The fact of the deformity was required to be attested by five of the nearest neighbors.

Throughout the Republican period the father, as domestic magistrate, had the right to punish his children, even with death, after a trial at which the kinsmen were present. In the Imperial period, exposure of children was forbidden, and the right of paternal punishment was reduced to reasonable disciplinary limits.

It was also within the power of the father to sell the child. Sale into slavery was unusual, however. In the later Empire it was allowed only in the case of new-born children, and when the father was in extreme poverty. Even then he retained the right of ransom.

A not uncommon practice was the pledging of the person of a child for the father's debt. Another analogous custom was for the father to sell his son's services for a number of years, although a so-called royal law forbade the sale of a married man. Another royal law prescribed that a son sold three times should be free from the father's further authority.

Under the rule of *patria potestas* in the early period, sons and daughters and their children had no property rights of their own. Whatever they acquired accrued to the head of the house. Later, in the Imperial period, the son and also the daughter secured property rights.

Patria potestas was nullified not only by the death of the father, but also by his loss of liberty or citizenship. If he were captured and enslaved by foreign enemies, that condition only suspended his paternal authority, and if he escaped or was ransomed, it was revived.

Paternal authority was also nullified under Roman law when a son became a flamen of Jupiter—one of the principal divinities of the pre-Christian era—or a daughter became a vestal virgin.

"RIGHT OF THE FIRST NIGHT".—A lascivious practice among various peoples during the feudal period was the much-discussed *jus primae noctis,* "right of first night", or as the French called it, *droit du seigneur,* "right of the lord."

The feudal lord had the patriarchal right to compel any man who had attained the eighteenth, and any girl who had attained the fourteenth, year to marry. He could prescribe to both men and women whom they were to marry, even in the case of widows and widowers. Early marriage of the serfs and many children were to the interest of the feudal lord, as this added to the number of his workers with resultant increase of his income and wealth. Moreover, it was an age without any conception of sanitation or hygiene; mortality rates—especially of infants—were very high, epidemics of plague and pestilence were wont to rage, and a high birth-rate was necessary even to assure a stationary population.

The "right" of a lord to enjoy the sexual favors of his female serfs was generally acknowledged in most feudal areas. If his lands were too extensive or if the number of his vassals was too great for him to give personal attention to all his subjects, he could delegate his right to a representative, who might be his major-domo or his managing overseer. In many places, however, the right was subject to waiver upon payment of a tax. The terms "bed tribute", "virgin tax", etc., had their origin in this way.

Jacob Grimm, whose exhaustive works on the society of the Middle Ages are among the most authoritative extant, gives the following description relative to the custom of *jus primae noctis:* "The groom shall invite the manager of the estate to the wedding and he shall also invite the manager's wife. The manager shall bring a cartload of wood to the wedding, and the wife shall bring a quarter of a roasted pig. When the wedding is over, the groom shall let the manager lie with his wife for the first night, or he shall redeem her with five shillings and six pence."

According to the record of the Swabian monastery, Adelberg, in the year 1496, the serfs living in the community of Baertlingen could redeem the right if the groom gave a bag of salt and the bride gave 1 lb. 7 shillings in a dish "large enough that she might sit in it." In other localities the brides could redeem the right by giving the feudal lord as much butter or cheese "as was the size of their seat."

Besides the feudal lands of continental Europe, the practice has been ascribed to the clan organizations of Scotland and Wales during the Middle Ages. In *The Fair Maid of Perth,* Sir Walter Scott relates: "The ancient laws of Scotland assigned such a privilege to every feudal lord over his female vassals, though lack of spirit and love of money hath made many exchange it for gold." The phrase "ancient laws" may have been used loosely by Scott instead of ancient custom, which would probably be a more accurate term.

With the passing of the custom toward the end of feudalism, the right appears to have been exercised for a time symbolically by the laying of a leg in the bride's bed.

PASSING OF THE PATRIARCHAL ORDER.—The patriarchal system may be said to have had its origin among the pastoral peoples of southeastern Europe and southwestern Asia. It reached its turning point and decline with the passing of feudalism. Remnants remained, as is always the case with a bygone social order, and many of our fundamental laws and mores are patriarchal in their implications. But the framework and substance have gone.

The patriarchy of the feudal period, of course, was not the patriarchy of the ancient Hebrews, Greeks and Romans. It was modified by time and circumstance, but it was essentially a patriarchal order in the character of father-right, paternal powers, subjugation of the female, masculine line of descent and inheritance.

Feudalism, already on the decline, received its death warrant in the cataclysmic convulsions of the French Revolution and the Napoleonic wars. The rise of industry changed the way of life, left its impress on religion and morals, stimulated science and invention, diffused education, created great centers of urban population, all of which, of course, affected the status of the family and the customs of courtship and marriage.

CHAPTER XII

Multiple Marriage

Polygamy.—The popular understanding of *polygamy* is the marriage of a man with two or more women, and for the sake of convenience the term has been so used from time to time in the previous chapters. It properly denotes, however, the marriage of either a man or a woman with more than one mate.

In the present chapter, which deals with multiple marriages of various kinds, the technically correct term of *polygyny* will be used to indicate plural marriage on the part of the man.

The reverse situation—the marriage of one woman with two or more men is termed *polyandry*.

There is a third form of multiple marriage or sexual relationship, combining polgyny with polyandry, which is variously termed group marriage, promiscuity or sexual communism, some features of which have already been described.

Multiple marriage in some form is everywhere practiced among primitive peoples, by at least part of the population. Far from being regarded as a licentious custom, or as a manifestation of moral laxity or form of self-indulgence, or as evidencing a lack of consideration for the feelings of women, it is everywhere in primitive societies looked upon as a laudable ideal and a great virtue.

Even the outlawing of polygamy, or polygyny, in Europe

came about at a later period than is generally suspected. Its prohibition was promulgated for the first time in any part of the world in the code of Justinian in the sixth century of the present era. It is true that the practice had fallen into decline in the most advanced countries of Europe before that time, but it was not legally or ecclesiastically proscribed.

POLYGYNY.—In this form of plural marriage the double standard of morality almost invariably applies because it is usually a male-dominated relationship. There are some exceptions in certain primitive societies, such as the American Indian tribes, in which women have held a position of relative equality with, or even economic superiority to, the men. The situation generally, however, has been that when a husband had two, three or many wives, he looked upon them as his personal property, and felt that the moral standards which were imposed upon women had nothing to do with men.

In practically all polygynous societies, and some have enjoyed a high degree of cultural development, the women are carefully shielded and guarded from contact with men other than the husband. If in spite of these safeguards and precautions, the wife is discovered to be unfaithful to her husband, she is punished without mercy. Death, enslavement or banishment is the usual penalty.

The husband, however, has no scruples about philandering on his own account. He may find it dangerous to trespass upon the harem of his neighbor, and therefore out of expediency respect his neighbor's sexual property. If prostitutes or unmarried or unguarded women are available to him, he may cohabit with them without qualm on his part, or without objection from his neighbors, who exercise the same privilege. Even the wives themselves may not be expected to object, because their training and experience have conditioned them to accept this situation as normal and proper—or at least inevitable.

The Biblical law clearly points to the existence of polygyny among the ancient Hebrews. Marriage with a brother's widow was required when no male children survived. The living brother was not exempted from the duty of marrying his sister-in-law because he was already married. Thus, for many centuries polygyny was an accredited institution among the sons of Israel. And, of course, Solomon had his numerous wives and more numerous concubines.

Monogamy as it evolved out of a patriarchal order of society has been traditionally founded upon the same double standard, until the influence of woman coming into economic and political rights on her own account has tended to greater equalization of the moral code. On general principles an only wife is much more likely to exercise an influence over a man than would be the case under polygyny.

As we have already seen, in classical antiquity when the position of the wife was generally an inferior one, true monogamy among the upper classes was very rare. The concubine was often a sort of secondary wife, paradoxically holding a preferred position as intellectual companion to the husband. Moreover, her very legal inferiority resulted in special opportunities to educate herself, which were denied to the wife.

In group marriage and in polyandry, the position of the wife tends to be higher, because the economic situation is quite the reverse of that existing among polygynous peoples. The matriarchal system, as we have already seen, is normally associated with such forms of marriage or has a traditional heritage from such a background.

Polygyny among peoples of some high degree of cultural development is now to be found mostly among the Orientals.

Owing to the limited number of women that are at a man's disposal—for the ratio of the sexes is approximately equal—and to the expense of maintaining more than one wife, polygyny is at present practiced only by the privileged and propertied classes.

PRIMITIVE POLYGYNY.—It has been pointed out that in the animal kingdom species are sometimes polygamous, sometimes monogamous, but that in general a gregarious life, a life of considerable association, favors polygamy. Man is of course a sociable being, and in the primitive state polygamy in one form or another has been universal.

Primitive life is physically hazardous, and although there is an approximate equilibrium in the birth ratio of the sexes, the conditions of savagery make prodigious demands upon the lives of the adult males. There are frequent wars, in which there is no place for captives; taking captives for the purpose of slavery came at a later period. Among many tribes there are adventurous and dangerous undertakings to procure food or materials of value, hunting and fishing expeditions that often involve a high mortality rate.

Notwithstanding a hardihood and natural invulnerability to many infections and to the shock of wounds that would be devastating to the more artificially conditioned civilized man, the natural hazards of savage life did take their toll, more so upon men than upon women, whose constitutional resistance is greater than man's. Even the prevalence of female infanticide failed to equalize the sexual ratio, so the excess of women was sufficient to permit polygyny, at least among the more privileged members of the population.

Polygyny may become restricted in savage society because a small number of the strongest and most feared men—the chiefs, the sorcerers, or the priests—so monopolize the available desirable women that there are not enough left over for the common man to marry several wives, if indeed he is able to marry at all. As an example, in Australia the older influential aborigines took possession of so many of the women of all ages that most of the younger men could not acquire a wife before the age of thirty. And thirty is a very advanced age for marrying in primitive society, where young men and women alike are considered eligible for marriage at about the age of puberty.

The situation in these circumstances is ameliorated to a considerable extent by the fact that this enforced celibacy does not necessarily demand male continence. Among the primitives under discussion and those of similar low culture, the husbands are much more jealous of their other property rights than they are of their conjugal rights. They may therefore be persuaded by the inducement of a suitable present, to lend their wives to the less fortunate bachelors. As a matter of fact, the practice of lending wives under such advantageous circumstances may be one of the incentives for establishing a monopoly. It is an example of the law of supply and demand at work in a primitive society.

Among the Melanesians of the Fiji Islands, the chiefs who lived in great state sometimes acquired several hundred women, of whom the greater number filled the position of servants to the master, and at the same time were concubines at the disposition of the warriors or of the guests. The titular wives whose children inherited were very few in number. They were acknowledged as daughters of the chief, and their situation, though less degraded than that of the concubines, was still very humble.

We are told that not only did these royal princesses, so to speak, resign themselves without difficulty to polygyny, but they were subjected to a singular duty—that of rearing for their husband a chosen concubine. The procedure has been thus reported: The bride takes with her a young girl who is still a child, but who shows promise of beauty, and who has been carefully selected from the lower class of the people. It is a virgin destined for her husband. She brings her up with the tenderest solicitude. When the girl is marriageable, the queen, on the appointed day, undresses her, washes her carefully, and even pours perfumed oil on her hair, crowns her with flowers, and conducts her thus naked to her husband.

Indeed, in those primitive societies which are masculine-dominated, the women are so thoroughly imbued with the fact of their own inferior position—in reality their status being as property rather than as persons—that they have no thought of rebelling against a condition of life which they have been trained to regard as normal and proper. Under these circum-stances the wife in polygynous communities not only does not resent the arrival of additional wives or concubines into the domestic menage, but often welcomes them as added work-ers to perform the hard labor of the household and its premises.

We are told that among the Zulus the wife first purchased strives and works with great effort to help her husband obtain sufficient means to acquire a second wife, as a helper, over whom she will have seniority and special privileges. The women cultivate the ground and attend to the primitive agri-culture which, with the preparation of the food, is part of the domestic work, so the labor is heavy and arduous. The hus-band seldom concerns himself with the agricultural labor of sowing, cultivating and harvesting performed by his wives, as long as it is sufficient to supply his food requirements. The men seldom do anything to the land but clear off the bush and timber, when that is required.

As a consequence, the greater number of matured and elderly men of this tribe and other African aborigines similarly situated have two or three wives. This again leads to a scarcity of wives available for the younger men—as in the case of the Australians—and results in infant betrothals and the sale of child wives. Livingstone reported that the number of wives was the measure of a man's wealth and social standing.

In some primitive groups there appears to have been a prescribed wife for each man, or at least his choice was restricted to a very limited number. The prescribed mate was a status-wife, who alone held the position of a true wife. The men might also capture a woman from an alien tribe who would be a worker, or work-wife. She might in time win the man's amorous interest, and thus become his love-wife, or its primitive equivalent.

Among the Trobrianders, Malinowski reports that while monogamy is the general rule, polygyny is not only allowed to men of higher rank, but in some cases it is even expected of them. Sorcerers of renown and headsmen of high rank are obliged to have a number of wives by virtue of their position. The chief or headman, in order to fulfil the obligations of his station, must possess wealth, and according to native social conditions this is possible only through plurality of wives.

The acquisition of the wives is a matter of political arrangement, rather than personal choice, or is so after his first marriage. From each sub-clan or village the chief takes a wife, who may be said to be the perpetual wifely link with the group in question, because, upon her death, another wife, her substitute, is immediately wed to him from the same village or sub-clan. All the male members of the bride's sub-clan contribute their share to her dowry upon her marriage to the chief.

The author relates as an example, the instance of a representative chief who began his sexual life in the ordinary way of the tribe, passing through the stages of complete freedom, and finally made a permanent attachment. His selection was a very presentable young woman of the tribe, who in later years possessed "charm, dignity and simple honesty." Five children resulted from the union. This wife remained his favorite; all the circumstances indicating it was a marriage of love and real companionship.

Even before his accession, however, the chief acquired other wives, each from one of the communities or sub-clans whose obligation it was to make this contribution to his domestic circle. Furthermore, upon the decease of his predecessor, this chief inherited the late chief's widows, who automatically and at once became his wives, and their children became members of his household. The majority of these widows were fairly old, some having passed through the hands of three husbands. The chief was not under obligation to cohabit with the inherited wives, but it was his privilege and right to do so if he wished.

POLYGYNY IN SOCIETIES FAVORABLE TO WOMAN.—The foregoing examples of primitive polygyny are concerned primarily with its practice in societies where women are held in inferior position. Polygyny, however, was also widely practiced by the North American Indians, among whom women held a favorable and often a dominant position in the political and economic life of the tribe.

The reason for the practice was doubtless the numerical preponderance of women, due to heavy loss of adult males in wars, and from the hazards of hunting and other pursuits of primitive life. The morality of savage society is invariably governed by practical considerations and the necessities arising therefrom. Celibacy has no place in primitive life—except as a religious or ceremonial custom—and if there is a preponderance of females, polygyny is practiced. If some unusual conditions should bring about a preponderance of men, polyandry then tends to become a factor in the marital relationship.

Among the Omaha tribe, the man never took a second wife without the consent of the first. Often, indeed, the initiative came from her. She might say to him: "Marry the daughter of my brother. She and I are of the same flesh."

To a large extent, polygyny had among many tribes of Indians an incestuous tinge. The wives of the same man were often relatives, habitually sisters, as we shall presently see.

Sometimes a man took as wives an aunt and niece of his first wife. Among the Californian aborigines a man not only married the sisters, but also their widowed mother. Among the Columbians every wife had her separate habitation, or at least her special fireside. Sometimes there was a chief wife having authority over all other wives.

SORORATE—THE CUSTOM OF MARRYING SISTERS.—Among many primitives it is the custom to marry off the eldest daughter of the family first, usually soon after puberty. Among forty or more of the North American Indian tribes, when a man married the eldest daughter of the family, he acquired by express privilege and right all her sisters as wives as soon as they reached a marriageable age.

This custom while widely practiced, however, was not obligatory. The man might waive his right in this respect, but if he insisted, his superior claim would be recognized by her clan. If the husband did not wish, or could not afford, to exercise his claim upon his wife's sisters, he allowed them to marry other men, but in order to do so his consent was necessary. When a bride-price was due, it was sometimes paid to him and not to the girl's relatives.

Among the principal tribes practicing this custom were the Omahas, the Cheyennes, the Crees, the Osages, the Blackfeet, the Crows, the Ojibwas, the Pawnees, the Spokans of Columbia, the Chawanons of Louisiana, and many others of lesser prominence.

Reports of the domestic life of these Indian families who practiced the sororate indicate it was an unusually harmonious domestic arrangement. The men were said to prefer to marry sisters for the very purpose of securing domestic peace. In some tribes it was claimed that the practice brought the husband "good luck." The fact that it tended to increase domestic felicity is in itself a piece of good luck, and so the abstract principle could well arise from this concrete result.

Sororal polygyny was also popular among the women because they realized that children bereft of their own mother would come under the care of her close kindred, and not fall into the hands of a woman of alien origin.

The acquiring of marital rights by a husband over a wife's sisters is a widespread principle in primitive societies generally. Briffault states that in Queensland, Australia, among the natives on the Pennefeather and Tully Rivers, a man is understood to have the same sexual rights over his wife's sisters as over his wife, whether they happen to be married or not. In Southeast Australia, when a man secures a wife from another tribe through elopement, her parents, after their anger has blown over and the matter has been amicably settled, turn over her sisters also to their son-in-law.

These practices seem to indicate that the sororate is a remnant of group marriage or a general form of clan promiscuity, giving the man sexual claim upon all the women of the group with which his own group has entered into a marriage agreement. Thus the sororate is a gradual breaking away from gross promiscuity—an important step in the evolution of marriage—and the marital alliance is generally restricted to the several sisters of a family.

Among the South American Araucanians when a man is able to obtain several sisters together as wives, he prefers it to marrying women who are not related to one another, because "this accords with their laws." The men of the Amazon and Rio Negro tribes also commonly married all the sisters of a family.

The custom is very prevalent throughout Africa, especially among the more primitive tribes and those whose social organization has been subject to the least modification in the contacts with civilization. Among the Bushmen a man usually marries several sisters or female cousins—that is, tribal sisters. The Kaffirs and Zulus, as well as the natives of Portuguese East Africa and Mozambique, also follow the practice.

If a man of the Herero tribe of western South Africa took a fancy to a younger sister and decided to marry her, he could not do so without also marrying her elder sister. Among the Basoga of East Africa, when the bride leaves with the groom for his home, they are accompanied by the bride's sister, who joins the household as a secondary wife.

The sororate has a long tradition among the primitives of Siberia and western Mongolia. Genghis Khan married two sisters, and the precedent was followed as an honored example by his warriors and khans. In ancient China and Japan, too, it was a recognized practice. The most common form of polygyny among the Malays of the Patani States was the simultaneous marriage with several sisters.

There is an analogy between the *levirate,* which obligated a man to marry his deceased brother's widow—described in a previous chapter—and the *sororate,* which demands or permits the marriage of a man with all of his wife's sisters. Both had their origin in primordial family life when sexual customs were at best little above a promiscuous level. As has been already stated, in primitive life and economy there is no place for the unattached female. The fulfilment of her biological destiny is inevitably taken for granted. She is expected to mate or fit into the sexual pattern prevailing in the community as soon as she reaches pubescence. This principle may be dignified by the term of "natural law", as it is universal in the primitive world.

This is the explanation of promiscuity, whether unlimited or restricted, of group marriage, of sexual communism as practiced by certain primitives; of hetairism, of the consanguineous form of marriage as practiced by the Iroquois and other American Indians, of so-called temple prostitution that came along at a later period, and of other plural marital practices.

Celibacy and chastity after puberty are concepts of a fairly high degree of civilization, although it may be a savage or a barbarous civilization. Then they are invariably associated with a special class of religious devotees, and have no part in the life of tribal womanhood in general.

Where the levirate and sororate prevail they are usually imperative customs and obligations. Whether the society be matriarchal or patriarchal in principle, the woman has no alternative but to conform to the pattern that has been devised to assure her of the fulfilment of her biological function. This is even more true of matriarchal than of patriarchal societies, as the former have a more positive instinctive feeling of the necessity of this functional complement of woman's life.

RESTRICTIONS REGARDING COUSIN-MARRIAGES.—Civilized society has in many cases, but not always, imposed restrictions on
the marriage of first cousins under the general prohibition of
incestuous marriages.

Primitive peoples have their ban on cousin-marriages, but
the prohibition is not uniform according to the degree of
relationship. Where cousin-marriage is permissible in these
societies, it is nearly always limited to those relations known
as *cross-cousins,* whereas *parallel* or *identical cousins* are prevented from marrying on account of the incest taboo.

The respective children of brothers are parallel or identical
cousins; as are the children of sisters. On the other hand, the
respective children of a brother and sister are cross-cousins.

Some primitive tribes not only permit cross-cousin marriage,
but prescribe it wherever possible. The Toda, the Vedda and
other peoples of Southern Asia, and the Fijians among other
Melanesians, follow this practice. The aborigines of the North
American Pacific coast region, some South American Indians,
and a number of South and East African tribes adhere to the
custom. While far from universal, it has nevertheless been
observed in every grand division of peoples throughout the
world. The practice is of course endogamous and leads to a
high degree of inbreeding, but other factors may serve to bring
new blood into the tribe.

If a man has no cross-cousins—if his mother has no brother,
or having one, he has no daughters—a substitute is then made
of some more remote relative reckoned on cross-kin lines.

One effect of this marital procedure is that when a man
weds the daughter of his mother's brother, or of his father's
sister, a maternal uncle will normally be his father-in-law, or a
paternal aunt his mother-in-law. As a consequence, in many
tribes practicing this form of marriage the men have a single

term to designate mother's brother and father-in-law. They likewise have another single word to indicate father's sister and mother-in-law.

Sexual Communism.—Sexual promiscuity in the form of what may be designated as "group marriage" has been touched upon in a previous chapter. This classification has been used to cover various forms of the group type of marriage, which may vary from absolute promiscuity, without incestuous restrictions of any kind, to others that have quite definite regulations.

As the term "marriage" scarcely applies to some of the conditions labeled *group marriage,* even under Westermarck's broad generalization, Dr. Rivers and other anthropologists have used as a substitute the term *sexual communism* as a more appropriate designation.

It has been pointed out that extensive sexual communism may coexist side by side with individual marriage. That is, one portion of the community may practice the former system, and the remainder of the community the latter.

As an example of the two types of sexual life coexisting in a given locality, we may mention the Bororo of Brazil. The older men are regularly married and live in their family huts. The bachelors occupy a special dwelling, where they jointly possess such girls as they capture or purchase from the village, and for whom they pay to their mistresses, brothers or maternal uncles.

Promiscuous practices of this kind among the Bororo, the Masai and others, which are openly sanctioned in the communities, do not conflict with the institution of individual marriage, which is the normal routine of life after the period of youthful profligacy. In brief, there is one system for the young, and another for the older members of the social group.

Among the Chukchee, reported by Bogoras, on the other hand, sexual communism is a general practice on the part of practically all families. There is, however, a certain method of selection which again shows how logically the primitive mind works according to its own lights.

Second or third cousins, or unrelated men desirous of entering into the arrangement, will form a group exercising marital rights over all the wives of the men concerned. It is not customary for brothers to enter into these agreements; nor are bachelors usually admitted into the group because it is based primarily on reciprocity. The union may include as many as ten couples.

The Chukchee "companions in wives" do not dwell together with their mates in a common household. They have their separate camps and the apparent object of the arrangement is to provide the men in their sojourns with temporary bed-companions. In actual practice, therefore, the Chukchee has but limited opportunity to exercise his potential rights under the mutual agreement.

The observer reports that the inmates of one and the same camp are seldom willing to enter into a group-marriage, the reason obviously being that the reciprocal use of wives, which in this form of marital collectivism is practiced rather seldom, is liable to degenerate into complete promiscuity should the members of the group live too close together.

It will be observed that this type of marital arrangement is not by any means unrestricted sexual license, but is governed by very definite regulations and limitations. Its most likely origin is in the old custom of reciprocity in the hospitality of wives, which is commonplace in many primitive societies.

The Dieri tribe of Australia has a very different form of community of wives, but theirs is likewise governed by definitely formulated rules from which they do not appear to digress. Under this arrangement the man may marry his mother's mother's brother's daughter's daughter, or his mother's father's sister's daughter's daughter.

These relationships seem almost too involved to be grasped by the primitive mind. However, the members of the tribe are very much concerned about the orthodoxy of following these lines of kinship. When a boy and a girl stand to each other in one of these relationships they are considered eligible for future marriage, and a childhood betrothal may be arranged by their mothers and maternal uncles. It will be seen that this tribe follows the principle of mother-right, so common among very primitive peoples. Normally there will be an exchange of girls by the two contracting parties, so that in each family a boy is provided with a mate.

A peculiarity of this system is that no woman is ever the betrothed wife of more than one man. After the marriage is consummated, however, the wife is free to become the concubine of several other men, married or single—but they must stand to each other in the orthodox relationship as already defined.

As the practice works out, brothers who have married sisters may share their wives, and a widower in exchange for gifts takes his brother's wife for his concubine. Furthermore, a visitor of the *proper relationship* may be offered his host's wife as a temporary concubine. Aside from these examples, concubines are assigned through formal allotment by the council of elders, which confers rights of concubinage on individuals who are potential spouses. Only men of distinction, however, are likely to have a number of concubines. The common tribesman is advised by the dominant elders to confine himself to one.

All of the instances cited above, which are the most representative of so-called group marriage, or sexual communism, as it has been practiced by primitive peoples in modern times, are by no means evidence of unrestrained sexual licentiousness. All of them have carefully defined, well-formulated codes, within the restrictions of which the members of the organizations are expected to conduct themselves.

It is the usual custom for each member of the group to have his own wife, and the wife her own husband, but a right exists under certain conditions, and subject to certain restrictions, for the interchange of women for cohabitation. This privilege of sexual intercourse, actually a survival of reciprocal hospitality, cannot properly be called "group marriage", and even the term "sexual communism" is really a misnomer. While their concept of conjugal fidelity is different from ours, their code is as definite in its own way as that applying to marriage in civilized societies.

What happened in the relative promiscuity that probably existed in the infancy of the human race is of course not known. It is probable that the formulated codes associated with these vestiges of sexual communism, as well as the evidences of paired mating in the animal world—indicating a "natural" tendency to selective mating—have influenced Westermarck's conclusion that there never existed unrestrained sexual promiscuity in the human race.

POLYANDRY.—The marital arrangement whereby one woman has two or more husbands, termed *polyandry,* is much rarer than polygyny. It may be remarked that physiologically, it is more natural that a woman should have a plurality of husbands than that she should be one of a number of wives.

The usual cause ascribed to polyandry is the chronic scarcity of women in a given community. It has been found to arise when the males of one race immigrate to a country which is racially different. The few women who accompany them must be divided among a larger number of men. This seems a logical reason to account for polyandry, but Briffault says there are objections to the categorical acceptance of this explanation, because of the conspicuous exceptions to the rule. In Tibet, for instance, one of the principal polyandrous countries, there is no numerical disproportion between the sexes. As polyandry has been practiced in Tibet from the earliest known times, we may attribute it to the survival of a very ancient custom that has not been obliterated by contact with antagonistic ideologies.

Among some primitive peoples whose activities require the men to be much away from home, polyandry is said to be necessary so that the wife will always have a protector with her. Thus the Mongoloids of the Himalayan Mountains sanctioned the marrying of one woman to four brothers. One of the brothers always remained at home while the other three were at a distance, serving in the army, taking care of roving flocks or attending to matters of trade.

While sporadic instances of polyandry have been found in various parts of the world, the great centers practicing this form of marital relationship have been Asia, especially Tibet, parts of India and Ceylon. A number of primitive tribes of India, nearly always addicted to female infanticide, have practiced polyandry. Female infanticide, indeed, has been given as an important factor accounting for the scarcity of women and leading to this institution.

Fraternal polyandry—a woman becoming the wife of several brothers—seems to be the most prevalent form of this marital arrangement, but it is not always so restricted.

Among the Todas when a man marries a girl she becomes on that account the recognized wife of all his brothers, and inversely these become the husbands of all the sisters of the wife. This is really an instance of polygynous polyandry. The first offspring of these marriages is attributed to the eldest brother, the second to the next brother, and so on.

Polyandry flourished in Ceylon up to very recent times, especially in the interior, and probably still is practiced to some extent. It has disappeared from the coastal regions because of the opposition of Europeans who are influential in the commercial life in those areas.

This form of marital union, in contrast to polygyny, does not seem to last in communities that have contact with civilization. Polyandrous marriage institutions have survived only among populations in isolated countries, of which Tibet is perhaps the best example.

Among the Nayars or Nairs of Cochin, Malabar and Travancore, polyandrous unions of a different, non-fraternal type prevail. According to the Nayar custom, every girl, before she attains puberty, goes through a marriage ceremony the essential feature of which is the placing around the neck of the bride a conjugal collar by the nominal husband. The marriage is consummated, the provisional husband receives the customary fee and departs, retaining no conjugal rights over the girl, who remains with her family.

Now duly married, the Nayar girl might take for husband whomever she likes, *except* the provisional husband of the marriage ceremony. The number of her husbands varies from four to twelve. Each of them is first presented to her either by her mother or by a maternal uncle.

These husbands remain a very short time, usually only a

few days, when they are free to participate in further conjugal endeavors of this polyandrous society. This, of course, introduces the polygynous element into the marriage system, which makes it plural on both sides.

The Nayar husbands generally are neither brothers nor relatives of other degree. Unions outside the caste, however, are the only ones reputed immoral. These are considered adulterous.

There are certain marital responsibilities and duties that accompany the rights and privileges. The several husbands are in honor bound to maintain the common wife. One undertakes to furnish the clothes, another to supply the rice, and so forth. Under these conditions each may in turn enjoy the conjugal relationship, and in order not to be disturbed in the exercise of his rights, it suffices the husband on duty to hang on the door of the house and on his wife's door his shield and his sword or knife.

In addition to the two types of polyandry—fraternal and non-fraternal, of which examples have been given, there are also characteristic kinds representative of the two orders of society—matriarchy and patriarchy.

In the matriarchal order the girl or woman does not quit her family or her gens. Sometimes she even is permitted the right of choosing her husbands, or this may devolve upon the mother or maternal uncle. The husbands may, or may not, be related to each other according to the mores of the people in question. However, the wife is scarcely dependent upon the husbands, since she remains with her own relations, works with them and bears children for them.

On the contrary, under patriarchal polyandry, the woman, captured or purchased, is almost entirely uprooted from her original environment. She leaves her maternal protectors to go and live with her husbands, to whom she belongs in the sense of a property relationship, and who demand strict conjugal fidelity, unless they authorize the exceptions as hosts.

CONCUBINAGE.—Concubinage may be described as a link between free sexual promiscuity and marriage. It represents an evolutionary step between prostitution and the monogamic union, although the institution of concubinage has largely flourished in polygynous societies.

Legal concubinage is indeed a sort of free marriage, sanctioned by custom and recognized by law, co-existing by the side of the formal marriage. It was at first a blending of polygyny with monogamy, and in the refinement and evolution of the relations between the sexes it ended by itself becoming monogamic in ancient Rome.

Roman concubinage was a free union between a man and a woman not wishing, or not being able, to marry. It was lawful to have as a concubine a woman with whom marriage was forbidden—an adulteress, an actress, a woman of questionable past, or a freed slave. Its monogamic character is shown by the fact that the Roman concubinate was, to all intents and purposes, a marriage of inferior status. A married man could not take a concubine; a bachelor could not have more than one at a time.

In its primitive phase, concubinage was simply the conjugal appropriation of slaves, especially of women captured from vanquished enemies. They were part of the spoils of victory. Moses authorized this practice, as set forth in *Deuteronomy*. It was an habitual custom among the Arabs, as it was among all nomadic herdsmen and militant tribesmen.

The Homeric warriors were given to the practice, as indicated in various passages of the *Iliad* and the *Odyssey*. In the former epic narrative, when Chryses comes to offer Agamemnon a rich ransom for his daughter, the mighty king callously replies: "I will not set your daughter free; old age shall find her in my dwelling at Argos, far from her native land, weaving linen and sharing my bed. Go, then, and provoke me not."

In the *Odyssey,* when Ulysses, unnoticed, enters his own house, and observes his female slaves making merry as they play with the suitors, his emotion is not merely that of an affronted proprietor, but that of a jealous man whose harem has been transgressed. His first impulse is to kill these women who have dared trifle with his honor, which he later does, and he hears "his heart cry out in his bosom, as a bitch, turning around her young ones, barks at a stranger and tries to bite him."

The canon regulating Christian marriage finally abolished concubinage as a legal institution, but like all established customs it continued to live on long after its ecclesiastical proscription.

Study of the sexual practices of mankind shows that concubinage in some form has flourished among all races, in all periods, and it still thrives under other names in our own time alongside of legal marriage. The presence in modern society of the mistress, the "kept woman", even the cultured counterpart of the classical Greek courtesan, are matters of common knowledge.

THE HAREM.—The very name of *harem*—meaning that which is sacred, set apart, forbidden—indicates its original religious character. From our Western lights, we are apt to look upon the harem as an institution degrading and humiliating to women, but such is neither the purpose nor the effect from the Mohammedan point of view. It is part of the whole Islamic concept of the relations between the sexes.

Probably the most objectionable features of the harem, from the social and ethical standpoint, are the idleness and vacuity of the life of the inmates and, in the royal households, the employment of eunuchs as supervisors and attendants.

The Koran enjoins that women shall be discreet in their association with the opposite sex, and forbids them to expose face or person except to a husband, father, son or certain intimate male relatives. The setting apart of a special apartment for women in the house is but one of these precautions, and undoubtedly antedates the time of Mohammed, as it is a deeply rooted Oriental idea, much older than the rise of Islam. The same thought is implicit in the *gynacontis* of classical Greece.

While within the household the social intercourse between husband and wife is quite free, the wife or the wives of a man, attended by servants, usually female, lead generally isolated lives. The women visit one another and spend most of their time in each other's apartments. Restrictions of various kinds are imposed on them when they leave these apartments. When appearing on the streets they must be veiled, and are generally accompanied by a male servant.

The harem is not necessarily a polygynous institution, for although a Mohammedan has by law of the Koran the right to take four wives, there are comparatively few householders who are able to afford this luxury. One wife, or a wife and a concubine, is the rule. It is mostly in the case of persons occupying a high official position that several wives are gathered under one roof.

It is an unwritten law that a Sultan has the right to seven wives and an indefinite number of concubines. The rather embellished stories of extensive harems maintained by the former rulers of Turkey are conceded to have been much exaggerated, and were due to a confusion between actual wives (or concubines) and female attendants and slaves, of which there were, of course, large numbers in a royal household.

The position of "chief" wife, who takes rank above the others, is carefully preserved under Mohammedan custom. If a man has several wives, they may prevail upon the husband to furnish each with a separate apartment, consisting of at least a bedchamber and kitchen. Within the harem the woman reigns supreme. There she entertains her female friends and, attended by servants, spends her days with her children. From the Western point of view, it must be an existence of great boredom and monotony, but as it is the only life these women know, it doubtless seems natural and normal to them.

Most of the traditional accounts of intrigue, cruelty, crime and immorality that have colored the stories descriptive of harem life in the past are concerned with the royal households, the voluptuous life of the numerous inmates, the vagaries of the eunuchs, and sometimes the gruesome methods by which their eunuchism was effected.

There are both white and black eunuchs employed to guard the more pretentious harems. The duties of the white eunuchs are usually confined to the outer gates and entrances; they are never permitted to see the women of the harem. The black eunuchs wait upon the women directly. Some of the women in the royal household may have several dozen black eunuchs each at their command.

The emasculation of the eunuch, of course, was done as a precaution to make him a safe guard of the harem, from the husband's standpoint. The Oriental eunuch was primarily a chamberlain—the guardian of the bedchamber. In the households of the Sultans and other Mohammedan rulers, eunuchs sometimes gained prominent positions and acquired great influence in the court. Due to this tendency, the term *eunuch* came to be applied in Egypt to any court officer.

There is a common belief that because of their mutilation eunuchs are effeminae, lacking in physical strength and vigor, and of cowardly spirit. The general run of eunuchs may suggest these traits. If so, there certainly have been striking exceptions, as there are instances of eunuchs who have been strong characters, able administrators and loyal supporters of the regime. Narses, one of Justinian's noted generals, was a eunuch.

CHAPTER XIII

Marriage by Capture

TAKING WIFE BY FORCE.—There are races still extant among whom marriage by capture frequently occurs. The practice has taken place in every part of the world and in all epochs. It is the natural accompaniment of primitive warfare and pillage, and with some tribes became the principal object of such warfare.

At this late date, however, it is impossible to say that in primitive society the capture of women has ever been the *usual* mode of procuring a wife, as suggested by some authorities, notably McLennan. But we do know that apparent remnants of the practice and symbolic or ceremonial capture are still an important part of the marriage rites among peoples all over the world.

Some writers suggest that the rites in question had their origin in the attempt to ward off the "evil eye"—a superstition that for untold centuries plagued the mind of man; also, that they are indicative of the modesty of the bride. Both of the latter factors are elements that have left their impress on customs governing the marriage ceremony, but there is no mistaking the evidence that the primitive usage of forcible nuptials likewise left its mark in the evolution of marriage.

The essential qualities of marriage by capture are taking the woman by force without her own consent and without the

consent of her kindred. The violent seizure and marrying of a
woman was legal in England until the reign of Henry VII,
when it was made a crime to abduct an heiress. A thirteenth-
century petition in the Rolls of Parliament declares that heiresses in every part of the kingdom were, by guile or force,
brought in the power of designing men. The capture of heiresses for the purpose of marrying them is recorded in Ireland
as late as the eighteenth century.

That the practice was of great antiquity in Ireland is indicated by an old poem of that country, *Duan Gircanash,* which
makes reference to three hundred women being carried off
into enforced marriage by the Picts from the Gaels. One of
the verses narrates:

> Cruithne, son of Cuig, took their women from them—
>   It is directly stated—
> Except Tea, wife of Hermion,
>   Son of Miledh.

Finding themselves thus deprived of their women, the Gaels
finally made an alliance with the aboriginal tribes of Ireland,
as we are told in the following quatrain:

> There were no charming, noble wives
>   For their young men;
> Their women having been stolen, they made alliance
>   With the Tuatha Dea.

In a previous chapter reference was made to practices in
medieval Italy which were based on the seizure of young
women of means for marriage. Armed retainers and guards
were employed by the wealthy families to protect their daughters from being abducted into marriage in this way.

Chrestien de Troyes, describing the social customs of
medieval France, states that if a damsel were accompanied by

a knight, it was the privilege of any other knight who might be attracted by the lady's charms, to give combat to the escort. If successful in winning the lady by arms, he might do his will with her, and no shame or blame whatsoever would be held to attach to him.

Marriage by capture occurred among the Southern Slavs down to the beginning of the nineteenth century. In the Albanian mountains it persisted down to very recent times. Other wild, free-living mountaineer peoples have likewise preyed upon the women of the more passive plainsmen within modern times.

The instance of taking women by force in connection with wars, and inducting them into marriage or concubinage, was a widespread practice of great antiquity; likewise when, owing to the scarcity of women in a given area, it has been difficult or inconvenient to obtain wives in the ordinary manner.

MARRIAGE BY RAPE.—As violence is inherent in the practices of so many savage and barbarous tribes, the rape of women of alien peoples is to them a natural and simple occurrence. Its incidence as an accompaniment of capture and marriage or concubinage is a sequel taken for granted.

The story of the rape of the Sabines has come down in the legends of the Romans as a classic example of the traditionally ancient method of obtaining wives.

In the *Book of Judges,* xx-xxi, there is the detailed narrative of how the tribe of Benjamin procured wives for themselves by massacring the inhabitants of Jabez-Gilead, including "every woman that hath lain by man", and capturing four hundred virgins.

Even this raid "sufficed them not", so the Benjaminites again set forth and, emulating the rape of the Sabines, each man seized and carried off one of the daughters of Shiloh to be his wife on an occasion when the women gathered for a festival in the vineyards near Bethel.

Other Biblical stories of like character are to be found in *Numbers* xxxi, 7-9, wherein we are told of the defeat of the Midianites by the Israelites, and the carrying off of all the cattle, children and women. *Deuteronomy* xxi also describes the Israelites taking as captives the women of the vanquished enemy, and bringing home to wive those who were beautiful and desirable. If the Israelite husband found "no delight in her," then he "shalt let her go whither she will."

The Australian aborigines have been given to the practice of violence and rape in connection with the acquisition of their women. The native who desires to carry off a woman belonging to another tribe prowls around the outskirts of the camp. If he happens to discover a woman without a protector he rushes on her, stuns her with a blow of his club, seizes her by her thick hair, and drags her thus into the neighboring wood. When she has recovered her senses, he forces her to follow him into his home community, where he violates her in the presence of his people.

Marriage by rape is symbolized in the nuptial rites of some aboriginal tribes. Among the Araunanians of southern Chile, while the prospective bridegroom's friends bargain with the girl's father, the groom himself slinks about the house and tries to catch the girl. As soon as he has grasped her he lifts her on his horse and carries her away toward the forest. The people of the neighborhood raise a loud clamor and try to prevent the flight. As soon as the man has reached the shelter of the forest, however, the woman is considered to be his wife. This holds true, even if the abduction be perpetrated against the parents' will.

A similar practice prevails among the Mosquito Indians.

After the arrangements for a wedding have been made and the bride-price paid, the bridegroom carries off the bride and is followed by the women kinfolk who stage a mock battle and pretend to rescue her. The couple finally escape and "go in hiding," the primitive counterpart of our honeymoon.

Among the Australians, a favorite custom was for two men to unite to commit a rape-raid upon an alien tribe. The men stole noiselessly into the camp at night; one of them wound round his barbed spear the hair of a sleeping woman, the other pointed his spear at her bosom. Awakened, she dared not cry out. The captors took her off, bound her to a tree, and then returned in the same manner to make a second capture, after which they returned in triumph to their own people.

The captives rarely revolted, for this method of capture was traditional in the lives of these people. From infancy, the girls became familiarized with the fate that awaited them, and the simulation of the rape was one of the games of the Australian native children.

The life of an attractive Australian girl was marked by a series of plots to carry her off, and often of successive rapes, which forced her to pass from hand to hand. In the process she was subjected to wounds received in the resultant conflicts, and also frequently to bad treatment inflicted by the women of the strange tribe into which she was introduced. Sometimes she was taken far away from the place of her birth, even hundreds of miles.

In these instances it was the duty of the tribe to which the ravaged woman belonged, to avenge her. As tribal obligations are the primitive equivalent to moral duties, skirmishes or battles frequently followed. More often, to escape serious damage for an offense to which both sides were addicted, the tribes held a meeting, and then the ravisher submitted to a symbolic retaliation or punishment agreed upon beforehand.

Armed with a shield of bark, he faced at about forty yards a group of ten warriors belonging to the offended tribe. Each of these threw two or three darts at him, which were almost always dodged or parried. The offense was thereby expunged, and peace re-established.

The same custom prevailed among the Papuans of New Guinea and the Fiji Islanders. The men carried off and violated unaccompanied women, and afterward arranged with the aggrieved tribe regarding compensation. Real or simulated rape was general, and even had an element of glory attached to it. A particular divinity presided over this rite. The ravished woman either fled to a protector or resigned herself, whereupon a feast tendered to the parents concluded the affair.

Marriage through force represents one of the great stages through which this institution has passed in its evolutionary development. Some authorities have referred to it as a form of "glorified rape," but it was to all intents and purposes a form of marriage, as usual and regular in its time and place as our own conventional marriage is to us.

Significantly, none of the North American Indian tribes ever made a practice of obtaining wives by capture, and in that respect were exceptional among all known primitive races. On the other hand, the practice was common among the South American and especially the Caribbean Indians of the West Indies. The strong endogamous habits of the North American aborigines discouraged marrying outside the tribe under any circumstances.

While females of the enemy were frequently taken prisoners by the more warlike tribes, the usual course was to hand over the female captives to the women to assist them in their labors. They were adopted into the families and usually treated with great kindness. We are expressly told that no cruelty or violence was visited upon them, and after adoption they were married in exactly the same way as the women of the tribe, and had the same choice and veto. This exceptional treatment of female captives by the North American Indians may well be attributed to the matriarchal traditions that pervaded their social order.

CAPTURED WIFE AN EVIDENCE OF VALOR.—The captured wife must have been a source of satisfaction to the ego of primitive man, as she was a tangible evidence of his prowess and might. She was in effect a trophy, attesting to his valor in warfare, and to his resourcefulness and strength in carrying her off.

From this feeling grew the conviction among savages that the members of the tribe married to captive women were more honorably married than those who had taken wives from within the tribe, which assured them a higher status in tribal prestige.

Another factor contributing to the desirability of the captured wife was the fact that as an alien she served the exogamous purpose of bringing new blood into the tribe. This element increased in importance as primitive man became more influenced by incest taboos, and more eager to obtain a wife from outside the tribe.

In the Babar Archipelago it was considered a glory to capture a woman from another village. Among the Negritos of the Philippine Islands marriages, until comparatively recent times, were never contracted within the tribe. As it was the exogamous practice to capture women from neighboring tribes, this custom led to endless wars.

Among the Chukchee, it is reported that a company of

young men would seize a young girl and carry her to the house of the one who wanted her for a wife. Not only the men of alien families, but even fellow-tribesmen and cousins followed this practice after having been refused by the father of the girl. The assault and the ravishing were not considered as grounds for implacable hatred and feuds. The parents would come and demand ransom, which was paid, usually in kind—one woman for another.

In the Purang district of Tibet, it was the custom when a young man wished to marry a girl, to await a favorable opportunity and, accompanied by one or two of his friends, carry her off by force. Thence on, his methods were more civilized than those of many of the peoples who practiced marriage by capture. While he kept the girl confined to a separate house, he provided her with good food and nice clothes, and remained nearby to coax her and win her love.

Should the girl prove unyielding and refuse to live with her captor, or if her parents did not desire the marriage, the matter was submitted to the village elders or the tribunal of the district chief for settlement. If they permitted the union, a day was set for the marriage, which took place amid much feasting and drinking of wine.

Among the Gonds, a Dravidian tribe, marriage by force is commonplace. The girl may not like the man, and her parents may not countenance his suit. That does not discourage the swain. He awaits his opportunity, as for example when the girl goes to fetch water from the river, and with the aid of his friends, carries her off by force. When caught the girl is closely guarded. After a time she becomes reconciled to the man, and thenceforth they are regarded as husband and wife.

In the mountains of Gazelle Peninsula of New Britain girls are forcibly abducted from their parents. Sometimes a man carries off another man's wife. If the men belong to different communities, it results in a feud. In other cases the matter is often amicably settled by some influential personage acting as arbitrator.

Among the forest tribes in the northeastern part of the Mongala basin in the Congo, it is said that a man carries off a wife by force, "betakes himself with her to the forest, lives there by hunting, and only returns to the village when the wife has a child and it is weaned." Upon returning home, he frequently quits his temporary wife, and gives her half the proceeds of their hunting in exchange for the child.

Marriage by capture has authorization in the ancient code of the Hindu Aryans. According to the Laws of Manu, one of the eight legal modes of concluding a marriage was the *rakshasa* mode, namely, "the forcible abduction of a maiden from her home, while she cries out and weeps, after her kinsmen have been slain or wounded, and their houses broken open." The sacred tradition permitted this mode of acquiring a wife to the Kshatriyas, or warrior caste.

MOCK RESISTANCE AS A SURVIVAL OF MARRIAGE BY CAPTURE.— The Roro tribe of British New Guinea have an unusual ceremonial touch in their marriage rites which suggests resistance to capture. On the wedding day a party of men belonging to the bridegroom's local group, but not including the bridegroom, surround the house of the girl's parents and carry it by mimic assault, with great fury and shouting. The bride thereupon rushes out and runs away as fast as she can, and although she is soon overtaken and caught, she defends herself to the best of her ability with hands, feet and teeth.

In the meantime a sham fight rages between the adherents of the bride and the groom. The bride's mother, in the midst of the commotion, armed with a wooden club or digging stick, strikes wildly at every inanimate object within reach, and shouts curses on the ravishers of her daughter. This availing nothing, she collapses, crying for the loss of her child. The other women of the village join in the weeping and lamentation. The girl's mother keeps up the appearance of extravagant grief for three days, and she alone of the girl's relatives does not accompany the bride to her father-in-law's house.

Among the Banyankole, in Northern Bantu, the bridegroom enters the kraal of the bride's family and is conducted to the hut in which the bride stands waiting. He takes her right hand and leads her from the house and out of the kraal to the assembled guests. A strong rope is produced by one of the bride's relatives and is tied to one of the bride's legs. Sides are then chosen by members of the bride's and the bridegroom's clans and a tug of war takes place. The bride's clan struggles to retain their sister, and the groom's clan strives to carry her off.

During this contest the correct procedure is for the bride to stand weeping, which she does, because she is taken from her old home and relatives. The groom stands by her, still holding her hand, and when the final pull is given in his favor, which is a foregone conclusion, he slips the rope from her ankle and hurries her to a group of friends a few yards away where a cowhide lies spread upon the ground. The bride sits upon this and the young men raise her up and rush off with her in triumph to the bridegroom's parents' house, pursued by friends and relatives of the bride.

The custom among the Mongols is as follows: The bridegroom—distinguished by the bow-and-arrow case he carries slung from his shoulder—and his party proceed to the bride's tent. Her brother blocks the entrance and demands of the strangers what brought them there. "We want to enter your tent," they reply. "Then you'll have to fight for it!" is the answer. The respective parties start to scuffle, shoving each other about a good deal. After a brief sham fight, the defenders give in and invite the assailants to enter the tent.

Strenuous but mock preparations to prevent the seizure of the bride, and a final sham capture, have been a traditional practice in many parts of Europe. A commonplace custom is to barricade or stop the bridal procession in its march. In Italy this is known as *fare la barricata,* and in Holland as *schutten* or *keeren.*

Some authorities have suggested that the stopping of the bridal procession originated as a protective measure against evil spirits, which so long tormented the mind of man, including the European, down to quite modern times. The use of loud and abusive language is a common practice among some of the European peasantry, so much so as to be considered a folk-custom. It is believed that the abuse was originally directed against the "evil eye" as a danger which menaced the young couple.

The barricading sometimes consists of throwing logs or similar objects, or even weapons, before the bridal carriage. More frequently, however, in later times, it became customary to throw a rope or string of flowers across the way. The bridegroom thereupon had to pay a ransom before the carriage was permitted to pass.

The barring of the wedding procession with a cord is also known in certain parts of England and Wales. In the latter country, in fact, until quite recent years, the resistance offered was more formidable. On the morning of the wedding day the groom with his party demanded the bride. Her friends gave a firm refusal, whereupon a mock struggle took place.

The bride, mounted behind her nearest kinsman, was carried off, pursued by the groom and his friends with loud shouts. When the participants had fatigued themselves and their horses, the groom was permitted to overtake his bride, and lead her triumphantly away. The mock capture of the bride was also formerly enacted in some parts of Ireland and Scotland.

Nansen, the Arctic explorer, states that on the east coast of Greenland the only method of contracting a marriage is still for the man to go to the girl's hut, catch her by the hair or anything else which offers a hold, and drag her off to his dwelling without further ceremony. Violent scenes often result, as maidens always affect the utmost bashfulness and reluctance to any proposal of marriage, lest they should lose their reputation for modesty. Meanwhile the woman's relations stand quietly looking on, as the struggle is considered a purely private affair, and the natural desire of the Greenlander to keep on friendly terms with his neighbor prevents him from attempting any interference with another's business.

Among the Eskimos near Smith Sound, there is no marriage ceremony other than that the young man is required to carry off his bride by main force. Here again feminine modesty demands a show of resistance, although the woman knows beforehand that her destiny lies with the bridegroom at hand. As he attempts to embrace her on the appointed nuptial day, she responds to the inexorable law of tribal convention by struggling with all her might to free herself, kicking, biting and screaming, until she is safely landed in the hut of her future lord, when she gives up the combat very cheerfully and assumes possession of her new abode. Marriage may only take place after the lover has killed his first seal, thus testifying to his manhood and maturity.

The Koryak have a characteristic custom, with some unique side features. When the bride's father decides it is time to get the marriage under way, he tells the bridegroom that he may seize the girl—that is, marry her. The mother warns the bride that the groom has obtained the right to take her.

Custom requires that the bride shall not surrender without a struggle, even if she deeply loves her groom. Should the groom find his bride undressed in a separate sleeping tent, which she is given before marriage, he would not touch her, considering the easy accessibility a wrong to himself. The bride's resistance is a test of her chastity. Accordingly, the bride, aided by her friends, ties up with thongs the sleeves and trousers of her combination suit, so that it cannot be taken off without untying or cutting the thongs.

On the day when the bridegroom obtains the right to seize the bride the latter goes about thus tied up, and tries to run away when the groom approaches her. The groom seizes an opportunity to catch her unawares, and tears or cuts the garments with a knife. He touches the bride in a most intimate manner, which is a symbol of the consummation of marriage; the young woman ceases to resist, and submissively leads the groom to her tent. The marriage ceremony is thus complete.

Among the Lisu tribes of the Burma-China frontier, the village elders on the wedding day proceed to the home of the maid, with the youths who will assist them in bearing the bride away. At first she makes a show of resistance, kicking and biting her carriers, while the members of her family cry to the ancestral ghost that their child is being borne away and that they are powerless to help her. Upon arrival at the village boundary, however, the struggling maiden is released, and she walks gaily to her future home with the wedding party.

Many European peoples have practiced ceremonial marriage by capture. In ancient Greece, especially Sparta, it had a strong tradition. A passage from Plutarch's *Life of Lycurgus* gives illuminating details on this point: "In their marriages the bridegroom carried off the bride by violence, and she was never chosen in a tender age, but when she had arrived at full maturity. Then the woman that had the direction of the wedding cut the bride's hair close to the skin, dressed her in a man's clothes, laid her upon a mattress, and left her in the dark. The bridegroom went in privately, untied her girdle, and carried her to another bed. Having stayed there a short time, he modestly retired to his usual apartment to sleep with the other young men, and observed the same conduct afterward, spending the day with his companions, and reposing himself with them in the night, nor even visiting his bride but with great caution and apprehension of being discovered by the rest of the family; the bride at the same time exerted all her art to contrive convenient opportunities for their clandestine meetings."

The ceremonial of capture was long observed in Rome in the plebeian marriages, which were not constituted by *confarreatio* or *coemptio*. The usual drama took place of the carrying off of the bride by the bridegroom, with the pretended resistance of the mother and other relatives.

In the higher class marriages the ceremonial of capture was simplified, but still very significant. The hair of the bride was separated with the point of a javelin, and for this symbolic ceremony a javelin that had pierced the body of a gladiator was preferred. Then the bride, conducted to the house of her husband, was to enter it without touching the threshold; she was lifted over it—thus completing the final symbolism of the capture and taking her by force into the home of her future master. The latter custom is very ancient, and worldwide. It is found, among other places, in India, Java, China, Egypt, and it is still commonly practiced among peoples of European tradition.

The ceremonial resistance by the bride abetted by her family and female friends is not only a relic of a former practice of genuine marriage by force or capture, but it also satisfies a fundamental feminine trait of coyness and sexual modesty. Whether this modesty be real or assumed in the individual case, its universal manifestation indicates an elementary characteristic normally present and instinctively asserting itself.

MARRIAGE BY ELOPEMENT.—The runaway marriage has a long tradition behind it, even though we are prone to look upon it as a modern escapade, typical of present-day youth. In primitive societies, elopement is sometimes resorted to as a means of defeating parental opposition—the same motive as in civilized society; at other times as a part of the nuptial procedure, either as a preliminary to the marriage or as a method of concluding it.

Elopement is in itself a sufficient act among some tribes to make the runaway couple husband and wife. We are told that the Dakota Indians had two kinds of marriage—buying a wife and runaway matches. It is the accepted principle that when the young people run away, they are to be forgiven at any time they choose to return, if it should be the next day, or six months afterward.

Sometimes elopements are arranged with the connivance of the bride's parents, who are too proud to admit that they would willingly permit their daughter to marry before a substantial bride-price has been paid.

Among the Havasupai of Arizona, if parents refuse to sell

their daughter to a suitor and the couple elope, the matter is ended as far as parental opposition is concerned. The ethics of the tribe prescribe that when cohabitation has taken place, the parents have no authority to declare the marriage void.

Likewise among the Thompson Indians, even if an irate father succeeded in bringing back a daughter who had eloped with her lover, he must deliver her up to the young man, as custom declared them already married.

Runaway marriage was especially prevalent among some of the Australian tribes, principally because that was the only way in which a man, with rare exceptions, could obtain a wife. Reference has already been made to the widespread practice among the Australians of taking wives by force from neighboring tribes. Due to the practice of child betrothal, and the monopolizing of women by the chieftains and other important personages, elopement offered the only means, aside from capture, for the young men to procure a wife.

It became a part of the business of the medicine-man to aid in the elopement of young couples, which gave sanction to the practice. If the parties were prohibited from marrying on account of the relationship that existed between them, the elopement was punished with great severity. Marrying under those proscribed conditions was a violation of the taboos, and in the belief of the tribesmen would bring ill luck and a train of evil magic upon the community.

On the other hand, if the eloping couple were not of a tabooed relationship, they could remain man and wife. In many cases the lover had to fight the man to whom the girl had been betrothed or promised, or, if she were already married, her husband. In some instances, a more general struggle occurred between the kindred of the two parties. The outcome of the struggle, in any event, decided whether the lover could keep the woman or not.

In the Wollari tribe, in cases of elopement with the wife of another man, it was the custom for the abductor to stand out before a number of the woman's kindred, who were armed with spears, he having merely a spear for protection to turn them aside. If he happened to pass through the ordeal safely, he was permitted to keep the woman.

Among the Toorkomans, marriage can be concluded with or without the consent of the parents. In the latter case, the young couple elope and seek refuge in a neighboring community. They are usually well received, such being the custom, and remain a month or six weeks. During this time the elders of the two communities negotiate an agreement with the parents. They agree on a price to be paid for the girl, who thereupon returns to the parental home. She must remain six months or a year, or even longer, before living with her husband, and during all this time he may see her only clandestinely.

The Mezeyn Arabs combine pursuit with elopement. The girl, in the so-called capture, evades pursuit and takes refuge in the mountains, where her friends have prepared provisions for her in advance. The bridegroom joins his future wife in her retreat, and it is there that the marriage is consummated. After this the couple return to the parental domicile, which the woman, unless she is pregnant, does not quit for a year.

Among the Soligas of India, when a girl consents to marry, the man runs away with her to some neighboring village, and they live there until the honeymoon is over. They then return home and give a feast to the people of the village.

Marriage by elopement is definitely recognized by the Chukmas of the Chittagong Hills. After a couple run away the parents of the girl can demand restitution on three separate occasions, but if the lover can successfully accomplish a fourth elopement, he has won wifely title to the girl.

A man and woman of the Muduvars of Southern India who do not succeed in obtaining the consent of their relatives to marry, run away into the jungle or a cave, visiting the village frequently to obtain grain and other food from sympathizers. When the parental anger aroused by their conduct has subsided, however, they quietly return to the village and live as man and wife.

SURVIVALS OF MARRIAGE BY CAPTURE.—McLennan reminds us that in the whole range of legal symbolism there is no symbol more remarkable than that of capture in marriage ceremonies. Among many races the symbol of capture occurs whenever it is necessary, in their tradition, that the bridegroom or his friends should go through the form of feigning to steal the bride or carry her off by superior force.

The marriage is agreed upon by mutual arrangement of the contracting parties, but a ceremonial capture or abduction of the bride follows as a matter of form to make the marriage valid. Variations of this practice are observed among peoples, ancient and modern, savage, barbarous and civilized.

If there is no preceding contract or agreement, in the event of a capture or marriage by use of force, then the case is one of actual abduction, and is not ceremonial or symbolical. Many instances of this kind have been cited.

The struggle, tears and screams of the bride among many peoples are recognized as a part of the formal marriage routine, but they are none the less considered absolutely necessary to prove her feminine traits of modesty and bashfulness.

In brief, the sham struggle and lamentation of the bride and her friends serve to show that the marriage was forced upon the girl and that she is entering it only under compulsion.

As we have seen in a previous chapter, the functions of the bridesmaids, the "best man" and groomsmen at the wedding, and the custom of the honeymoon, a hasty departure after the wedding—symbolizing the act of carrying the bride away—derive from practices inherent under conditions of marriage by capture and by the use of force.

The wedding ring itself, in one of its aspects, is regarded as a symbol of man's absolute authority over his newly acquired spouse—a sublimated relic of the fetters which were placed upon the captive woman of primitive times as evidence of her bondage.

CHAPTER XIV

Marriage by Purchase

MARRIAGE BY CONSIDERATION.—Marriage by purchase, or by consideration, has undoubtedly been the most widespread of all forms of marriage, at least within historic times. It has been practiced by peoples of all races, and all degrees of cultural development from the primitive to those possessing a high degree of civilization. It may be said to be the general and normal mode of acquiring a wife in all stages of culture above the lowest and below the most advanced.

This form of marriage is implicit in patriarchal society, so marriage by purchase was inherited by European civilization from three direct sources—the Hebraic, the Roman and the Greek.

The religious traditions of the Hebrews—imparted by the Old Testament theology; the legal traditions of the Romans—which formed the basic structure of Western jurisprudence; the philosophic traditions of the Greeks—which shaped the intellectual tendencies of the modern world—all of these jointly contributed to the concept of marriage that came down from antiquity, survived almost unaltered through the Middle Ages, and, with certain modifications, remains with us today.

So firmly established was the ancient tradition that woman is essentially the property of her lord and master, devoid of rights and privileges—except those extended by the grace of masculine "chivalry"—that it was not until the nineteenth century, even in advanced countries, that she obtained elementary legal rights, and the twentieth century was well under way before she secured political equality, even in theory.

It is a primary principle among the lower races that consent to marriage is not given for nothing. In most cases some consideration has to be offered to the father or other relatives of the bride, either in the form of property of some kind, or of service, or of exchanging another woman for the bride.

Far from being considered a degrading practice, even by the women themselves, the payment of a consideration for the bride is looked upon as attesting to the legitimacy of the union, and therefore to the "honor" of the woman. The respectability of a wife is often measured by the price which has been paid for her.

Among the Yakut, a wife for whom nothing has been paid is regarded as a social outcast. The women of the tribe do not think European women quite respectable, since they can be had for nothing, and even offer a dowry to a man as an inducement to marry them. In West Africa a wife who had not been properly purchased was considered a lewd and wanton woman.

Aside from capture, the alternative of paying a price of some kind for the bride is elopement, with all the personal hazards that this involves in most primitive communities. It is true that some tribes have cultivated a tolerance with respect to the eloping couple, usually making a noisy pretense of retaliation, of which examples were cited in the preceding chapter. Generally speaking, however, the runaway bridegroom is treated as an abductor, or holder of stolen goods.

The value of the property given as a consideration, of course, varies greatly among different peoples. It may range from an apparently trifling amount of food to articles of relatively great value. We are told that among the upper classes of the city of Mecca, virgins were sold as wives for from forty to three hundred dollars each. The value indicated was probably greater to them than this amount would be to us.

In some cases the bride-price is given in the form of a present or gratuitous offering. The bridegroom may even receive a gift in return—the equivalent of the dowry.

Among the North American Indian tribes, property of relatively minor value was given in the form of presents, which were really more or less optional. There were, however, some exceptions. In the Shastika tribe of California, twelve ponies might be paid for an attractive bride, and that represents value in any society. Among the Hupa tribe in the same territory a man's standing in the community depended on the amount of money which had been paid for his mother at the time of her marriage. If the sum was large, he was the peer of any in the tribe.

In Africa, the purchase of wives is very extensive. The price may vary from some food, blankets or furs to trophies of great value. A chief, for instance, sometimes pays a hundred head of cattle or more for a bride. There may be involved in this the prestige and pride of the chief, who would consider it a reflection on his exalted position if his bride were worth less than such an amount.

In one part of Uganda, the customary price which men of high degree give for a wife consists of a hundred goats and sixteen cows. A suitable consideration for a poor man to pay is three or four bullocks or six sewing needles. Among the Bangala, a free man marrying a free woman was formerly required to give her parents four slaves, two male and two female, and no money or goods would be taken in lieu of them.

Cattle and goats are the usual medium of exchange in paying for the bride among many Africans. Ten or twelve cattle
was an average price for the ordinary Kafir bride. Among the
Herero a "bear market" prevailed in the price of wives generally, and a rich man or a dignitary gave no more for a wife
than a poor man, which of necessity was little. It was the custom that when a woman went to live with a man he transferred to her father or guardian a large ox, a heifer, a large fat
sheep, and a ewe with a lamb, but the most valuable of these
animals were at once strangled and eaten at the feast which
was the only ceremony attending the union.

A bridal price as high as three thousand roubles, equivalent
to about fifteen hundred dollars at that time, is reported to
have been paid among the Baskir of Asiatic Russia. A poor
man, however, could obtain a mate for a cartload of wood or
hay.

In general the price is influenced by a number of factors: by
the personal qualities of the bride, by the social position of the
respective families, by the age and desirability of the bridegroom, by the sexual ratio of the population, by the economic
development of the community, and by other local considerations that might seem unimportant to us.

Occasionally there is a fixed price established by custom or
law, which must be paid regardless of these factors. Almost
always, a divorced or widowed woman may be secured at a
lower rate than one who has never been married before. A
female who is under the age of puberty, or far above it, also
usually commands a lesser price than one who, in the eyes of
primitive peoples, is just ripe for marriage.

Marriage by consideration still prevails among the Chinese,
a highly civilized people. The persons who negotiate the mar-

riage specify the precise amount which is to be paid for the bride, and until this sum is handed over by the bridegroom or his family, the marriage cannot take place.

In Mohammedan countries every marriage is supposed to be accompanied by the payment of a sum of money to the father of the bride. As the custom has developed, however, this payment is turned over to the bride as a marriage portion to protect her in case the husband dies or divorces her. A further step forward is indicated in many instances by the transfer of the bridal price into a gift made directly to the bride.

In its literal sense, marriage by purchase was a custom that contributed to the degradation of woman, or it might be more accurately expressed as a practice inherent in the degraded position of woman. It placed her in the category of a non-personal commodity, for barter or sale, which in certain primitive societies and in ancient civilizations was literally the case.

The position of the wife in classical Greece, where this practice prevailed, is indicated by a significant wedding custom. As soon as the bride entered the house of her new lord and master, she ceased to exist for her family. They had sold her, and there was no longer any claim upon her. This was symbolically expressed by burning before her husband's house the gaily decorated carriage that had brought her there. The last tie linking her with her parents had been destroyed.

Among the early Teutonic and English peoples marriage took the form of a sale of the bride by the father, or other legal guardian, to the bridegroom. The *beweddung* was a genuine contract of sale. Sale-marriage was the common form of nuptials. The marriage ring at this period was evidence that the bride-price had been paid.

In England the York and Sarum manuals in some of their forms direct the bride, after the delivery of the ring, to fall at her husband's feet, and sometimes to kiss his right foot. The early Church's acceptance of these folkways and incorporating them into the ritual led Pollack and Maitland in their *History of English Law* to refer to "that curious cabinet of antiquities, the marriage ritual of the English Church."

In Russia it was also the custom for the bride to kiss her husband's feet as a visible sign of her subjugation. Subsequently, in France, the custom underwent the refinement of having the bride let the ring fall in front of the altar and then stoop at her husband's feet to pick it up. Once more a primitive demonstrative action became symbolized by a perfunctory gesture.

Marriage by purchase was an undisguised business transaction among the Russian peasantry down to the time of the revolution. An observer reports the procedure as follows: The father of the suitor, usually accompanied by a relative, visits the girl's parents and says, "We have a purchaser; you a commodity. Will you sell your ware?" Then ensues the bargaining, which we are told differs in no respect from a negotiation over the sale of a cow.

In ancient Russia a marriageable girl was called a *kunka,* from *kuna* (marten), because her parents might exchange her for marten-skins, the usual medium in those old days. The Scandinavians spoke of "the fairly bought wife" (*kona mundi keypt*).

The purchase of the bride was customary among the ancient Celts. In Ireland the bride-price (called *coibche*) consisted of various objects, such as articles of gold, silver, or bronze, clothes or horse-bridles, cattle or swine, land or houses. Install-

civilization, with its high-pressure selling of automobiles, electric refrigerators, vacuum cleaners, and other household commodities.

In Timorlaut, so long as the bride-price is not paid in full, the wife is entitled to stay with her parents and is not completely subjugated to her husband, nor does he possess a right to the children. Among the Central African Banyoro, a poor man unable to produce at once the cattle required for his marriage, arranges to pay for them by installments. Children born in the meantime belong to the wife's father, and each of them must be redeemed with a cow.

We are told that in Tenimber the father of the girl has often to wait a long time for the ivory portion of her price, but he hands over the bride to the purchaser on payment of other items of the bargain. The husband thereupon takes up residence in his father-in-law's household, where the wife and her children remain as hostages until payment is made in full.

Marriage by Exchange.—The theory that one doesn't give something for nothing, which the primitive has applied in delivering his daughter in marriage for a bride-price, also finds expression in the custom of marriage by exchange. Thus the wife is obtained in exchange for a female relative.

Perhaps the most common practice in this form of matrimonial procedure is the exchange of girls by their respective parents as wives of each other's sons, or in some tribes the exchange of sisters or other female relatives by the young men themselves. In these cases it is not merely the blood-sisters of the men that are exchanged, but also clan-sisters, when the former are not available. The terms "sister" and "brother" in tribal life are not restricted to children of the same parents, but often include all members of the clan or tribe of the same generation.

Among the Narrinyeri of South Australia, it is considered disgraceful for a woman to take a husband who has given no other woman for her. If there are no daughters in the family as a basis for exchange, the right to give a daughter away is often purchased from the nearest male relative who has a sister to spare.

The practice of exchanging women as wives prevails among the Kiwai Papuans, as it does in New Guinea, the New Hebrides, the Solomon Islands and Sumatra. In the western islands of Torres Strait the exchange of "sisters," in the tribal sense, was the common method of obtaining a wife. As practiced by some tribes, a bride-price is called for in addition to the exchange—the bridegroom in this case paying his father-in-law a stipulated sum.

It is said that the Sumatrans, instead of paying the *jujur,* or bride-price, sometimes exchange one virgin for another. A man who has a son and daughter gives the latter in exchange for a wife to the former, and the man who receives her disposes of her as his own child or marries her himself. Peoples practicing marriage by exchange are often polygynous.

As another instance, a brother may give his sister in exchange for a wife, or, lacking a sister, will substitute a cousin for the purpose. Moreover, it is not unusual to borrow a girl from a friend or relative in order to exchange her for a wife, the borrower pledging himself to replace her in due time, or to pay her *jujur* when called for.

MARRIAGE BY SERVICE.—A custom closely identified with marriage by purchase—but having certain significant differences—is that of serving the parents of the bride for a specified time as a means of paying for her. It often happens in cases where the prospective bridegroom is without means to make a cash purchase. In these cases, it is literally marriage by purchase, the payment being made with the husband's labor instead of property.

In some instances, however, it is a requirement in itself, in addition to paying the bridal price, even if the bridegroom is wealthy. In these cases, the whole principle of the marriage is usually different from marriage by purchase.

The Biblical classic of this kind is set forth in the story of Jacob (*Genesis,* xxix), who went to his uncle Laban's house and fell in love with his cousin Rachel, whom he saw as she brought her father's sheep to a well.

We are told "Laban had two daughters, the name of the elder was Leah, and the name of the younger was Rachel. And Leah's eyes were tender, but Rachel was beautiful and well favored. And Jacob loved Rachel, and he said, I will serve thee seven years for Rachel, thy younger daughter. And Laban said, It is better that I give her to thee, than that I should give her to another man: abide with me."

Jacob thereupon served seven years for Rachel, when Laban gathered together all the men of the place, and had a great feast. When Jacob retired to the nuptial bed, Leah was substituted for the beautiful Rachel, and in the morning the bridegroom discovered he had been tricked. Upon complaining to Laban, Jacob was given Rachel at once, as a second wife, but had to remain seven years longer in Laban's service to pay for her. It is clearly indicated here that cohabitation was recognized as the real act of marriage; having slept with Leah, Jacob was *ipso facto* her husband, even though no ceremony uniting him with her had been performed.

In primitive matriarchal societies the man obtains marital status with a woman by contributing his services to her family. In the absence of personal property and transferable wealth, that was the sole form of economic contribution he was able to make. This seems to be the origin of marriage by service, although it is found—probably as a holdover—in patriarchal societies, as in the instance cited from *Genesis*.

In the matriarchal form of society, the husband continued in the same economic role as long as he lived, or at least as long as he remained married to the woman in question; whereas, under the patriarchal system, the term of service was for a specific period, until the bride-price was paid.

The practice has been followed among a number of South American aboriginal tribes. The young bridegroom of the Canelos Indians of Ecuador has to clear the ground for his father-in-law's chacra and yuca crops. Among the Brazilian Indians a young man has to work for several years with great diligence for his wife's people before he reaches independent status. The bridegroom of the Arawaks of British Guiana works for his father-in-law, and the young couple often remain with him until an increasing family makes a separate establishment necessary.

Among the Yucatan Indians the young husband serves his father-in-law for a period of four or five years. If he fails to complete the required term of service, he is turned adrift and the woman is given to another man.

Among some of the South American tribes the custom of service was a competitive test that began in the courting stage. When several suitors were desirous of marrying a girl, they would all *serve* for her during a period of two or three years. The suitors would work for her father and family, cultivate his garden, cut wood, fish and hunt and supply the household with such things as their skill was able to produce. The swain who proved most active, and whose contributions were most abundant, was selected as the girl's husband.

That there is often some obscure principle involved in the

service, and that in these cases it is not purely a form of payment, is evidenced by the continuance of the practice even where the man makes such a payment. The Awok of northern Nigeria, the Koryak, and the Chukchee of Northern Asia, follow this custom. The man pays a bride-price for his wife, but in addition he must work for a certain time in the service of his prospective father-in-law.

This personal service cannot be waived by outright purchase. Even a rich suitor who owns flocks in his own right is obliged to serve several years as herdsman for his wife's father. Not only is he placed in the position of a servant, but he is often treated more harshly than an ordinary servant. The whole idea behind the personal service appears to be a test of strength and character to determine whether or not, in the eyes of the bride's family, the suitor is worthy of their daughter.

Marriage by service in its more conventional form is widely practiced by aboriginal tribes of India, Indo-China and China, by the Ainu of Japan, in many islands of the Indian Archipelago, in Africa and South America. The period of service seldom lasts less than a year, and may last as many as ten, twelve or fifteen years. During this time the prospective bridegroom may or may not have marital relations with the bride. He may even have to serve after his marriage as well, perhaps until a child is born, or even longer, according to local custom.

The Chukchee call the practice of marriage by service by a term which means "serving as a herdsman in payment for the bride." So firmly is this term established that it is used even by the maritime natives of the same tribe, although they have no herds, and the bridegroom simply lives in the household of his bride, and works for her father for a stated period.

The preliminaries to an ordinary marriage among the Kuki-

Lushais of Assam have been described as follows: A man hav-ing taken a liking to a girl offers a present of liquor to the parents and talks the matter over with them. If they find the man acceptable as a son-in-law, he takes up his residence with them for three years, working in the *jhums,* and becoming practically a bond servant. At the end of the probational period he is allowed to marry the girl, but even then he is not free, as he has to remain on for another two seasons, working in the same manner as he did before.

At the end of five years, he is at liberty to build a separate house and start life on his own account. Two rupees is the amount usually paid the parents of the girl, the sum evidently representing a nominal payment to bind the contract, the long period of servitude being the real consideration.

Likewise among the Bisayans of the Samar and Leyte islands of the Philippines, the suitor has to serve in the house of the bride's parents two, three and even five years before he is free to take the bride home. And money cannot purchase exemption from this onerous restriction. Other tribes in the same group and islands of the Indian Archipelago regard service as a regular or necessary preliminary to marriage.

A year's service suffices for the bridegroom of the Kenai, an Eskimo people of Alaska. It is the custom for the suitor to go to the house of his prospective father-in-law; without any ex-planation, he starts to heat the bathroom, bring in water, and prepare food. If his suit is not rejected he remains as a servant in the house a whole year, after which he is rewarded by the father-in-law for his services, and he takes his wife home with him.

Among the Makaranga of South Africa, a young man too poor to acquire a wife by the payment of cattle makes an arrangement with the father of the girl to live with her and to serve him. As the children from this union do not belong to their father until the full *ikazi*—that is, the bride-price consisting of cattle—has been paid, the father of the woman has sole control over all that are born.

Marriage by servitude was not uncommon among the North American Indians, and the custom fitted well into their matriarchal system. As a matter of fact, the new husband might truly be said to have been absorbed into the wife's family, and in a sense he rendered lifelong service to her people. Even the marriage was not fully confirmed until the birth of a child. Prior to that event, among most tribes, the wife could dismiss her husband at her pleasure; or, even afterward, for cause. Any children born of a marriage so terminated belonged to the wife's family, not to the husband. There is no evidence that a woman under any circumstances left her clan to join that of her husband.

The net result of marriage by servitude is placing the husband in a position subordinate to the wife, or at least to the wife's family, in which he is so long treated as a servant. It is readily seen that the wife married under these conditions acquires a certain independence which is not the case in the instance of marriage by purchase.

Invariably, the serving husband could be turned out if he proved unsatisfactory, either as a worker or as a mate. In fact, the period of service seemed to have been designed as a test of his worthiness. In those instances where the wife was finally taken away from her parents, she often had the right, if ill-treated by her husband, to return to her family. This was rarely, if ever, the case in marriage by purchase, an institution in which woman was regarded purely as property, or as a slave, which of course is tantamount to property.

Marriage by service did, therefore, have the moral virtue of lessening the rigid and sometimes cruel subjection to which woman is so often liable in savage and barbarous societies.

BRIDE-PRICE PAYABLE TO THE BRIDE.—A considerable step forward in the evolution of the marriage relationship is indicated when the bride-price becomes the property of the bride. The effect of this is that the bride, instead of being purchased as a chattel, is given a present.

Of course, this does not mean that the status of the married woman is suddenly transformed from one of extreme subjugation to that of marital bliss. The custom of the bridegroom making a gift to the bride prevailed at a stage in patriarchal society when woman was still under the masculine strong-arm, to insure against her becoming entirely dependent upon her father in the event of her husband's death, or her divorcement. In brief, this practice was primarily in the interest of the patriarchal father. It was, however, a decisive step forward for the woman.

This practice has long been customary among the Jews and Mohammedans, both of whom held woman in low regard. In order to protect the wife in the event of her becoming widowed or divorced, it was established by the Jewish Law that before the nuptials the husband was to make out an obligation in writing, which entitled her to receive a certain sum from his estate in the case of his death, or in the event that the marriage was terminated by divorce.

This obligation was known as *kethubhah* (marriage deed). The minimum amount fixed under the obligation was two hundred silver *denarii* upon marriage to a virgin, or one hundred upon marriage to a widow. As security for the wife's claim under this agreement, all the property of the husband, both real and personal, was mortgaged. The origin of this

The dowry was also in vogue during the classical period of Greece, at least among families of wealth and distinction. It was in fact a criterion of honorable marriage, as distinguished from concubinage. Isaeus said that no decent man would give his legitimate daughter less than a tenth of his property. At the time of Aristotle it is estimated that nearly two-fifths of the whole territory of Sparta belonged to the women as their dowers.

In Rome, even more than in Greece, the marriage portion became a mark of eminence for a legitimate wife. It was the legal right of a woman to demand a *dos,* or dower, from her father, but it was at first given to the husband to help defray the expenses of the new household, representing the wife's interest therein.

Later, under the development of Roman law, the wife's *dotal* property was fully protected and she was recognized as the sole owner. The husband's right to the use of this property was restricted to the time during which the marriage lasted, and safeguards were imposed prohibiting him from alienating or mortgaging any funds comprised in the *dos.*

The dowry as a marriage portion may have the meaning of a return gift to the bridegroom. It may also imply the very equitable arrangement that the wife as well as the husband is expected to contribute to the expenses of the joint household. In countless instances, it has been a practical means by which a father has bought a husband for his daughter. This has been particularly the case where marriageable women have outnumbered the marriageable men in a given population, and where women of wealthy but socially inferior families have sought husbands of high rank, social prestige or title.

It was the custom among the ancient Mexicans, when a couple started housekeeping, to make an inventory of all the effects the man and wife brought together—the furnishings for the house, land, jewels and ornaments, etc. This inventory was kept by the bride's father, and in the event of a divorce— which was common if the couple did not get along well to- gether—the goods were divided according to the portion that each had brought.

The Laws of Hammurabi, King of Babylon about 1955 B.C., provide that the wife's marriage portion be returned to her if the husband puts her away (divorces her), or "if she has been economical and has no vice, and her husband has gone out and greatly belittled her," and she in consequence leaves him. On the wife's death, this portion passes to her children, and, in case she leaves no children, it reverts to the house of her father. This is contingent, however, upon the bride-price being returned to the husband. If the latter does not get the bride- price back, he is entitled to deduct it from the marriage portion, and give the balance to his father-in-law.

In practically all cases the husband had the privilege of using the wife's marriage portion and enjoying the profits that may have derived therefrom, without the right of impairing the principal. Of course, notwithstanding some of the pre- cautions taken by law, as already cited, there were abuses under these circumstances, where the husband literally squandered or dissipated his wife's dowry, and rarely could anything be done about it, unless the wife's family retained a mortgage on the husband's property, which was sometimes done.

William Boulting in his book, *Woman in Italy,* gives an instance of the patriarchal power of the father in the year 1488. A Genoese blacksmith promises his daughter to another man following the same trade, with a dowry of 400 lire, pay- able in four years. Meanwhile he agrees to take his prospective son-in-law into his shop and support him. Should there be any indecorous conduct between the affianced couple, however, both shall be sent away and the father set free from every obligation.

At this period the destiny of a daughter could be determined by a father in his will, and the widow and the dead man's other trustee could delegate their authority over her. Another case is cited of a Genoese undertaking by legal contract to give his daughter as a wife to another citizen upon her attaining the marriageable age of twelve, and, in pledge of fulfilment, the prospective son-in-law receives a house.

We are told that two Genoese (acting as matrimonial brokers) declared they had received authority from a widow to marry her daughter to whatever Genoese citizen may appear most desirable, with a dowry of 100 bezants, in addition to the trousseau. If the future couple were present at their betrothal it was certified in the presence of witnesses by the gift of a ring and a kiss. The kiss was especially important, as "the recipient was supposed to be half-deflowered thereby."

The significance of this statement lies in the fact that among the higher class Italians of that period, girls and young women were carefully guarded and kept from any but the most formal contact with members of the opposite sex. If a man publicly kissed a young woman, it would be regarded as a violation of her virtue, for which the only honorable reparation was marriage; otherwise, she would be looked upon as a ruined woman, and no self-respecting man would ever marry her.

Dowries of many kinds and forms are recorded, but nowhere do we find one sought with more frankness and self-assurance than by a receptive male Colonial, who inserted the following advertisement in the Boston *Evening Post* of

February 23, 1759, one of countless numbers of similar solicitations that were to follow:

> To the Ladies: Any young Lady between the Age of Eighteen and Twenty-three, of a Midling Stature; brown Hair, regular Features and a Lively Brisk Eye; of Good Morals and not Tinctured with anything that may Sully so Distinguishable a Form; possessed of three or four hundred pounds entirely her own Disposal, and where there will be no necessity of Going Through the tiresome Talk of addressing Parents or Guardians for their Consent: Such a one by leaving a Line directed for A. W. at the British Coffee House in King Street appointing where an Interview may be had will meet a Person who flatters himself he shall not be thought Disagreeable by any Lady answering the above description. N. B. Profound Secrecy will be observed. No Trifling Answers will be regarded.

A. W., while lacking the finesse of a Romeo, was obviously a business man who knew what he wanted and wasted no time or words in getting to the point. Many well-known alliances between American heiresses and representatives of European nobility—in which an immense dowry was cashed in for a title—make the above advertisement look like a gem of sentimentality.

CHAPTER XV

Trial Marriage

ANCIENT FORMS OF TRIAL MARRIAGE.—In making a survey of the social traits and customs of mankind, we must come to the inescapable conclusion that "there is nothing new under the sun." Some years ago there was a great to-do and controversy over the question of *trial marriage,* which was roundly denounced in many quarters as an ultra-modern innovation that threatened the family, the home and all that our time-honored moral code holds dear.

Studies in anthropological lore remind us that trial marriage is older even than our time-honored moral system, and under one subterfuge or another has survived every change in man's mode of marriage, and crops up under various names or in divers forms at all epochs.

In using the broad term *trial marriage* in the present instance, it is not intended to convey, at the moment, that all such forms have been regularly concluded in a legal manner. That phase of the subject will be discussed under a special subdivision later in the chapter.

Trial marriage, in its historic sense, is represented by a temporary sexual mating, or a sequence of temporary sexual matings—often found in primitive society, and not unknown in modern life—terminating in a regular legal marriage when a satisfactory partner has been found through this form of experimentation.

Often these temporary matings, as noted by anthropological observers in their reports, have combined tender and idealistic love with the strong physical passion of youth. The matings while they lasted have been a sincere and heartfelt mingling of two enamored souls, resembling in this respect the un-consummated "puppy love" frequently seen among adolescents in our own society.

Some phases of this subject have been discussed under their more formal classifications in previous chapters. In the earlier stages of our Western civilization these forms of mating were especially common among Teutonic, Celtic and Anglo-Saxon peoples. They have passed under such names as *Probenächte, fensterln, Kiltgang, handfasting, bundling, sitting-up, court-ing-on-the-bed, tarrying, night-visiting, night-running,* and *queesten.*

Some of these customs as practiced in certain areas did not always reach the stage of sexual mating, but most of them were definitely of that character, and all of them were recognized as such in most places, especially where they had a long traditional background in the local folkways.

All of them had the common trait of fidelity to the temporary mate, as the custom was generally practiced, thereby distinguishing them from promiscuous sexual episodes. In all cases, they were socially approved practices in their respective communities, and there was no stigma of moral reproach attached to those who engaged in the custom. It was assumed that the couple had serious intentions, and would eventually conclude a formal marriage if they found themselves suited to each other.

On the other hand, if they definitely broke off relations, their past experience was not held against them and they normally formed new contacts. If pregnancy resulted from the free union, the couple were expected to marry in order to legitimatize the offspring. Among primitives, marriage is often not required in case of pregnancy, unless both parties are agreeable to the union, as there is no distinction made between legitimate and illegitimate children, and premarital pregnancy usually brings no opprobrium and does not disqualify the woman for future marriage.

TRIAL MARRIAGE AMONG PRIMITIVES.—The Eskimos of the Ungava district often took wives "for a period." Among the Icelanders it was customary for a man and a woman to decide to live together for a year, and when that time expired, if both parties agreed, they became husband and wife. If not they separated, and neither was the less thought of for the experience.

Many of the North American Indian tribes, and the West African Negroes followed the same custom. Natives of some of the islands of the Indian Archipelago are regularly betrothed to each other for a longer or shorter time, sometimes for not more than a month, and at others for a period of years.

In Tibet temporary marriages are recognized as conventional unions, and may be contracted for six months, a month, or even a week. Marriages among the Abyssinians are likewise contracted for a period, at the end of which the husband and wife separate and go their separate ways.

Ammianus Marcellinus reported that among the ancient Arabs marriages were often entered into for a limited time of definite length, and at the termination of this period the wife might withdraw if she so desired. Thus it was an optional arrangement, which is really an identifying characteristic of trial marriage, because when both parties to the union are satisfied it continues and normally becomes permanent.

Apparently there is something in the Arabian philosophy

to which marriage by trial appeals, as this form of marital alliance still exists in certain parts of Arabia. We are told that in Mecca marriages of short duration are contracted by pilgrims who remain there for longer or shorter periods of time. Egyptian women make a practice of going there to enter into such unions.

Temporary marriages are recognized by the Shi'ah Moslems, and may be contracted for any fixed period—a day, a month, a year, or any other stated length of time. This temporary agreement of marriage, termed *mut'ah,* establishes no right of inheritance in either principal, although children born of the union are legitimate and inherit from their parents the same as offspring of a permanent marriage.

The wife is not entitled to any maintenance unless the contract so stipulates. The husband has the privilege of refusing procreation, which he does not have in permanent marriage. Another striking difference between the permanent and temporary contract of marriage is that in the latter the husband has no power to divorce his wife, although the marriage may be dissolved by the mutual consent of the parties before the specified period has expired. This form of temporary marriage still exists among some of the Islamic peoples, but it is held to be unlawful by the more orthodox Sumnis.

Among the ancient Egyptians marriages were not definitely concluded until after a "trial year." Reference to this usage is constantly found in legal contracts. Very often a child was born before the formal marriage was concluded, as it was not thought proper to marry until the trial period was over.

Some of the Ceylon natives used to contract marriage provisionally for fourteen days. After that they were either confirmed or dissolved.

The young people of the Trobriand Islands, British New Guinea, after puberty gradually enter into definite sexual alliances, which are invariably temporary and may be terminated and others undertaken, until a final permanent union is concluded. They are often undertaken with all the idealism and enthusiasm of youth. Professor Malinowski states that the adolescent gets definitely attached to a given person, wishes to possess her, works purposefully toward that goal, plans to reach the fulfilment of his desires by magical and other means, and finally rejoices in achievement.

The boy develops a desire to retain the fidelity and exclusive affection of the loved one, at least for a time. The feeling, however, is not associated with any idea of settling down to one exclusive relationship. The young people generally wish to pass through other experiences until they feel they have found the mate that is most completely compatible to them.

Two lovers living together in a *bukumatula* (the bachelors' and unmarried girls' house) are not bound to each other by any ties in tribal law or imposed by custom. They come together under the spell of personal attraction, and are kept together by sexual passion or personal attachment. They may part at will. In this way, however, a temporary liaison often develops into a permanent liaison, ending in marriage.

The *bukumatula* is an institution sponsored by tribal custom and etiquette that offers shelter and privacy to young couples in their amorous pursuits. A limited number of couples—from two to four—live together for longer or shorter periods under this temporary arrangement. Actually the couples live here only at night, as sleeping quarters, spending the day-times and taking their meals in association with their respective family households.

The institution of the *bukumatula* is characterized by the

following features: (a) individual appropriation—the partners of each couple belonging exclusively to one another; (b) strict decorum and absence of any orgiastic or lascivious display; (c) the lack of any legally binding element; (d) the exclusion of any other community of interest between a pair, save that of cohabitation.

The Chippewa, and other American Indian tribes, countenanced prenuptial freedom of intercourse, which took the form of nightly visiting. It was not indulged in with the specific view to marriage, but might lead to matrimony. Formal marriage was entered into by way of negotiations between the families.

It is significant that among the tribes practicing this custom, which was extensive, the women were observed as in "no hurry to get themselves married." They were versed in the use of methods that enabled them to avoid bearing children, and they were thereby enabled to postpone marital ties until it was their pleasure to settle down to formal married life.

Here again we see the matriarchal influence of Indian social life. The women were not the property and pawns of the men, to be disposed of at their will. With respect to the sexual freedom permitted the women, this also is characteristic of the matriarchal traditions wherever they prevail in primitive society. The women have a sexual freedom under the rule of mother-right that is comparable to that enjoyed by the men under patriarchal rule.

It was the custom among all the North American Indian tribes for a man, when he went out on a prolonged hunting expedition, to arrange for a young woman to accompany him, both for sexual companionship, and also to assist him with the carrying, cooking and preparation of the products of the hunt. The woman received an equitable share of the profits, and the whole transaction was on a mutually advantageous business basis. Upon the conclusion of the expedition, the temporary association was terminated without obligation on either side.

The aboriginal Indian commonly passed through many mating associations, most of them temporary arrangements to meet certain contingencies in his active life. There was no formality either in forming the temporary union, or in parting. It was the understood folkway of Indian tradition. One early explorer reported: "They laugh at Europeans for having only one wife, and that for life; as they consider that the Great Spirit formed them to be happy, and not to continue together unless their tempers and dispositions are congenial."

Among the Lolo of Upper Tonkin a form of experimental mating is indicated by a girl spending one night with the suitor at his house. She then returns to her own home and continues a life of sexual freedom. If in the course of time she goes back to her suitor in a pregnant condition, she is received as his wife, although he fully realizes that he is unlikely to be the father of the child. If she does not return to him, the betrothal lapses.

It might be said that premarital pregnancy in most primitive tribes (unless they are under patriarchal influence) is in no way a reflection upon the character of the girl, and does not adversely affect her chances of marriage. On the contrary, it may well make her a more desirable wife—because she has demonstrated her fertility.

The Rev. Merolla da Sorrento wrote that the natives of the lower Congo were accustomed to cohabit with their wives for some time before they married them, "to try if they could like them, and after the same manner the wives experimented with their husbands."

At Quoji on the West Coast of Africa, it was customary for girls from the inland districts to visit the coast in quest of a husband. A girl would cohabit for ten days or two weeks with a bachelor, and then return home. If she bore a son, she would send a message to the man informing him of the fact, and, if he was interested, he entered into negotiation with her parents to arrange for marriage.

The advanced races of Mexico and South America practiced experimental marriage. Among the aboriginal Mexicans a young man would request the father of a girl to let him and his daughter live together for a certain period. This would be the equivalent of the modern courting period, and was looked upon as a thoroughly conventional procedure. If the young woman became pregnant, the man was under no obligation to marry her, and if he did not do so, the association was completely dissolved.

The ancient Peruvians likewise sanctioned a regular system of trial marriage. The arrangement was binding for a period of one year only. At the end of that time both parties were free to enter into other engagements if they chose to do so. Previous sexual experience was considered so essential a preliminary to marriage that a woman who had married without this normal requirement was not esteemed as respectably wedded, and she was likely to be taunted for this shortcoming if the marriage did not turn out successfully.

The Indians of some of the South American countries were so confirmed in their adherence to the custom of prenuptial experiments that the Spanish missionaries lamented over their inability to do anything to overcome the practice. The native couple commonly lived three or four months together, which they called *amanarse,* that is, to habituate themselves—before they married. As a consequence, the first question asked at the marriage ceremony was whether the couple were *amanados,* in order to absolve them of the sin before they received the nuptial benediction.

Among the Akamba premarital relations among the young people usually leads to marriage, but with his practical disposition the native takes care to see that he gets an industrious wife. If his temporary mate is lazy he continues his association with her as long as it pleases him, but he marries someone else.

A boy of the Munshi tribe of Northern Nigeria may live with a girl as her husband if he gives her mother ten cloths and a pig, with the understanding that any offspring of the union shall belong to her family, and that, unless he can within a reasonable time make an equivalent exchange, he must give up his wife.

Trial marriage takes on a unique form among the Samoyeds of the Great Tundra, where the wife has a turn-in value. She may be returned to her parents at any time within a year, and the money paid for her is duly refunded.

TRIAL MARRIAGE IN EUROPE.—So ancient are many of the folkways in the realm of the sexual relations that they go back to, and indeed are intimately bound up with, the early European custom of private marriage, without benefit of clergy, which the Church finally outlawed. But the spirit of the earlier informal matings remained and asserted itself in numerous forms of temporary unions.

These free unions which have been widely practiced in many of the European countries, particularly among the peasantry, were essentially experimental in nature—trial marriages in fact, regardless of what term they were known by in their particular locality. There can be detected in them an element of instinctive caution against forming too hasty a permanent union until actual experiment has demonstrated the harmony or the fruitfulness of the alliance.

The ancient and unrelenting proscription of divorce by the Church, which became reflected in the legislation on the subject in most European states, tending to make marriage practically, if not theoretically, indissoluble, helped to foster these forms of trial marriage.

Again it must be emphasized that these folk customs met with the approval of the people in their time. They were sexual mores that had developed out of the necessities of their social life and experiences. These free unions were by no means promiscuous episodes. They demanded obligations of the principals. They were usually rendered legal before or after the birth of a child. Even if there was no prospect of children, the union generally terminated in legal marriage if the experiment proved that the couple were compatible mates.

THE CUSTOM OF TRIAL NIGHTS.—A very old custom of the Teutonic countries was known as "trial nights." The German author J. Fisher, in his work *Uber Probenächte* (1780), described the practice as widespread among the peasants of most German communities. He cautioned, however, that one should be very much mistaken if from this custom one drew the conclusion that the girls were lacking in womanly modesty and without restriction offered their favors to lovers. We are told that "the country girl knows just as well how to be careful in offering her graces and with 'moderation spice the enjoyment,' as any lady at her toilet table."

Trial nights might be held every night, Sundays and feast days and their evenings, until both parties were assured of their mutual fitness to marry, or until the girl became pregnant. Among these country people with their simple customs it seldom occurred that a man abandoned a pregnant girl. Such an act would expose him to hatred and contempt on the part of the entire local population.

It often happened that by mutual consent a couple separated after the first or second trial night. The girl thereby ran no risk of losing her reputation, for a new lover soon appeared, willing to begin a new romance with her. Only in case the girl had trial nights with many men without result was her good name endangered, as then the village people began to suspect there was something wrong with her in the way of bodily imperfection. The country people found the custom so innocent that often when asked by the preacher concerning his daughters, a farmer with a father's pride replied that they had already begun to hold trial nights.

Writing of the marital custom of Sweden, Ellen Key states that the majority of the population began married life with the free union, which is finally legalized, if successful, and automatically dissolved if the parties find themselves misfits. Failure in one trial union is not held as a moral lapse, and the individuals make another alliance in the hope of finding a partner who will prove satisfactory for permanent marriage.

Engagement, according to Swedish law of 1734—which was based on the amatory customs of the country—was equivalent to marriage if the woman became pregnant. It was stipulated that marriage should then be concluded by proper ceremony, but even without that formality the woman was declared to be the lawful wife of her paramour, and had legal dower right to his property.

Freedom of sexual relationships in Russia is an ancient tradition, and under the regime of the czars seems to have been the only freedom that did exist. It is conceded that some of the free unions in modern times were largely the result of the rigid laws against divorce. It was common for unhappy married couples who were unable to secure divorce, to separate and form new unions without legal marriage.

In Yorkshire, England, until comparatively recent times trial marriage existed. The only commitment was the solemn declaration on the part of the groom: "If my bride becomes pregnant I shall take her."

The so-called "Island custom" of Portland, England—which is one of the most unequivocal examples of trial marriage in modern times—has been described in some detail in a previous chapter. Variations of the practice, not so clearly defined in many of its aspects, were fairly common in almost all parts of rural England.

The French working classes of the larger cities carried on the ancient system of free unions, notwithstanding the opposing influences of the Latin patriarchal tradition. In the late nineteenth century we are informed that in an average Paris arrondissement nine out of ten legal marriages were the ratification of free unions, and early in the present century at least half of the marriages were of this kind.

HANDFASTING A SCOTTISH PRACTICE.—Scotland, which has originated so many quaint customs, has made its contribution to trial marriage under the name of *handfasting*. The term means literally "pledging the hand," and was the equivalent of the betrothal, with a good deal of the latitude in intimacies that went with that status among many of the European peoples.

In old Scotland it was only necessary for a man and a woman to make an oral pledge while holding each other's hand, after which it was quite proper and legal for them to live together for a year and a day. At the end of that period, they could, if they so desired, be permanently married, or, if either of them objected, the union was forthwith dissolved. If there was a child as a result of the union, it had to be supported in this case by the one who objected to concluding the marriage.

The custom has been described by James Brown, in *A History of the Highlands* (1853), as follows: "The law of marriage observed in the Highlands has frequently been as little understood as that of succession, and similar misconceptions have prevailed regarding it. This was, perhaps, to be expected. In a country where a bastard son was often found in undisturbed possession of the chiefship or property of a clan, and where such bastard generally received the support of the clansmen against the claims of the feudal heir, it was natural to suppose that very loose notions of succession were entertained by the people; that legitimacy conferred no exclusive rights; and that the title founded on birth alone might be set aside in favor of one having no other claim than that of election. But this, although a plausible, would nevertheless be an erroneous, supposition.

"The person here considered as a bastard, and described as such, was by no means viewed in the same light by the Highlanders, because, according to their law of marriage, which was originally very different from the feudal system in this matter, his claim to legitimacy was as undoubted as that of the feudal heir afterward became. It is well known that the notions of the Highlanders were peculiarly strict in regard to matters of hereditary succession, and that no people on earth was less likely to sanction any flagrant deviation from what they believed to be the right and true line of descent.

"All their peculiar habits, feelings and prejudices were in direct opposition to a practice which, had it been really acted upon, must have introduced endless disorder and confusion, and hence the natural explanation of this apparent anomaly seems to be that a person who was feudally a bastard might in their view be considered as legitimate, and therefore entitled to be supported in accordance with their strict ideas of hereditary right, and their habitual tenacity of whatever belonged to their ancient usages.

"Nor is this mere conjecture or hypothesis. A singular custom regarding marriage, retained till a late period amongst Highlanders, and clearly indicating that their law of marriage originally differed in some essential points from that established under the feudal system, seems to afford a simple and natural explanation of the difficulty over which genealogists have been so much puzzled.

"This custom was termed *handfasting,* and consisted in a species of contract between two chiefs, by which it was agreed that the heir of one should live with the daughter of the other for twelve months and a day. If, in that time, the lady became a mother, or proved to be with child, the marriage became good in law, even though no priest had performed the marriage ceremony in due form; but should there not have occurred any appearance of issue, the contract was considered at an end, and each party was at liberty to marry or *handfast* with any other.

"It is manifest that the practice of so peculiar a species of marriage must have been in terms of original law among the Highlanders, otherwise it would be difficult to conceive how such a custom could have originated, and it is in fact one which seems naturally to have arisen from the form of their society, which rendered it a matter of such vital importance to secure the lineal succession of their chiefs.

"It is perhaps not improbable that it was this peculiar custom which gave rise to the report handed down by the Romans and other historians, that the ancient inhabitants of Great Britain had their wives in common, or that it was the foundation of that law of Scotland by which natural children became legitimatized by subsequent marriage. And as this custom remained in the Highlands until a very late period, the sanction of ancient custom was sufficient to induce them to persist in regarding the offspring of such marriages as legitimate."

Because of this social heritage of a limited free union, called *handfasting,* the tradition of non-sacerdotal marriage has been associated with Scotland down to recent times. The term, a "Scotch marriage," was once proverbial. By the early law of Scotland a declaration by a couple before witnesses that they were husband and wife was sufficient to make them so legally.

The custom of elopers from England going to Gretna Green, over the Scottish border, and there marrying according to Scotch law informally in a blacksmith shop, has resulted in giving the name of the village a special meaning in our language. Thus, any place that becomes well-known as a convenience for easy, runaway marriages is called a "Gretna Green."

But while the mere declaration by the couple that they were husband and wife was a valid marriage in Scotland, the Scots made one exception to the rule, namely: "A statement of a couple that they are man and wife *made to an innkeeper to obtain lodgings,* does not prove marriage." This may have been a wise precaution to prevent unintentional bigamy.

We have seen in a previous chapter that marriage without the services of a clergyman was for three-quarters of the whole Christian era the most common form of marriage throughout Europe. It could truly be stated that the couple married themselves, by repeating the required formula in the presence of witnesses. This was an authentic marriage, recognized as valid by the Church and as legal by the State, until the Council of Trent, in the middle of the sixteenth century, made sacerdotal marriage mandatory. Thereafter the services of a priest were necessary to make the marriage valid in the eyes of the Church. It might be said, however, that even before the Council of Trent, the Church was using its influence toward this end, and many of the more formal marriages were performed in church or were blessed by a priest. But among the common people, the private, non-sacerdotal, or even clandestine marriage sufficed.

Moreover, the old form of private marriage held out long in some sections of the Christian world, notably in Latin America and in Scotland. Some sects have preserved this form of marriage down to the present day. The Quakers, having no ordained clergy, allow the couple to marry themselves by a public declaration in the presence of the congregation.

George Fox, the great Quaker, uttered the dictum, "We marry none, but are witnesses to it." Under Quaker influence, the Commonwealth of Pennsylvania in 1885 passed a statute expressly authorizing a man and woman to solemnize their own marriage.

COMPANIONATE MARRIAGE.—During the latter half of the 1920's a nation-wide controversy took place in the United States over a suggested plan for solving some of the problems of modern marriage. The proposal, termed *companionate marriage,* was advanced by Judge Ben B. Lindsey, then of the Juvenile and Family Court of Denver, Colorado, as the result of his long experience with and intimate knowledge of family and marriage problems.

It should be stated that companionate marriage is not a new kind of marriage, nor is it a "trial marriage." Companionate

husband cannot take back the wife until she has been married to another and is again free. The divorced wife, however, is required to have returned to her the dower she brought with her to the marriage.

The Koran also specifies that the husband shall have four months' grace to retract his decision; also, if the repudiated wife is suckling an infant, the husband, or, in his default, the next heir, shall supply her needs during the two years that the suckling normally lasts.

It is decreed in the Koran that repudiated wives shall not marry before three menstrual periods; nor shall they dissimulate a pregnancy. The Islamic law authorizes the husband to sell a divorce to his wife for the cession of a portion of her dowry.

There are three graduated formulas of repudiation: (1) the disaffected husband simply says to the wife, "Go away," and if he has said it only once or twice, he may retract his decision; (2) if he should say, "Thou art to me as one dead, or as the flesh of swine," it is forbidden to take back the repudiated wife until she has been married to another, and again divorced or left a widow; (3) this formula is so solemn that it entails a separation forever; it is, "Let thy back be turned on me henceforth, like the back of my mother."

The woman with child can be repudiated, but she has a right to an "allowance during pregnancy." Custom also permits voluntary divorce, at the proposal of the wife, for a redemption paid by her to the husband. Sometimes the initiative comes from the husband, who, realizing that his wife desires her liberty, says to her: "I repudiate thee, if thou givest me this *pallium* of Herat, or this horse, or this camel," as the case may be. In effect, this is a divorce by mutual consent, and the two part as friends.

DIVORCE IN ANCIENT CIVILIZATION.—The *Code of Manu* of ancient India gave the husband exclusive right of repudiation. While the woman had no such right for any cause, the husband might divorce his spouse under any of the following conditions enumerated in the *Code,* viz:

"A wife given to intoxicating liquors, having bad morals, given to contradicting her husband, attacked with an incurable disease, as leprosy, or who has been a spendthrift of his wealth, ought to be replaced by another . . . A sterile wife ought to be replaced in the eighth year; the wife whose children are all dead, in the tenth year; the wife who only bears daughters, in the eleventh; the wife who speaks with bitterness, instantly . . . For one whole year let a husband bear with the aversion of his wife; but after a year, if she continues to hate him, let him take what she possesses, only giving her enough to clothe and feed her, and let him cease to cohabit with her."

Among the orthodox Hindus, however, marriage is a religious sacrament which cannot be revoked. A woman convicted of adultery may be deprived of her status and turned out of her caste, but even in this case divorce in the usual sense is an impossibility. She is forbidden to form a new alliance, and often remains in her husband's house with the status of a slave. This orthodox law is now often disregarded by certain castes, who have found the restriction too onerous in this modern world.

The ancient Hebrews, as indicated in the Old Testament, gave the husband the privilege of divorce for such cause as (*Deuteronomy,* xxiv), "when she find no favor in his eyes, because he hath found some unseemly thing in her." He has only to hand her a "bill of divorcement," and send her out

of his house. He then may not take her again, either if she is repudiated by another husband or becomes a widow.

Even at a later period when the wife acquired the right, theoretically, to sue for divorce the procedure required that the husband write her the bill of divorcement, or the *get,* as it was known, to free her from the marriage. The wife could never divorce the husband.

The school of Hillel, a renowned Jewish scholar and jurist immediately prior to the time of Christ, maintained that the least reasons were sufficient to justify a man to divorce his wife; for example, if she did not cook his food well, or if he found any other woman he liked better. The rival school of Shammai took the view that "a man must not repudiate his wife unless he find in her actual immodesty."

In Chaldea a man could divorce his wife merely by saying, "Thou art not my wife," by returning her dowry, and giving her a letter to her father. If she said to him, "Thou art not my husband," she might be drowned for the seditious remark.

The right of divorce in primitive Greece was left exclusively to the husband who could avail himself of it freely. In classical Greece the right remained, but under more restrictive regulations. It was necessary in repudiating a wife to restore her dowry, or pay interest at the rate of nine oboles. Thus was a character of Euripides prompted to cry mournfully: "The riches that a wife brings only serve to make her divorce more difficult."

Under primitive Roman law the right of repudiation was likewise allowed to the husband and denied to the wife. "Romulus," says Plutarch, "gave the husband power to divorce his wife in case of her poisoning his children, or counterfeiting his keys, or committing adultery, and if on any other account

he put her away she was to have one moiety of his goods, and the other was to be consecrated to Ceres."

According to the ancient law, when the woman was divorced on account of a crime, she lost all her dowry. Later, only a sixth was withheld for adultery, and an eighth for other crimes. Eventually divorce by consent (*bona gratia*) became the custom, and both parties had liberty of divorce.

Divorce evolved rapidly in Rome, and in time became very easy to obtain. Seneca makes reference to women counting their years, not according to the Consuls, but to the number of their husbands. Juvenal speaks of a woman who was married eight times in five years. Other instances are cited of men and women having had a score or more of spouses in rapid succession. It is only fair to say that these were exceptional instances, and attracted attention because they were extremes.

Constantine, after embracing Christianity, restricted divorce to such causes as: for the husband, if the wife was an adulteress, a preparer of poisons, or a procuress; and to the wife if the husband was guilty of murder, prepared poisons or violated tombs. Emperor Justin, in reviving the liberal law, stated: "If marriages are made by mutual affection, it is only right that when that affection no longer exists, they should be dissoluble by mutual consent."

In the latter days of the Roman Empire, before it became subject to the influence of the Church, woman had obtained under the law an enviable position in the marital relationship, which was unprecedented. Marriage was looked upon as a sort of private partnership in which the parties were equal and shared all rights—a condition far removed from woman's earlier status as masculine property, without any rights, which was still the prevailing condition in most other societies.

Marriage being founded on mutual affection and consent, the law permitted the parties the right to dissolve it when that affection had turned into aversion, either by consent or by one of them giving formal notice to the other, exactly like any other partnership, and no judicial or other inquiry into the causes of the divorce was necessary.

Later, under the Christian doctrine of indissoluble marriage, and the low opinion of the female sex that was inherent in the dominant Pauline philosophy, the position of woman again reverted to its ancient lowly status of utter subjection by the male. It took many hundreds of years before woman again recovered even in part the rights, based on moral and legal equality, which were hers in the latter days of the Roman Empire.

Among the ancient Germans and Scandinavians, the man alone had the right of repudiation, although divorce by mutual consent was permitted by the folk laws of these peoples.

It is said that the primitive Irish made divorce unnecessary by instituting marriages for one year, at the end of which the wife could be repudiated by the temporary husband and even ceded to another for a fresh year. These experimental marriages were made and terminated at festival periods, incident to the sowing and harvesting seasons, namely, on the first of May and first of November in each year.

The Anglo-Saxons, under Kings Ethelbert to Canute, had formulated laws governing marriage and divorce. Marriage was by purchase, but the position of the wife evidently was not quite analogous to chattel. There was the admonition: "And let no one compel either woman or maiden to him whom she herself mislikes, nor for money sell her; unless he is willing to give anything voluntarily."

Marriage by capture was penalized in the following statute: "If a man carry off a maiden by force, let him pay L. shillings to the owner and afterwards buy (the object of) his will of the owner."

"If she be betrothed to another man in money, let him make 'bot' with XX shillings."

The laws permitted divorce, apparently by mutual consent or upon the will of either party, usually without express reference to the cause, except for infidelity on the part of the wife. Adultery on the part of the husband was punishable by fine, but was in itself not a cause for divorce.

By strict legal theory in ancient times adultery was not a crime which a man could commit against his wife. When he was punished—which sometimes happened—it was not for unfaithfulness to his wife, but *for violating the rights of another husband*.

If the wife were guilty of adultery, however, it was not only grounds for divorce, but she was subject to physical mutilation by forfeiture of her ears and nose.

DIVORCE IN THE MIDDLE AGES.—The domination of religion over marriage and divorce is a characteristic of Western European civilization that began during the medieval period. As we have already observed, marriage had been from time immemorial governed by the folkways of the people, and was not considered within the province of religion except in a very incidental way, until the Council of Trent made the sacerdotal marriage mandatory.

Prior to that time in Western Europe, and in all other parts of the world, marriage was governed by secular laws and customs, and the dissolution of marriage was determined by the same principles.

According to *St. Matthew,* Christ taught that a man might

put away his wife for adultery, but for no other reason. St. Paul ruled that if a Christian is married to an unbeliever and the latter departs, the Christian "is not under bondage." Under the influence of early asceticism, however, the Church put marriage under increasing arbitrary restrictions; and eventually took the position of making a valid Christian marriage indissoluble—at least after it had been consummated.

At the same time the Church gave cognizance to a process by which the union—if it had been unlawful from the beginning on the ground of some canonical impediment, such as certain proscribed relationships, earlier engagement of marriage, or even "mental reservations at the time of marriage"— could be invalidated.

This procedure implied that a marriage which really never had been valid was officially declared to be void. In practice it led to the possibility of dissolving marriages that in theory were indissoluble.

DIVORCE LAWS IN ENGLAND.—The Founders of the English Church, which decreed the national laws for marriage and divorce, were more conservative than the reform element in Continental Europe. Luther called marriage a worldly thing to be left to the state. Calvin put marriage on the same level as house-building, farming or shoe-making. The general Reformation tendency, however, was that divorce should be granted only for adultery and malicious desertion. A more liberal party, including Zwingli, influenced by Erasmus and leaning toward the views of Roman Imperial law, advocated divorce for various causes. A smaller minority, represented by Bucer, would permit divorce when the married couple ceased to love each other.

At the beginning of the Reformation some of the leaders adopted the principle of self-divorce, as it prevailed among the Jews and as accepted by some of the early Church Councils. Along this line Luther maintained that the *cause* of divorce itself effected divorce without the necessity of any judicial decree, although a magisterial order was required for re-marriage.

The English Reformers, under Edward VI and his advisers, took a liberal view of marriage and were prepared to carry out many desirable reforms, but the early death of the young King frustrated these plans. The reaction under Queen Mary killed off the more ardent reformers. Queen Elizabeth, who followed, proved equivocal and illiberal with respect to marriage and divorce, and the conservative Church party again came into the ascendency.

As a result of the English Civil War, the Puritans put through the marriage Reform Acts of 1644 and 1653, asserting "marriage to be no sacrament, nor peculiar to the Church of God, but common to mankind and of public interest to every Commonwealth," completely secularizing the marriage laws. Milton's views on marriage and his classic treatise, *Doctrine and Discipline of Divorce,* doubtless did much to bring about this result.

The Restoration abolished this reform, and reinstated the old Canon-law traditions. Once more English marriage became what A. P. Herbert called "Holy Deadlock." It was not until the civil divorce law of 1857 that the legal principle of the indissolubility of marriage was at last abandoned. Even then divorce could be granted only to a husband whose wife had been guilty of adultery, and to a wife whose husband had been guilty of the same offense and certain aggravating circumstances.

THE TREND OF LIBERAL DIVORCE LEGISLATION.—The influence of the eighteenth-century school of philosophy, which emphasized the concepts of human freedom and natural rights, led to more liberal legislation on divorce in Continental Europe. France, in the wake of its liberating Revolution, enacted a divorce law in September 1792, proclaiming in the preamble thereto that facility in obtaining divorce is the natural consequence of the individual's right of freedom, which is lost if marriages are made indissoluble. Divorce was granted on the mutual desire of the two parties, and even at the wish of one party on the ground of incompatibility of temper, as well as on many other grounds.

This was the most radical reform in legislation governing the marital bonds that had been promulgated since the passing of the Roman Empire. Some countries of the Western World, and some of our own states, still retain divorce laws reflecting the traditional ecclesiastical point of view. South Carolina stands unique in granting no divorce under any conditions, and is today the only Protestant community in the world that holds marriage indissoluble.

Otherwise the world-wide trend generally has been toward a more rational divorce code. Divorce by mutual consent is at present permitted under certain conditions in several countries. The Scandinavian nations were the modern pioneers in this respect. Nevada and certain other American states are nearly as liberal as Scandinavia. Under the laws of Soviet Russia the grounds for divorce are either mutual consent of the parties, or the desire of one of them.

CHAPTER XVII

Romantic Marriage

LOVE ENTERS MARRIAGE.—We cannot, of course, with our civilized background and cultural veneer, venture to re-enact in our imagination the drama of courtship and mating that intrigued the primordial man and maid. Our patterns of conduct, our education, our conditioned impulses and inhibitions, preclude an understanding of the total elemental emotional experience of this hypothetical couple who vouchsafed us an ancestry.

We may justly and correctly infer that they were drawn together by the dynamic attraction of one sex for the other that is universal throughout nature. We may feel reverberating in the specialized nerve centers of our being a counterpart of the physical upwelling that drew them into consummate embrace. But still we cannot visualize the psychological reactions and subtle shadings of feeling that without a doubt accompanied the physical act.

At a much later period in the pedigree of man we know that the relations termed marital were based, not on the attraction of one individual for another, or on the feeling or affection of one individual for another, but on violence, purchase and barter. Neither love nor romance was considered, nor can they be conceived as compatible with brute force, rapine and trading in human life on a property basis.

These systems, which seem so remote and unreal to our minds, accustomed to other practices, prevailed by far the greater part of recorded time. What happened in the eons of prehistoric time during which man was on his slow, upward trek from sub-human divergence, we have no means of knowing and it would be futile to hazard a guess.

Even under the blighting conditions that would seem to stifle all tender sensibility and sentiment, we discover evidence of these emotions and feelings striving to assert themselves. In primitive Greece, which held women generally in subjection, and wives and daughters specifically within the confines of the *gynacontis,* romance struggled to express itself. We find the names of lovers inscribed in trees—even as we do today; and the use of flowers is referred to as a medium of testifying to a love that otherwise must have remained mute.

We have no way of knowing about the more ordinary methods used to signify the heart interest of one individual for another—when opportunity presented itself. Human nature being what it is, there must have been the impulse to give the sign of amatory attentiveness that needs no formal language to express.

Even the very restrictions, which were formidable, must have been an incentive to overcome the obstacles. Often the obstacles were insurmountable. Nowhere was romantic interest more frowned upon than in the true patriarchal societies. Daughters and sons alike were under the absolute control of their fathers, and the latter arranged all betrothals and marriages.

The feelings of the young people were not consulted or considered. The girls were usually betrothed and married so young that they were settled in the rigors of domestic life before they had an opportunity to develop romantic inclinations.

Marriages were planned to strengthen the family position, to increase its economic importance, all of which helped to make the patriarchal father a more powerful influence in his community.

In societies of matriarchal character and tendency—which were invariably of a lower cultural level—women were more free, had greater privileges, and consequently young people of both sexes enjoyed much more liberty in their choice of a mate. The North American Indian race is the most classic example of this kind, among whom the amatory life of both the men and the women was permitted a large measure of satisfactory fulfilment.

EARLY LOVE STORIES BELONGED TO FOLKLORE.—Love stories are not a rarity in our cultural heritage, but they are spun from the warp and woof of folklore and legends. They are the dreams of young humanity, wish fulfilments of primitive man. They belong to the realm of idealization and unreality. When in rare instances they derive from reality, they are veritable tragedies of love frustrated—not fulfilled—as in the story of Abelard and Heloise.

The love story of a Robert Browning and Elizabeth Barrett would have been inconceivable in an earlier age. Even in that case a patriarchal father—the spiritual prototype of ancient Greece and Rome—all but frustrated the romance, and doubtless would have if the couple had been less determined and resourceful.

The realistic love story, the narrative that has its counterpart in real life, is practically unknown before the latter part of the eighteenth century, and with rare exceptions it was not until considerably after this period that it became of importance in literature, either qualitatively or quantitatively.

What passed for love in antiquity, and in the medieval

period, was either idealization or eroticism, if we can judge by the literature that reflects those periods, and there are still plenty of representative specimens.

The imperishable masterpieces of Dante, Plutarch and Boccaccio were not love stories of real life, but inspired tales that ranged from idealized allegories and sublimated yearnings to erotic episodes and amorous adventures.

The records of the days and nights that constitute *The Decameron* are no more love stories than are the *Testaments* of François Villon—that engaging rogue and natural genius who left so stirring an account of his unquenchable and eminently readable lechery.

Villon did posterity a service when he penned the verses setting forth his vagaries, for aside from their interest as narrative poetry, and their value as the exhibitionism of a gifted knave, they throw a valuable sidelight on the manners of his times. Still, they are not *love* stories, although they were prompted by the only love that Villon knew, a lusty eroticism.

Boccaccio's fame lies chiefly in his authorship of the erotic classic associated with his name, into which he has crystallized the legends of untold generations in the form of enduring literature. That his work has superlative merit is best indicated by the fact that many of the great masters of the written word—Shakespeare, Dryden, Keats, Goethe, among them—have borrowed liberally from him in form, manner and matter. But still Boccaccio did not create realistic love stories because the type of human experiences which inspires them had not found expression in his age.

THE DEVELOPMENT OF CONJUGAL AFFECTION.—It required the social awakening resulting from the impact of ideas of eighteenth-century philosophy, as inspired by the French Encyclopedists, among others, to bring new values to and enhance the sentiments of human relationship. The ideas were slow in germinating, but they finally penetrated into the social fabric and individual consciousness sufficiently to create a concept of new standards in human values.

Always, however, there was the struggle with those who represented and typified the past, the bulwarks of traditionalism; the resistance of institutions and regimes which had their roots in a bygone age had to be overcome.

Nevertheless, out of this struggle of ideas there emerged greater freedom, tolerance, opportunity and enlightenment. In political life it resulted in the spread of democracy; in industrial and economic life it placed a new emphasis on the human equation. It broadened the scope of education, reducing illiteracy in some countries to a negligible quantity. It stimulated the physical sciences, leading to inventions and technical discoveries that have revolutionized the world mechanically. It developed the sciences of medicine, laboratory research and sanitation, reducing plagues and epidemics, and mitigated the scourge of many dreaded diseases. Sciences such as jurisprudence, on the other hand, lagged behind because they are rooted in ancient precedent, and are less responsive to reason.

Inherent in this philosophy which stemmed from reason, love of individual freedom and the humanizing of justice, was a concept of the integrity of the human being as such. Legal and social disabilities that had handicapped women and deprived them of rights and opportunities were gradually overcome, but always against the same type of opposition as in the past.

The awakened consciousness that recognized woman in the abstract as a qualified human being, entitled to equality in the social sphere, also acknowledged increasingly the individual woman as entitled to reciprocal rights in the marriage relationship.

Another great forward step was made from the time when love meant only erotic passion. Lasting conjugal affection is based on esteem, confidence and respect, no less than on sexual attraction; indeed the former qualities normally outlive the latter.

One cannot respect, honor and esteem a person of grossly inferior status, a submerged personality who intellectually and spiritually lives in a different world. Without those coalescent forces of reciprocity of feeling and mutuality of interest, based on recognition of each other's individual integrity, there is no foundation for a deep and lasting love.

Conjugal affection makes insistent demands upon the objects of its beneficence. It requires a spirit of co-operation and accommodation to harmonize sentiments that otherwise might become discordant. It requires self-discipline and good-fellowship, as well as good sense, to bring into working unison two personalities, with their individual temperaments, tastes and idiosyncrasies. Based on esteem, confidence and honor, enthralled by the biological magnet of sexual affinity, conjugal love is the highest fulfilment of human needs, desires and aspirations.

Index